A

MASTER ON THE

PERIPHERY OF CAPITALISM

A Book in the Series

Latin America in Translation/En Traducción/Em Tradução

Sponsored by the Duke-University of North Carolina

Program in Latin American Studies

Post-Contemporary Interventions

Series Editors: Stanley Fish and Fredric Jameson

A

Master on the

Periphery of Capitalism

Machado de Assis

Roberto Schwarz   *Translated by John Gledson*

Duke University Press

Durham · London

2001

© 2001 Duke University Press

Printed in the United States of America on acid-free paper ∞

Typeset in Galliard by Keystone Typesetting, Inc.

Library of Congress Cataloging-in-Publication Data appear

on the last printed page of this book.

CONTENTS

INTRODUCTION

John Gledson

In 1880, the brazilian writer Joaquim Maria Machado de Assis (1839–1908) began to publish his fifth novel, the *Memórias póstumas de Brás Cubas,* in the *Revista brasileira;* the following year, it appeared in book form. This is one of the major events of Latin American literary history. The first great novel to appear in the region, the *Memoirs* (as the book will be referred to here) need not be read for extraneous reasons — because of its importance in the history of literature, say, or because it is Brazilian, because its author was mulatto, because it gives a portrait of a slave-owning oligarchy, or any number of other motives. We can read it "simply" because it is a great work of art, with a unique atmosphere that imposes itself on the reader from the start, an artistic unity and tone, a brand of humor that may have affinities with other books but that is also sui generis and still has its effect today, whether the reader is Brazilian or not. As Roberto Schwarz comments, in the originality of its prose it could be compared to works by great innovators like Henry James or Proust. Since then, of course, there have been numerous attempts to pin down and explain this elusive quality, which is all the more extraordinary in that the novel appeared, or so it seems, out of the blue. Nothing even approaching it in quality or style was being published in Brazil at the time. Machado himself had published four novels in the 1870s — the last of them only two years before the *Memoirs* — which are still read today, but for which we have to make allowances: they are, on the surface, conventional enough stories of star-crossed love, doomed to failure either because of jealousy (*Ressurreição* [*Resurrection*], 1872) or because of the protagonists' different stations in life (*A mão e a*

luva [*The Hand and the Glove*], 1874; *Helena,* 1876; *Iaiá Garcia,* 1878).
Usually they involve the female protégée of a rich family and the heir to the
family fortune: the basic situation is something like that of *Pamela* or
Mansfield Park.

In 1990, Roberto Schwarz published this book, the first to give a
convincing account of this extraordinary literary event. Previous explanations were often biographical or "philosophical" in nature, or combined
the two, often in simplistic ways. Machado, a successful and hard-working
civil servant, had to ask for leave from work in Rio de Janeiro, to recover in
the spa town of Nova Friburgo from an illness that apparently threatened
his sight. Some have speculated that the sharply satirical, sarcastic tone of
the *Memoirs* was brought on by increased pessimism. Others have given
overriding importance to literary influences, most obviously that of Laurence Sterne, mentioned in the opening note "To the Reader," on the
novel's digressive, quirky organization. None of these explanations was
ultimately satisfactory, if only because they were one-sided, concentrating
on either style or content when what was needed was something that
embraced both. For some years, Schwarz had begun to elaborate a much
less naive account of the process of change, which focused its attention on a
combination of social and literary causal patterns. The central ideas of this
work began to take shape in the period around 1964; they were elaborated
and researched in the following turbulent years, eight of which (1969–77)
Schwarz spent in exile in Paris.[1]

In 1977, on his return to Brazil, Schwarz published *Ao vencedor as
batatas* [The Winner Gets the Potatoes], which reached the threshold of
the 1880s without crossing it, though it promised to do so.[2] In an "Explanation to the Reader," he said, "This is the first half of a study of Machado
de Assis. Because it has a relative independence, and the second half might
take time to finish, I preferred not to wait, and to publish the chapters that
follow straight away." *Ao vencedor* was a considerable success: its arguments,
about nineteenth-century culture and literature in general and Machado in
particular, had a striking originality, and, what was more, fitted the novels
of the 1870s to perfection, allowing one to read them with new understanding, even a sense of revelation. Not exactly an easy book to read, but
written with a density and verve that force one to combine patience and
pleasure, it was far and away the most influential book of literary criticism — not just on Machado — to have been published since the fundamental shift in Brazilian culture that began to take place in the late 1950s and
early 1960s.[3] When *A Master* did appear, thirteen years later, it was an

immediate success: partly because the wait had been long, but partly also because of the irresistible conjunction of the first great book by Brazil's greatest writer, and the critic universally acknowledged to have risen to the challenge Machado poses to literary criticism, theory, and history. Although more demanding to read than *Ao vencedor*—a difficulty with its own logic and necessity, and its corresponding rewards—*A Master* soon went into a second printing and remains, without a doubt, the central point of reference for the study of Machado, with implications for the study of Brazilian and Latin American literature, of Third World literature in general, and of the nineteenth-century novel, particularly in the complex and long-drawn-out shift from, *grosso modo,* realism to modernism.

The great achievement of *A Master,* I think, is to explain an apparent paradox: how is it that a writer so rooted in his own time, writing in a slave-owning cultural backwater, is also, in many ways, so *advanced?* Schwarz's great perception, which lies at the root of a good deal of his achievement, is that the modernity paradoxically arises, to a considerable degree, out of the backwardness, and does not merely happen in spite of it. The primary object of this introduction is to set the scene, especially in terms of the Brazilian context, to help understand how, in the words of the title, there came to be a "master writer on the periphery of capitalism."⁴ The book can, of course, be read on its own—more precisely, with a copy of the *Memoirs* at the ready—but its peculiar density will, I hope, be made less daunting by a previous airing of some of its contexts and arguments.

In the opening pages of *A Master,* Schwarz says, "The possible correspondence between Machado's style and the particularities of Brazilian society, slave-owning and bourgeois at the same time, occurred to me a little before 1964. The idea carries within it the concern with dialectics prevalent at the time, and added on top of that came the swift reversal of the following period" (3). The obvious implication is that this book and the one that preceded it have strong links with recent Brazilian history, 1964 being the year of the coup that put an end to the illusions of populism and marked the beginning of more than twenty years of military rule. Some understanding of this process illuminates the reading of *Ao vencedor as batatas* and of this book.⁵

The most defining moment of all is, not surprisingly, the military coup itself, though it should be remembered that in the first few years of the regime, roughly until the coup within a coup that brought the hard-line right to power in 1968, intellectual life still flourished, though within increasingly circumscribed boundaries.[6] The context was one of increasing polarization: the parameters of thinking about class divisions within Brazilian society, and about Brazil's place in the world, were changing. In particular, the relative ease with which the army and their backers had taken charge was, for many, an occasion for rethinking the ways the rich and powerful successfully imposed themselves on the poor and how this might have been historically determined.

In a very useful and informative recent essay, "Um seminário de Marx" [A Seminar on Marx], Schwarz recounts the regular meetings held by a group of young teachers and students at the University of São Paulo in the late 1950s, in order to read Marx's *Capital*.[7] Under the circumstances, marked by the explosive radicalism of the Third World, studying Marx was a polemical act in several senses. It implied a criticism of American and Soviet imperialism, attacked the conformism of the kinds of social science exported from rich countries, cast doubt on the conventional Marxism propagated by the Communist parties, and for good or ill expressed a desire to find a way forward suited to the group's own aspirations. I should underline, too, that Marxism's insistence on the reality of social classes and the need for studying them had an unexpected effect: it challenged the usual use of European historico-social categories, including Marxist ones, in the description of the Brazilian experience. It became obvious that it was a mistake to use the same terms to describe, for instance, colonial and classical slavery, or the plantation system and European feudalism, or the Brazilian and European middle classes; the same applied to the working classes in different circumstances. As a consequence, it was clear that it was mistaken to think that the line of "progress" of European civilization, from slavery to feudalism and so on to the bourgeois order and then, hypothetically, to socialism, was part of the nature of things and therefore bound to be repeated in Brazil. It was also apparent, however, that the relative particularity of the social development of Brazil — or more generally of any country emerging from colonial domination — did not mean a completely autonomous kind of development but something more "complementary" in nature. Just as colonization had not created societies identical to those in the metropolis, decolonization, when it came — since it happened in the context of a new world order, in effect a new and extremely lopsided international division of labor — was far from creating conditions of equality between nations. The ex-colonies did not have, and did not even move toward having, the same internal constitution as the metropolis. These metropolitan countries, however, perforce became their models — the unreachable objective they were always aiming for. In other words, even though it appeared within the progressive left, this study of Marxism ended up by questioning the universal, straightforwardly inevitable certainty of progress.

All of this may seem fairly familiar to us now, but awareness of these things, a product as much of the political and economic concerns of the time as of the study of Marx, began to change the orientation of academic study. Schwarz mentions two characteristic books produced by members of this group, Fernando Novais's *Portugal e Brasil na crise do antigo sistema colonial, 1777–1808* [Portugal and Brazil in the Crisis of the Old Colonial System] and Fernando Henrique Cardoso's *Capitalismo e escravidão no Brasil meridional* [Capitalism and Slavery in Southern Brazil] ("Um seminário," 93–96). The titles are both symptomatic of the new perspectives: the first placed Brazil in its position vis-à-vis the world economy, particularly the incipient Industrial Revolution in Britain, seeing the system as a whole. The second (whose author cowrote one of the most important texts on dependency theory and is now president of Brazil),[9] tried to work out the relations between two systems that, according to a simplified Marxist model, should not coexist — this in the southern state of Rio Grande do Sul, in the nineteenth century.

In "Um seminário de Marx," Schwarz tries to combine Cardoso's work with another book that appeared at the same time, Maria Sylvia de Carvalho Franco's *Homens livres na ordem escravocrata* [Free Men in a Slave-Owning Society]. Although Carvalho Franco was not a member of the Marx seminar, as Schwarz notes, her work "breathes the same critical, ideological, and bibliographical atmosphere" (97). Though based on different areas of Brazil and different parts of the economic system (the production of dried meat to feed the slaves in the first case, and the lives of the dependents and hangers-on around the big coffee plantations in Guaratinguetá, in the Paraíba valley in São Paulo state in the second), they both investigate the impasses and cruelties of a society in which the slave system was harnessed to capitalist, profit-oriented production. It is the latter book, though, that takes us closer to our subject, largely because Carvalho Franco deals with the free but "dependent" class who had, so to speak, direct experience of this interface, and that is central to Schwarz's own vision of Brazilian history and its connections with literature. After a theoretical introduction, which does indeed breathe the same intellectual atmosphere we have been describing, we are suddenly launched into the extraordinary world of these dependents, who, in Schwarz's own words, "have the whole of Brazil to drop down dead in" (*Ao vencedor,* 99). Principally, it is one of apparently gratuitous, explosive violence, all the more shocking for being conveyed in the deadpan language of the legal cases Carvalho Franco uses as her basic source material, and which is produced by the extreme instability of these people's lives: they were free, but without rights or possessions, and subject to the whims of the owner class.[10]

Carvalho Franco, through her analysis of these legal cases and the total economic and social structure of which they were a part, made what had seemed marginal into something central and representative of the larger whole. It should be said, too, that her concentration on violence has obvious parallels with the deeper process of changing self-awareness in Brazilian society mentioned above. As people were brought face-to-face with institutionalized torture, they began to question a long-standing tradition — of which Gilberto Freyre is doubtless the dominant figure — that saw the country's history in a more conciliatory mode.[11] One of the principal results of this process was to bring the country's enormous poor population, urban and rural, into greater focus. The result has been an explosion of historical and sociological studies. In the literary field, one of the most notable collective efforts was edited by Schwarz: a collection of essays on some thirty authors titled *Os pobres na literatura brasileira* [The Poor in Brazilian Literature] in 1983. The section on Dona Plácida in *A Master* was originally published in this book, in a slightly adjusted form.

One of Schwarz's first great achievements, set out in his essay "Misplaced Ideas," first published in 1972 in French[12] and later appearing as the first chapter of *Ao vencedor as batatas,* is to have seen the practical and theoretical importance of a dissonance that in nineteenth-century Brazil was a simple fact of life: Brazilian society was based on a tripartite division of society into masters, dependents, and slaves. This society had its own logic, obviously, but this did not prevent its having the European system as its model: something that meant it was possible not to "see" things that nevertheless lay on the surface. This is nowhere more crucial than in Machado's work — Machado himself, it is worth mentioning, was brought up as a dependent in a "big house" on the outskirts of Rio de Janeiro. The middle group, covering a wide spectrum of more or less humble occupations, many of them shadowed by the permanent threat of destitution, were numerous both in the countryside and in the city: though free in legal terms, they were in fact very often more or less completely subjected to the owner class. One can already see the absolute contrast with the European "norm," where that middle group corresponded to the bourgeoisie, free in much more than a legal sense, and the engine of much of the social change of the time. In Brazil, the adjective "bourgeois" is more suitably used, as indeed Schwarz uses it from time to time, to describe the oligarchy who imitated European (especially French and British) middle-class culture. In none of the relations between the classes in Brazil could there be said to exist any kind of freedom. This is blindingly obvious in the case of the slaves, but in that of the dependents, itself conditioned by the existence of slavery, which meant that the market for free labor was at best limited, *favor* — or, to use a common word in this context, *clientelism* — mediates. That is, those who are free under the law still depend on the decisions — the caprices — of those with wealth and power.

This same intermediate, free but poor class became the object of directly literary analysis in an article first published in 1970 by Antonio Candido, which is mentioned more than once in *A Master*. Titled "Dialética da malandragem," and translated as "Dialectic of Malandroism," it is an analysis of the *Memórias de um sargento de milícas* [*Memoirs of a Militia Sergeant*] by Manuel Antônio de Almeida, first published in serial form in 1854–55. Almeida himself, who died tragically young in a shipwreck, was one of Machado's early friends and mentors. In one sense, we could hardly be further away from the horrors of Guaratinguetá. We are now in the city of Rio de Janeiro, "in the king's time" — that is, after the arrival of the King João VI and the Portuguese court in 1808, in flight from Napoleon's armies. A comic romp, set in a world of small shopkeepers, barbers, petty thieves, and the like, and whose hero is the roguish scamp Leonardo, the novel has been thought of as a kind of late Brazilian flowering of the picaresque, or as a precursor of later realism. Candido shows that these affiliations do not stand up to analysis, and that the origins of the novel's structure and meaning can be found much closer to home. It takes place, in fact, in the same narrow space described by Carvalho Franco, now given greater elbowroom by the novel's urban setting. The plot and framework of Almeida's book are, according to Candido, a kind of "structural reduction" of the situation of this class, itself representative of the nation, which not surprisingly finds echoes in later, twentieth-century works. The word *malandragem* itself, which the translation rightly refuses to render in an English word but whose closest equivalent would be "roguery," refers to a peculiarly Brazilian kind of trickster or prankster, the *malandro,* a poor (often black) man who refuses to work, living off his wits and cocking a snook at respectable society.[13] Despite appearances to the contrary, he is not simply the representative of a carefree, easygoing society, but its product — the antislave, so to speak, and thus the product of a slave society.

Schwarz is in many ways Candido's heir and greatest admirer; *Se-*

qüências brasileiras begins with four articles dealing with him. As the acknowledgment in the preface to *A Master* says, Candido's influence on Schwarz is not only powerful but diffuse. Yet there are differences too, which show Schwarz in creative tension with his mentor. The ones that concern us most center precisely on "Dialectic of Malandroism"; they also serve to bring Schwarz's own ideas more closely into focus. What he admires most is the close connection Candido establishes between social and literary structures. At a time when a more formalist kind of structuralism was becoming fashionable, and the military regime's pressure on the universities against anything that could be thought of as subversive might well have seemed to tend in the same direction, there is a kind of courage and faith in the structural interdependence of social and literary matters in this article, and consequently of the value of literature as a means of understanding society and history at a deeper level, which have always been among Candido's hallmarks. In this article, though, they are taken one stage further, to the postulation of a form of dialectic. I say "a form of" because Schwarz obviously felt its precise nature to be problematic. In an article first published in 1979, two years after the appearance of *Ao vencedor as batatas*, and cautiously titled "Presuppositions (Unless I'm Mistaken) of 'Dialectic of Malandroism,'" he tries to make the issues at stake more explicit. Because it shows Schwarz sharpening his own analytic tools, this article is worth a little detailed consideration.

Schwarz is full of praise for Candido's article, which reveals a "confidence in art's value as a means to knowledge" and an opposition to the compartmentalization of knowledge brought about by such things as the modern university system, vogues like structuralism and formalism, and what he calls the "instrumentalized" vision of much of modern official Marxism — that is, its subjection to external imperatives, mainly political ones. In the end, however, he finds that Candido, no doubt consciously and for motives of his own, which may well have to do with a fundamental sympathy with and commitment to the text he is studying, or with a "deliberate reticence" with regard to certain Marxist currents whose influence he doubtless feels (Candido has famously said that he is 50 percent Marxist in times of normal politics, 90 percent in times of oppression), refuses to stray beyond certain limits.[14] Thus, the social and historical realities the *Memoirs of a Militia Sergeant* give shape to are of two different orders, according to Candido. One, as we have seen, refers to a social group who, from seeming to be marginal, have become unexpectedly central. The other pertains to a cultural continuity, that of the *malandro*, which Candido identifies throughout Brazilian social and literary history, in the seventeenth century in the poetry of Gregório de Matos, or in the twentieth with works like Mário de Andrade's *Macunaíma,* and in a vein of popular literature that surfaced, again, in the comic and satirical journalism of the Regency (1831–40), a period of political and social upheaval that corresponds to Almeida's youth. Without fear of excessive schematization, one can say that Candido's article brings two traditions together but leaves the potential opposition between them unresolved—perhaps deliberately. One springs from the Marxist-orientated historical analysis of the interface between capitalism and slavery and emphasizes the importance of violence; the other, coming from a quite different source and an earlier generation, places the emphasis on trickery, on a healthy disrespect for order as a value, and, at the extreme, on accommodation. The two most important representatives of this earlier generation, who systematized these ideas—both of considerable stature though with differing perspectives—are Gilberto Freyre and Sérgio Buarque de Hollanda.

At one point in "Dialectic of Malandroism," Candido compares the *Memoirs of a Militia Sergeant* to Hawthorne's *The Scarlet Letter.* Whereas the former represents the free-and-easiness of Brazilian society, its relaxed flouting of systems and rules, the latter represents the harsh authority of the law; in that sense, they are representative of Brazil and the United States, one with a tradition that could be described as popular/Catholic, the other bourgeois/Protestant. Such attempts to define national character make Schwarz wonder if they are not parts of an ideological model that "supposes separate national histories, in the framework of a concert of independent nations, whose differences, according to this view, are part of humanity's rich heritage" ("Presuppositions," 153). As is frequently the case with Schwarz, he is anxious not to allow himself to be the victim of any "instrumentalization," or of the "fetishism" to which any kind of intellectual argument is prone: in other words, he wants to keep the dialectic going. As he says at the very beginning of "Presuppositions": "In literature, the basis of Marxist criticism lies in the dialectic between the literary form and the social process. These are orders easy enough to proclaim, but difficult to obey" (129).

The strong links and tensions between Candido and Schwarz are most sharply brought out in these articles on Manuel Antônio de Almeida: however, they directly concern Machado as well. In his classic history of Brazilian literature between 1750 and 1870, *Formação da literatura brasileira* (Formation of Brazilian Literature), Candido explicitly stopped short of dealing with Machado, which is all the more striking in that he deals with the period, before 1870, when Machado was already a considerable presence on the literary scene, though he had not yet written his first novel.[15] Of course, Candido is not incapable of writing about Machado in illuminating ways: his essay "An Outline of Machado de Assis" is the best general introduction we have, and is available in English. But there is a real sense in which Machado raised discussion of Brazilian literature and its relation to Brazilian society to a new level of self-awareness — and so, if we are to understand his full import, he requires a new kind of treatment, particularly in a book that takes the growth of that self-awareness as its subject. As we will see in the context of the second chapter of *Ao vencedor as batatas,* this process can be traced in Machado's predecessors: with Machado himself, it makes a further, crucial leap. This is most explicit in an article of 1873, written for a magazine published (in Portuguese) in New York, titled "Instinto de nacionalidade" [The Instinct for Nationality], and whose most famous and crucial words Schwarz quotes on the first page of *A Master*. In this article, Machado argues the right of Brazilian authors not to have to limit themselves to local or national realities but to talk about anything they want — but they will also talk about these things *as Brazilians,* with the corresponding "intimate feelings" Machado mentions yet fails to define too closely. The daring of these claims of "local" reality's right to universal significance should not be underestimated, even though it may seem strange that anyone would want to deny a Brazilian's claim to it against that of, say, a Frenchman. Still, in his celebrated article "El escritor argentino y la tradición," published in *Discusión* (1932), Borges has to argue the same point.

The obverse of this is that, once we become attuned to Machado, and in particular if we approach him with as few preconceptions as possible, he can make many twentieth-century writers look juvenile: in particular, he can be said to transcend the side of Candido's unresolved opposition that has a greater affinity with Freyre and Buarque de Hollanda by simply not taking it into account. There is no real belief in conciliation to be found in Machado, and very little if any of the popular culture on which Manuel Antônio de Almeida's balance depends.[16] As Schwarz perceives, quoting Walter Benjamin on Baudelaire, what makes Machado so readable today is not so much some abstract universal quality transcending time and place but the fact that the problems he dealt with — corruption, clientelism, imperialism, and many others — are still in place.[17]

One of the crucial instruments that allowed Schwarz to, in some sense, take Antonio Candido's thinking to a further level of analytic acuity and deal with the new stage of national self-awareness represented by Machado de Assis is his now famous theory of "misplaced ideas," in Portuguese "as idéias fora do lugar." The essay outlining this notion, as has been said, was first published in 1972 and became the first chapter of *Ao vencedor as batatas*. The phrase has become part of common currency in Brazil, often quoted out of context, but its overall usefulness as a means of dealing with Brazil's subordinate, dependent status on the level of ideas and ideology cannot be doubted. One of its sources is the Marx seminar, in which, it will be remembered, one of the subjects of discussion was the "fit" between Marx's categories and Brazilian history and reality.

Ao vencedor's opening sentence sums up an argument put forward in a Brazilian pamphlet in 1863: "Every science has principles on which its system is based. Free labour is one of the principles of Political Economy. Yet in Brazil the 'unpolitical and abominable fact' of slavery reigns" (13; *Misplaced Ideas*, 19). Schwarz argues that since Brazilian reality did not fit in with the liberal ideologies of the time and could not be described in their terms, it always appeared as somehow displaced in relation to them and vice versa (that is, those ideologies themselves do not emerge unscathed from the confrontation). If Brazilians only see things according to foreign models, they will not see what is in front of their noses, while, conversely, if they do pay attention to what is going on there, an important and prestigious part of European thinking will seem irrelevant — a daring notion in the context of the time. His great achievement was to readjust the focus and allow us to see these things with a new clarity. Commenting on the clientelist system, which complemented slavery, Schwarz puts it this way: given the power of European ideologies, "no one in Brazil could have the idea, nor the strength to be, let's say, the Kant of relations of favor, giving universality to this social form" (*Misplaced Ideas*, 23). Or, in Machado's own words, from an article published in 1879, just before the *Memoirs*: "It is external influence which determines the way things go: for the moment, in our own context, the power of inventing new doctrines does not exist."[18] Brazilians, then, did not see their social system in its own immediate terms but in those of another system, precisely that of bourgeois, liberal Europe (principally Britain and France), whose lack of correspondence to local truths was perfectly plain to Machado. It is important to remember that we are not discussing the rights or wrongs of any particular ideology but the way in which each ideology relates to the facts of the case. As Brazilian slave owners and their apologists were eager to point out, European factory workers were scarcely free, and perhaps no better off than the slaves who toiled in the sugar and coffee plantations; nevertheless, the system they worked under was that of the free labor market and thus ideologizable, so to speak, in those terms. The Brazilian facts were shorn of any ideological justification, and in this vacuum, although the current ideologies of the liberal nineteenth century operated, they had a different "secondary" relevance and revealed a shallowness of their own. Besides having other functions, they could be, and frequently were, used to show off how up-to-date one was.

Machado knew all about this national peculiarity, a fact which is key to understanding how he transcends his predecessors, such as José de Alencar or Manuel Antônio de Almeida, among the last writers dealt with in Antonio Candido's *Formação*. In stories and novels, the phenomenon of "misplaced ideas" makes frequent appearances, most famously perhaps in the story "Teoria do medalhão" [Education of a Stuffed Shirt] (1881), in which a father tells his son how to get by in the world, and in fact, achieve considerable success, by having a collection of useful phrases, suitable for all eventualities; what he must take care not to do is take any of the substance of these ideas seriously. In the later "Evolução" [Evolution] (1884), another version of the same idea but that embodies it in a plot, we meet Benedito, a successful practitioner of these skills (he is even the ideal age for a *medalhão,* forty-five): "Morally, he was what he was. Leopards don't change their spots, and Benedito was a good man—or, more exactly, he was placid. But, intellectually, he was less original. We can compare him to a much-frequented inn, where ideas of all sorts and descriptions were lodged, and sat down at the table with the host's family. Sometimes, it so happened that two enemies, or people who didn't much like one another, were there together: nobody argued, and the owner imposed mutual tolerance on the guests. That was how Benedito managed to combine a kind of vague atheism with two religious brotherhoods he founded" (*OC,* 2:704). The story revolves around a phrase, wonderfully typical of the nineteenth century at its most naively optimistic: "One can compare Brazil to a child crawling on all fours: it will start walking properly only when it has lots of railways" (704). The narrator says this to his friend—and then wonders to see how Benedito, over a few years, manages to persuade himself that he was the one who coined the phrase. The process is slow, "evolutionary," one might say, but conclusive. It is a brilliant study, always in a comic, satirical vein, of the adaptation of all kinds of ideas to new and unexpected uses in their Brazilian context. We could notice here too a characteristic combination of ambitious generality—progress and evolution; could one think of two more important ideas, more central to nineteenth-century thinking? — and comic trivialization. As Schwarz says, Machado is a master of these complex meanders.

When I first came across the notion in the late 1970s, the great attraction of misplaced ideas was that they blurred outlines, particularly national borderlines: they removed the need to posit some "essential" Brazilian-ness — *brasilidade* is one of the awkward words used to describe this mythical beast — without making the country a simple reflection of the metropolis. Nevertheless, it was also the subject of polemic in the 1970s, after the first publication of Schwarz's essay, and was attacked by no less a figure than Maria Sylvia de Carvalho Franco, who published an article arguing that "as idéias estão no lugar" [the ideas are in place].[19] As in the case of Antonio Candido, it is worth looking at this point of tension to clarify the usefulness of Schwarz's ideas. At the time, he replied in a fascinating interview — which, partly because its tone is conversational, reveals something of Schwarz's habits of mind — in ways directly relevant to *A Master*.[20] Carvalho Franco argues against the dualism that, according to her, lies at the core of the notion:

> Metropolis and colony, backwardness and progress, development and underdevelopment, traditionalism and modernization, hegemony and dependency — are some of the variants of this theme that we come across in theories of Brazilian history.
>
> Any of these oppositions — from the way they were formulated by nationalistic Romanticism to present-day dependency theory — carries with it the implicit presupposition of an *essential* difference between metropolitan countries, the headquarters of capitalism, the hegemonic nucleus of the system, and the colonial peoples, underdeveloped peripheral and dependent. (61, emphasis in original)

Following the argument, Carvalho Franco claims that *things,* goods, do obey this dualism, because the absorption of merchandise by dependent countries "is inherent to the very nature of international markets and the division of labor" (62). But do ideas follow the same rules? she asks. How do they enter Brazilian society?

> By the force of social prestige, of the ornamental attraction of the "superior" culture? By the diffusion of ideas that migrate from consciousness to consciousness, indifferent to the radical difference between the foundations, there and here: differences that have been postulated precisely so that the ideas can be made to look out of place? On one hand, we would have bourgeois ideas and reasonings eagerly

adopted for no reason at all, and on the other, Brazilian clientelism and slavery, incompatible with them. To set up this opposition is, ipso facto, to separate its terms and to lose sight of the real processes of ideological production in Brazil. (62)

The key here is surely the word "essential": if we postulate too rigid a difference between the metropolis and the periphery, there is a real danger that the two will become incommensurable.

It is just this essential difference that "misplaced ideas" seems to relativize. Nevertheless, the danger pointed to by Carvalho Franco is real. Everything depends on the uses the concept is put to, and the care, tact, and knowledge with which this very useful tool is used.[21] It is interesting that, in contrast to Carvalho Franco's title, the original phrase has no verb: that is, unless I am mistaken, Schwarz is saying not that ideas in general, much less in essence, are out of place, but that there are such things as misplaced ideas.

This is made clearer in the interview mentioned above. Schwarz begins by stating that "foreign ideas can help us to understand our own world" (33): he is not, then, proposing that Brazil and Europe are in some sense incommensurable, which would be patently absurd. A great deal depends, he avers, on the context we are dealing with: in Guaratinguetá, "the ideological influence of contemporary Europe would not be the decisive element" (36). In literature, however, ideas can be given shape, in novel plots and situations, for instance, which often have deep roots in contemporary ideology and, as such, can be quite genuinely exported. As Schwarz notes, "they came from Europe every fortnight, by steamship, in the form of books, magazines, and newspapers, and everyone went down to the harbour to wait for them" (34). This assimilation of ideas to things, which denies Carvalho Franco's distinction between them, is more serious than the comic vision of intellectuals anxiously awaiting the next cargo and points to one of Schwarz's strongest affinities within the field of Marxism. As he proclaims in the same interview: "Along with the Frankfurt School, I believe that the principal ideology of modern capitalism lies in the mass of available goods, and in the organization of the productive process, while ideas properly so-called have taken a back seat" (37). We will see later that such notions, in which Adorno's influence, in particular, can be felt, have an important part to play in establishing the status of the narration in the *Memoirs*.

The best place to see the usefulness of "misplaced ideas" as an analytic tool in the writing of literary history is in the second chapter of *Ao vencedor as batatas*, "A importação do romance e suas contradições em Alencar" [The Importing of the Novel and Its Contradictions in Alencar], whose subject is Machado's predecessors, primarily José de Alencar, most famous for such "Indianist" novels as *O guarani* (1857) and *Iracema* (1865) but who also wrote novels with urban settings. It is important to realize that Brazil, given its necessarily subordinate cultural role, produced a surprising number of authors who achieved popularity in the novel, the most representative form of the period. This in itself is one of the explanations of Machado's success: he was not starting from square one, though his relation to his predecessors is not one of simple influence, as Schwarz points out. Rather it was complex and apparently contradictory, made up of affection, conscious adaptation, satirical mockery, and desire to see things in their true dimensions. Three novelists in particular are involved: Joaquim Manuel de Macedo, Manuel Antônio de Almeida, and Alencar. The first, the most innocent of all and the one for whom Machado had least respect, was the most prolific: tuned in to the atmosphere of his local, carioca audience, he was enormously popular (though fast becoming out of fashion by the 1870s). He is famous above all for *A moreninha* (roughly, The Little Dusky Beauty) (1844), a story of childhood sweethearts who meet again as adolescents that is still widely read today. As Antonio Candido notes, this novel, set in the context of the local "bourgeoisie," and which is "so flat and trivial in social and human terms," also has a Romantic plot, with all the trimmings: "so much so that we wonder how it's possible for such ordinary people to get mixed up in the goings-on the author submits them to" (32). It is a simple example of "misplaced ideas" in a literary context: the Romantic, melodramatic, "imported" plot and the humble characters, true to a Brazilian setting governed by the restrictions present in relations between masters and dependents, clash.

Most of this chapter of *Ao vencedor* is dedicated to an analysis of *Senhora* [A Lady], the last of José de Alencar's "urban" works, published in 1875, when Machado de Assis had already published two novels. *Senhora*, along with much of Alencar's other fiction, exemplifies the same duality between ordinary local characters tied up in the world of dependence and favor, and a Romantic plot with its more absolute demands, as *A moreninha*. However, there has been some development, a kind of raised self-awareness, between Macedo and Alencar, and this is what attracts Schwarz's attention. What he wants to study, as he says, is a kind of semi-conscious dialectical process in which form and content interact, and move "from being an involuntary reflex action to becoming a careful elaboration, from incongruity to artistic truth" (65). The process has two sides. On one hand, it is patent that Alencar was, at some level, aware of the incongruity and nevertheless prepared to justify it in local, even nationalist terms. He defends Seixas, his principal male protagonist, from attack by a woman friend, who saw the character as weak, far beneath the stature needed for a Romantic hero. In a note appended to his novel, Alencar insists that he "shapes his characters to fit in with local Rio society," and that the incongruity is part of that fit: "your colossal figures would look like stone guests [*convidados de pedra,* an allusion to the Don Juan story] in our [Brazilian] world" (*Senhora,* 841; see *Misplaced Ideas,* 64). On the other hand, in Alencar's novels themselves, it could be said that the problem is not so much solved as exacerbated: his plots are even more marked by European, bourgeois values than those of his predecessor, because he takes those values more seriously. Thus, Alencar's incongruities are seen at one moment as a defect in the composition, at the next as something inferior in terms of a Romantic, European model, and finally as a positive achievement in terms of a Brazilian realism.

In the second chapter of Macedo's second novel, *O moço loiro* [The Blond Young Man], two girls discuss the dilemmas of young heiresses: how are they to know if their suitors are genuine or just after their money? Even here, Macedo has to insist that these girls are more aware than the run-of-the-mill marriageable girls of the time, in being able to discuss such matters. In *Senhora,* this self-awareness produces the entire basic structure of the plot. Aurélia, the heroine, is turned down by Seixas when she has no money; when she inherits, she decides to attract him with the promise of money, marries him incognito, only to accuse him of mercenary motives, humiliating him until he is finally "redeemed," both in the moral sense and in that of paying a debt. In both Macedo and Alencar, then, we have an unrealistic opposition between the free individual and money, which in the European novel, in Balzac or Dickens, for instance, would be entirely realistic — a prime example of an imported ideology, since it presupposes the bourgeois notion of that same free individual, whereas in real Brazilian terms, the patriarchal family intervened to arrange these things according to different values. Alencar, then, does not resolve the opposition between the two elements, local and European; and, as a result, *Senhora*'s plot has a peculiar artificiality and unreality, which is doubtless an aesthetic defect. As Schwarz posits: "This process is a complex variant of the so-called dialectic between form and content: our own, local material only reaches sufficient density when it includes, *on the level of content,* the irrelevance of the European form" (p. 51, my emphasis). This irrelevance is, then, first, with

Macedo, a matter for simple excuses; with Alencar, it appears in this form of exacerbation or exaggeration; later, Machado will include it in another, much more suitable guise — that of parody. The short stories I looked at above, both from the 1880s, are prime examples of the mature writer dealing, precisely, with the irrelevance of European forms on the level of content. From Alencar to Machado, we move from unintentional to intentional humor.

Alencar died in 1877, and with his last novels we are on the threshold of Machado's first great achievement, the *Posthumous Memoirs*. All that was needed, in a sense, was that turn to parody. The truth, of course, is a great deal more complex than this. In tracing the fascinating development that led to the *Memoirs,* more than once we will follow a process with its own logic, only to realize that Machado had to take a jump, had to do something quite coherent but also immensely daring in artistic *and* in social terms, to lift his work to a higher level of consistency.

The remaining part of *Ao vencedor as batatas,* more than half the book, deals with three of Machado's first four novels. We are going back in time, since, as has been said, *Senhora* was published in 1875; *The Hand and the Glove,* the first of the three, appeared in 1874. Rather than involuntarily dramatizing the incongruity between two differing systems, local and European, Machado took a more realistic route, creating the plots of these three novels within the overall context of the clientelism and patriarchalism that, along with slavery, constituted the dominant Brazilian social forms. Schwarz does not dedicate a separate chapter to the first of Machado's novels, *Ressurreição:* it might seem that this is because class conflict of any kind is absent from its pages, but that would be an unfair criticism, and, as we will see, the novel plays an important role in the process Schwarz describes. Often taken as a predecessor of *Dom Casmurro* (1899), along with the *Posthumous Memoirs* (Machado's most famous novel), *Ressurreição*'s central character, Félix, is a pathologically jealous man, who ends up refusing the young widow Lívia because, although he knows she has been falsely accused of flirting with another, the accusation "might have been" true.

In *The Hand and the Glove,* the first of the novels dealt with at length, Guiomar, a girl of poor origins but with a baroness for a godmother, is courted by three men — Estêvão, a sensitive poet; Jorge, the baroness's nephew; and Luís Alves, an ambitious young man with a practical turn of mind. Guiomar chooses Alves, because the two of them are kindred spirits (thus the hand and the glove), and manages to persuade her patroness that it is the right choice. Thus, ostensibly, the family can adjust itself to a certain kind of social mobility, there is room for the poor to better themselves, and nobody loses out except those, like the poet and the nephew, who are too effete to make their own way. As we can see, Machado adopts a kind of conformist realism that is not without its cynical side, and that conciliates no fewer than three ideological positions, clientelism, romantic love, and a kind of social Darwinism: the baroness is satisfied, the lovers are happily married, while in the struggle for life the fittest survive. As Schwarz maintains, there is a certain freedom in examining the family structure, within the overall conformity.

In some passages and phrases from the novel, this conciliation of contradictions creates a kind of tension in the prose, which needs only a tiny push to signify the opposite of its actual meaning. Here is part of an example, brilliantly analyzed by Schwarz himself (the subject is Guiomar):

> I wouldn't wish to give the impression that she is one of those souls swayed and blinded by passion, nor make her die of a silent, timid love. She wasn't at all like that, nor would she do such things. Her nature demanded the flowers of the heart, but one shouldn't expect her to go and pick them in wild, barren places, nor from the branches of a modest bush planted opposite some rustic window. She wanted them to be beautiful and flourishing, but in a Sèvres vase, placed on rare piece of furniture, between two windows in a city street, and with the said vase and the said flowers flanked by cashmere curtains, which should, in their turn, sweep their edges along the rug on the floor. (*Ao vencedor,* 77–78; *OC,* 1:251–52)

As the passage proceeds, perhaps especially when we come to the "said" vases and the "said" flowers, it becomes increasingly hard to believe that Machado empathizes with his heroine, much as he may approve of her. There are, without a doubt, real problems of irony, even of hypocrisy here.[22] As Schwarz points out, Machado in his youth was a card-carrying liberal: he may well have conformed because he had to, and molded his language to conform overtly, while hinting at something more critical. But his intentions are less important than the prose itself, which can simply affirm that things that are normally seen as opposites, like love and social ambition, in this particular case exist in harmony; as a result of this unusual union, the prose can take on the rhythm of the passage quoted, full of ifs, buts, and qualifications, and, particularly here, of extended, treacherous similes and metaphors, made for an ironic, covertly aggressive relationship with the reader. We are only inches away from the prose of the *Memoirs,* and indeed, an image there submitted to the most sarcastic treatment, the flower of the bushes, appears here in a somewhat more innocent guise.[23]

The three novels Schwarz deals with in *Ao vencedor as batatas* do not form a simple, linear progress toward the achievement of the *Memoirs,* but something made up simultaneously of advances and retreats; the process is, in fact, more dialectical, so that adjustments in one area — that of the novel's overall ideological context, say — can have unexpected knock-on effects in others, like that of the characterization. *Helena* (1876) is a good example. Here, in one sense, there is a step backward. We are in a similar position of that of *The Hand and the Glove,* that of a girl adopted by a household, though the situation itself is more complex: where Guiomar is simply the beneficiary of the baroness's favor, Helena is the illegitimate daughter of a counselor (i.e., an important politician in the imperial regime), who is recognized by him in his will, and so, after his death, becomes part of the family. But Helena is not, like Guiomar, ambitious for herself and to that extent disrespectful of family values: on the contrary, she is determined to be accepted by Estácio, the counselor's son and now the head of the family; by his aunt, Dona Úrsula, a lady of traditional values; and by others. Abnegation is the order of the day, then, and suddenly, ambition is replaced by Christianity, a religion for whose doctrine the mature Machado probably had little time but that is needed here for structural purposes and embodied in the (rather negative) figure of Padre Melchior. As Schwarz says, given the links between Christianity and paternalism — especially the injunction to be charitable to those less fortunate than ourselves — its presence produces no obvious clash. This could be called a retreat, in that it simplifies character and produces an unrealistic degree of virtue — the heroine, Schwarz says, is "the most exemplary and uninteresting person in the book."

The most important step forward, which again takes us to the threshold of the *Memoirs,* is in the character of Estácio. Where Jorge, the heir to the family fortune in *The Hand and the Glove,* is a wastrel and a weakling overshadowed by Luís Alves, Estácio synthesizes, to use Schwarz's word, the most important conquests of the preceding novels: the weaknesses and uncertainties of Félix in *Ressurreição,* and the social substance of *The Hand and the Glove.* "With the figure of Estácio," Schwarz declares, "Machado was beginning to sail the waters of modernity" (101). Estácio, too, on the surface is a model Christian, a harmless young student of mathematics, anxious to do his duty. However, he is also in love with his half sister, as she, covertly, is with him. As Schwarz rightly argues, the novel owes something to Romantic literature, in which incest is a frequent motif, but the real function of these motifs is superficial. In the end we find out, ludicrously enough, that Helena is not the counselor's daughter after all, and that Estácio's love was therefore innocent — by which time it is too late, for Helena is dying of her impossible situation. But the true focus of the novel's interest lies in the combination of social and psychological factors in a single character. Estácio, a relative innocent, does not know that he loves Helena and knows that he ought to respect her, but when the chips are down, he is ready to use his personal power as head of the family to control her. We are thus in the presence of the workings, the inner conflicts, the processes of rationalization, the young man as he struggles with his conscience, only to find the justification for what he wanted to do anyway. Here, Machado's appreciation of the ultimate readiness of those in power to impose their will, and to find the reasons afterward, can be clearly seen. In the following quotation from *Ao vencedor,* we are (again, by another route) moving very close to the world of the *Memoirs:*

> we can see above all that Machado's reflections on psychological matters (the Christian surface matter would disappear in the next novels) already here make the representation of paternalism more complex. Where before we spoke of power [*arbítrio*] as being the despotic will of the stronger party, here we have an analysis of power itself, which, when it does not hold on firmly to Christian values, turns out to be a tangle of different kinds of servitude. Now, if it is characteristic of paternalism that, on the side of the relationship where the power resides, there is no clear frontier between social authority and personal will, and if this latter is a more or less contradictory collection of desires, of blind spots and unfounded justifications that the individual cannot admit to himself that he has, the situation of the weaker, inferior party takes on another dimension. His or her social integration comes about via a direct subordination to the servitudes and emotional confusions of their superiors — which have their own authority, and which it would be ingratitude not to respect. (103)

As Schwarz says in the next sentence: "I hope the reader recognizes the dark clay [*o barro escuro*] that is molded into Machado's mature work." This passage leads straight to the world of the *Posthumous Memoirs,* where two words, caprice and volubility, appear time and time again, forming the basis not only of Schwarz's analysis of the psychology of the oligarchic, owner class, and the unhappy position of those whose lives are lived in its shadow, but of the whole style and structure of the novel. Right on the first page of *A Master,* we are faced, almost as an axiom, with the argument that this volubility is *both* "(a) rule for the composition of the narrative and (b) the stylization of a kind of conduct characteristic of the Brazilian ruling class." In the wake of *Ao vencedor as batatas,* that seemingly daring, even over confident definition of the style *and* the content of the *Memoirs* as sides of a single coin becomes much easier to accept.

Iaiá Garcia (1878) is the last of the four novels written before the appearance of the *Memoirs:* here one can sense, more than ever, that Machado has reached a kind of limit, and that radical change was necessary if he was to continue writing. The novel begins in 1866, at a moment of crisis in the Paraguayan War (1865–70): Valéria, a rich widow, wants to her son Jorge to enlist, for reasons that are ostensibly patriotic but that turn out to have motives closer to home — she wants to prevent his attraction to Estela, the daughter of Sr. Antunes, her late husband's factotum, leading to anything as serious as marriage. Immediately, then, we are back in the world of masters — mistresses, more frequently, since, as Schwarz notes, the male head of the household is usually removed, to provide something of a power vacuum and give the plot room for maneuver — and their dependents. The attitude of these dependents has reached a kind of culmination, or cul-de-sac, a result of the situation outlined in the passage on *Helena* quoted above: it should be said that Christianity has once again been removed from the equation. Given their situation of complete subordination to caprice, all these characters can do to maintain what shreds of dignity are left to them is to be as negative as possible without actually disobeying. Thus, in the first scene, Luís Garcia, a hard-working minor civil servant who "owes favors" to Valéria, and whom she wants to help her persuade Jorge to enlist, tries all possible means to extract himself from the situation. Estela, meanwhile, is subjected to a more advanced stage of the dominant male's "caprice" — virtual rape, as Jorge tries to kiss her in the grounds of an abandoned house belonging to Valéria. The shame involved in her rejection of him is what finally leads him to enlist. While he is away, the widow decides to marry the two dependents, Luís Garcia and Estela: it is a successful marriage mostly because both characters, out of necessity, can have no positive ambitions and are resigned.

Schwarz's main focus lies on the plot consequences of this completely disenchanted vision of the respective positions and attitudes of the owner class and dependents. One can see the problem that Machado faced: where caprice reigns, on the side of the owners, there can be no coherent, logical action; where mere negative resistance is the rule, no real action at all. And this is in fact what happens in the novel. When Jorge comes back from the war, his mother is dead, and he begins by thinking that Luís Garcia, who has heart problems, might die and leave the way open for him. However, after a few chapters in which Estela still removes herself from his company, he switches his attention ("between two cups of tea") to Luís Garcia's daughter, Iaiá.

It would be possible to go into more detail about Schwarz's brilliant analysis of the plot of this "humorless" novel, with its heavy, dead-end atmosphere, but the central point has been made. What is most important to my argument, and to Schwarz's, is that here we have the beginnings of an explanation of why Machado is, or at the very least appears to be, so modern. The Romantic plots with which Machado began, even though, given his remarkable sense of his own artistic integrity, he had always adjusted them and subjected them to the different presuppositions of the Brazilian social structure, were now completely threadbare. Suddenly, though the leap might seem daring, Samuel Beckett is on the horizon:

> Without ignoring Machado's tone of resigned decorum, he was openly taking on the somber lucidity of the true atheist, and was extending it to the appreciation of daily existence, whose mythological support he was in the process of dismantling. These are very considerable first steps, even though they result in literary failure, in the direction of a pessimistic, dissonant modern art, a vein that even today has not run out, as can be seen in Beckett, and that paradoxically also continues the antimythological work of the Enlightenment. (142)

These sudden changes in perspective, from detailed analysis to wide historical perspectives, become familiar to Schwarz's readers and are part of the excitement of reading him.

Nor is this the only way in which modernity makes its presence felt. On the level of the characters' psychology, too, we can see in the capricious decisions of the owner class patterns that are not simply irrational but determined by something we could well call the unconscious — in other words, we are suddenly well on the way to Freud. There is, in fact, a real question of historical influence here; in the chapter on *Helena,* where the repressed character of Estácio involves the same problems, Schwarz quotes, in a note, from one of Machado's newspaper columns (*crônicas*) of the time, in which he talks of "one of these inexplicable natural phenomena, which a modern philosopher explains by the unconscious, and the Church by the temptation of evil" (101). There are two candidates for this "modern philosopher," Eduard von Hartmann, the author of *The Philosophy of the Unconscious* (1869) and Arthur Schopenhauer, both of them important precursors of Freud.[24] Machado had both in his library, and this is not the only evidence of their influence on him.[25]

We are, yet again, on the threshold of the *Memoirs*. This summary of *Ao vencedor as batatas* has shown, I hope, how it forms part of a whole with *A Master*. In the style, characterization, and plot structure of Machado's three earlier books one can see the process leading to the writing of the *Memoirs*, an event that has always had an air of miracle about it. All that was needed — though it was still a considerable feat — was to "dar a volta por cima" [make the jump to seeing things from above] in Schwarz's words: no longer from the perspective of the dependents, but from that of the masters. We should also bear in mind that the facts of historical development played their part in this. It was almost impossible to imagine plots in which the dependents would be free of their masters' whims, since even with the end of slavery in 1888 the old system remained, in essential aspects, in place, and a free labor market remained what Joaquim Nabuco called it, an El Dorado.[26] At the end of *Iaiá Garcia*, Estela takes a post as a schoolmistress in the interior of the (then) Province of São Paulo, a long way from Rio and from its present reality — but Brazilian society itself did not change, even with the abolition of slavery in 1888, and Machado's fiction had to reflect that fact.[27]

Given the logical progression I have expounded here, it is almost easy to imagine Machado being forced by his own literary development into the change, thought at least two crucial elements are still missing: the voluble, digressive, Sterne-like narration and the handing over of that narration to a member of the upper class. The combination of these two, of course, is the stroke of genius analyzed at length in this book. Even here, certain precedents can be cited, as Schwarz makes plain in *A Master:* the digressive newspaper column of which Machado is an acknowledged master, and a certain comic, insouciant, popular tradition present in the drama of Martins Pena and Manuel Antônio de Almeida's *Memoirs of a Militia Sergeant* (156, 159–60). Even Sterne was not quite the unknown quantity in Brazil that one might imagine.[28] Still, there is an irreducible element of sheer daring and genius, if only in the combination of these elements, and the uncompromising pursuit of his aim of artistic truth that must provoke our admiration even today — nor would Schwarz deny that, though his main thrust, quite rightly, is a rational attempt to explain the "miracle." In his interesting recent book, *Atlas of the Novel, 1800–1900,* Franco Moretti quotes Schwarz's characterization of Latin American (and other) literature combining local realities and foreign ideologies, but prefers to update it from the Brazilian modernism of the 1920s to more recent "magical realism." The astonishing fact is that he could, as Schwarz shows, have gone back in time to Machado de Assis in 1880.

There is a gap of some fourteen years between the publications of *Ao vencedor as batatas* and *A Master.* Despite this, the unity between the two books is very real and stems both from Schwarz's original plan and from the consistency of his thinking, which has remained true to its (predominantly Marxist) roots. Nevertheless, there are genuine shifts of emphasis, which spring from two sources: from the shift from a diachronic subject matter to a synchronic one, since we are no longer dealing with the process leading up to the *Memoirs,* but with the achieved masterpiece itself; and to a lesser extent from critical works that have been published in the interim.

As we have seen, a double change took place between *Iaiá Garcia* and the *Memoirs:* the handing over of the narration to a member of the upper class, and the adoption of a fragmentary, deliberately playful style and structure, "after the manner of Sterne and Xavier de Maistre." These two things are inseparable, and the definition of "volubility" given in the first chapter is itself justified by this fact. The key discovery of *A Master* is that the capriciousness of the style expresses the capriciousness of a class. At the same time, it will not escape the reader's attention that Schwarz is much less interested in the author, Machado de Assis, than he is in the total structure and style of the novels he is studying, which have a meaning and a reality of their own. This is not a denial of the author's intention, or even of an interest in the links between Machado's life and his art: rather, it is a belief in the objective, historical validity of a literary form in which the author gives expression to forces that transcend him.

This basic belief has not changed over the years, but in *A Master* it faces a new situation. There is nothing in the book, from the title onward, that is not "written," or at any rate narrated, by Brás Cubas. Even in the third edition, when he added a short preface, Machado was very careful to maintain his own, ironic distance from the text: "I will say no more, so as not to enter into a critique of a dead man, who portrayed himself and others in the manner that seemed best and most suitable to him" (*OC,* 1:510). In a sense, this makes Schwarz's task easier, for we are faced with a total, in a sense even a closed, aesthetic artifact, with a unity of its own: at one stage, in passing, he refers to the "prose-in-itself," something that has an independent existence, with its own characteristics and logic. But there is also a sense in which this is an illusion, for Brás is, as we have seen, condemning himself out of his own mouth. Thus, there is always in the background the shadow of the real author, Machado de Assis.

It is here, it seems to me, that the Marxist tradition has been particularly useful to Schwarz. When he says, in the preface to this book, that "My work would also be unthinkable without the—contradictory—tradition formed by Lukács, Benjamin, Brecht, and Adorno, and without the inspiration of Marx," he is merely asserting what any reader soon discovers, if not from the text itself, from the footnotes. By the word "contradictory," he is pointing out that Marx's inheritance does not mean adherence to a strict party line—Schwarz has always been anti-Stalinist—and is not, to use his own words in another context, "a straitjacket for the intelligence." Indeed, it should perhaps be underlined that Schwarz's whole approach to literature is the reverse of dogmatic.[29]

We saw earlier that, in the same interview in which he defends the concept of misplaced ideas and argues that there is a considerable "ornamental" aspect to Brazilian culture, Schwarz notes how things can take on the role of ideas, how consumer goods, according to the Frankfurt school, become the primary ideology of present-day capitalism. In the process of being "misplaced," the reverse process also takes place. Ideas turn into things—they are "instrumentalized," "reified" almost independently of their content. Adorno, whose concern with the culture industry is well known, perhaps best exemplifies this argument: it can be well illustrated from article on the sociology of music, "Ideen zur Musiksoziologie," quoted by Schwarz more than once, translated by him in 1968 for a left-wing Brazilian periodical, and later republished in a collection of essays by the school. Adorno says, for instance:

> The social meaning that lives in music in itself is not identical to its social position and function. The harmony between these two spheres is by no means secure, and today the contradiction between them is essential. Great music, music complete in itself, whose level of consciousness was once self-sufficient, can become ideology, a socially necessary appearance. Even the most authentic of Beethoven's compositions, which are true, or, according to Hegel's terminology, an unfolding of the truth, have been degraded by musical circulation, and transformed into cultural goods that give prestige to the consumer, as

well as the emotions the music doesn't contain, and the very essence of music is not indifferent to this degradation." ("Ideen zur Musik-soziologie," 259–60, my translation from the Portuguese)

The parallel between this degradation of music from being something complete in itself to being a mere social object and the ornamental, degraded use of ideas in Brás's narration is plain. It also provides us with a convincing account of the degree of authenticity that that narration has: it is complete on its own terms, the representative of a kind of culture, but at the same time secondary, bound by social necessities, and to that extent inauthentic.

By an unexpected twist, it is precisely these features of Brás's narration and style that make the *Memoirs* so modern. Brás's satire is not only turned on himself and on his class; there is a sense in which this "misuse" of some of the most prestigious European ideas of that time and ours is reflected back and turns the spotlight on those very ideas. "We are laughing here at nothing less than the achievements of the modern Western world" (35). For Schwarz, Western values are an essential, if in a sense a negative, part of the basic, defining situation of the *Memoirs*. This point is made numerous times, and its origins plainly lie in the notion of misplaced ideas: while Brás acts according to one set of values—those of his own slave-owning, paternalist society—the world of liberty, equality, and the Rights of Man weighs on him "like a remorse." This, too, has paradoxically "modern" consequences, since it makes for a permanent sense of inner dislocation and a lack of that secure sense of the individual conveyed, say, by the novels of Balzac—the classic expression of bourgeois realism, above all according to Lukács. We are moving in the direction of narrators we cannot trust, and where, in a crucial phrase, "mistrust of the artist's power of representation . . . does not abolish reality, but displaces it into the very act of representing"—in other words, the language becomes not only a means of referring to reality but part of that reality itself. Machado doubtless never read Henry James, but like him, he creates what Schwarz calls "situated narrators," who write, always, from a defined and limited standpoint.

Of course, Schwarz's attempt to define the status and implications of the narration in the *Memoirs* is not the first, though it seems to me to be by far the most successful, not least because, as I said at the beginning of this introduction, it gives us a real, historical explanation for the novel's modernity. To conclude, I want to take a brief look at some other attempts, most if not all of which appeared between *Ao vencedor as batatas* and *A Master,* that seem to make a useful contribution to an ongoing discussion, and most of which are mentioned in this book.

Many can usefully be thought of under the category of parody, so long as the word is understood in a wide enough sense. Indeed, in the interview on "misplaced ideas" I have already quoted more than once, Schwarz is asked if "the use of parody as a privileged mode of expression [risks] leading to an excessively contemplative position." Provocatively, he replies: "I don't see why it should. Parody is one of the most combative of literary forms, as long as that is the intention. And anyway, a little contemplation never did anyone any harm. . . . Proust, Joyce, Kafka, Mann, and Brecht were all consummate parodists" ("Beware Alien Ideologies," *Misplaced Ideas,* 40). He could have added Machado de Assis.

An important beginning was made in 1972 with the publication of an article by José Guilherme Merquior, "Gênero e estilo nas *Memórias póstumas de Brás Cubas*" [Genre and Style in *Memória póstumas de Brás Cubas*], in which he argued that the novelty of the *Memoirs* was attributable to a genre switch. Machado had started to practice Menippean satire, in the tradition of Erasmus or Swift, or the late Greek writer Lucian of Samosata; the idea was given more flesh in *O calundu e a panacéia* [roughly, The Sulks and the Panacea], by Enylton de Sá Rego, published in 1989, primarily on Machado's quite conscious debt to Lucian.[30] It is important to realize that Machado knew what he was doing: lingering prejudices against "provincial" culture are, or should be, dispelled by a glance at the catalog of what remains of his library.[31] In chapter 5 of this book, Schwarz adds to our awareness of this by his own discovery that the *Memoirs* contains some detailed parodies of scenes from Alencar's urban novels, *Lucíola* and *Sonhos d'ouro,* in which even telltale details fit. What is vital is that he shows that this was an important creative process: at the same time that he mocks his predecessor's melodrama and unrealistic psychology and morality, Machado remodels Alencar's situations to suit his own purposes — parody, certainly, but now beginning to be understood in a wider explanatory context, for Machado has seen the realist potential in Alencar's absurdities.

We are beginning to build up a picture in which parody is not just an isolated exercise but a major constitutive element in the creation and structure of the *Memoirs,* whether at the level of style or situation — even, most intriguingly, at that of plot. It is, for instance, among other things, obviously a parody adultery novel. My own work as a critic, highly influenced by *Ao vencedor as batatas,* has contributed, too, to uncovering a somewhat parallel situation in the context of Brazilian history. In two books published in 1984 and 1986, I set out my findings concerning the numerous Brazilian historical references in Machado's work, arguing that they have a kind of order, reveal a consistent pattern of thinking on the subject, and are also most ofted coded, sometimes in quite abstruse ways; obviously, it was pleasant to find that Schwarz adopted my "method" in the context of the *Memoirs*. In recent years, it has become increasingly clear to me that, in the context of Machado's historical references too, unless some notion of deliberate parody enters into the account, their function will not be fully understood. Like Alencar's novels in this sense, the conventional markers of Brazilian history provide a story that can be used as a structure, but only on condition that they are simultaneously placed in quotation marks, so to speak, seen as an imitation of European (primarily French) history, and lacking the latter's conventionally accepted order and meaning. In other words, narrative structure and parody are intimately bonded, in several departments and levels.[32] It is not hard to see how much Machado's familiarity with the operation of misplaced ideas has to do with this apparent ease in inhabiting a world that might seem a mere shadow of its European "model."

A further, telling example of this same syndrome, which shows that its context is not exclusively Brazilian, is the reuse, again in critical vein, of situations and characters from the Portuguese novelist Eça de Queirós's novel *O primo Basílio* [*Cousin Basílio*]. Perhaps the best example of this parodic reworking of Eça's material can be found in the comparison of Juliana, the maid who discovers Luisa's letters to her lover and blackmails her, and Dona Plácida, the unfortunate dependent forced into the role of go-between in the *Memoirs*. As Machado says, the discovery of the letters is a mere accident and reduces the moral of Eça's novel to "The careful choice of one's servants is a condition for having a peaceful adulterous affair" (*OC*, 3:907)! The role and character of Dona Plácida might almost have been constructed on the basis of that sentence.

Machado was violently opposed to Zola on ostensibly conservative grounds. In fact, as Schwarz observes, he sounds out depths of sordidness that make naturalism look innocent in comparison (*Ao vencedor*, 156). As Schwarz points out, the chapters dealing with Brás's upbringing *compete with* naturalism: in other words, there was a sense in which Machado was quite consciously entering on the stage of world literature, where he belongs. He is gradually coming to be recognized as one of the great novelists of the late nineteenth and early twentieth centuries, and it is to be hoped that this book, and its publication in English, will further that recognition.

Inevitably, his belated arrival will cause changes. Schwarz refers more than once to the German literary historian and disciple of the Frankfurt school Dolf Oehler. His two books, published in German in 1979 and 1988, and which have unfortunately not been translated into English (though both are available in Portuguese), center on Baudelaire and Flaubert. In particular, they focus on their deliberately suppressed awareness of the crucial importance of the June massacres of 1848, the moment at which the clashing interests of the Parisian bourgeoisie and the working classes came into the open — the moment, too, when, according to Marx in "The Eighteenth Brumaire of Louis Bonaparte," history repeated itself as farce. In the despair following the events of 1848–51, an element of aggression and parody, and a recourse to secret, coded references to events everyone knew about but that bourgeois ideology had repressed, became a vital constituent of the best literature. In Baudelaire's poetry, in particular, this led to the sarcastic and coded identification of his lyrical subject with the "most abject side of the ruling class" — precisely Machado's trick in the *Memoirs*. To talk of possible influence would be at the very least an absurd simplification, although, unsurprisingly, Machado had read Baudelaire: what we are talking about are trends in literature that obey deeper forces. As Schwarz mentions in writing about Oehler in "Machado de Assis: Um debate, "what happened with two of the greatest writers in Western culture, Baudelaire and Flaubert, also happened to a certain extent with Machado — which makes one doubt that the dynamic is simply a Brazilian matter" (63). Schwarz's contexts seem primarily Brazilian, but (as I argued in my introduction to *Misplaced Ideas*), they refuse to be circumscribed in this way. The "master on the periphery" leads us, in fact, to change our perceptions of what happened in the hegemonic centers of European culture.[33] Thanks to this book, we no longer need simply assert that the *Memoirs* is the first great Latin American novel: we can understand why, and why views of the development of modern literature are incomplete without it.

My primary object has been to render Roberto Schwarz's text as accurately and accessibly as I could. This is not limited to the text itself: wherever possible, I have tried to point the way to English translations of the works quoted and have provided, in the glossary, a brief summary of the writers, figures of intellectual and historical importance, and one or two literary works and genres referred to, where they are not common knowledge — in practice this means that the vast majority are Brazilian. All such cross-references are indicated with an asterisk (*).

Schwarz is a very self-conscious, spare, and tight writer, acutely aware of the logic of his arguments. In his own account of his aims, he says that he is trying to get something of the force of the great dialectical writers — he mentions Marx, Adorno, Sartre, and Benjamin — into his work ("Machado de Assis: Um debate," 81). This can, obviously, be a challenge to the translator, the more so since the grammatical structures of Portuguese and English are not the same. To give one common example, relative pronouns in Portuguese are marked for gender, either masculine or feminine, and thus make their antecedents that much more easily identifiable. Sometimes, the only solution in translating into English is to break up a sentence. The inevitable result is a certain loosening of the tension of the original — but I have preferred to sacrifice that rather than logic or sense. In one aspect, I have made a particular effort to be faithful: a particularly attractive feature of Schwarz's style is an occasional "lapse" into a colloquial phrase, which often produces a release, even a laugh, as much the product of its accuracy and rightness as anything. I have always tried to find an equivalent, so that if the reader is surprised by such things, s/he can be assured it is deliberate.

One word should be commented on: "volubility" (*volubilidade*), which is central to the whole argument. The English word has one more meaning than its Portuguese equivalent, its most common one, that of "talkative." It should be made plain, then, that that is *not* the sense meant here, which is "changeable."

There are three English translations of the *Memórias póstumas de Brás Cubas,* two of them currently available: one from the 1950s by William Grossman, titled *Epitaph of a Small Winner,* and a recent one by Gregory Rabassa, *The Posthumous Memoirs of Brás Cubas.* Either can be used; I have preferred to give my own translations in the text itself. References are given by chapter number. Since the chapters are often quite short, this seemed the most practical expedient. For those who wish to consult the Portuguese, three editions can be particularly recommended: the critical edition used by Schwarz and published by the Comissão Machado de Assis (Rio de Janeiro: Instituto Nacional do Livro, 1960), which contains the numerous variants between the first edition in episodic form in the *Revista brasileira* and the later editions in book form; the Livraria Garnier edition (Rio de Janeiro/Belo Horizonte, 1988) and the Clássicos Scipione edition (São Paulo, 1994). These last two have very reliable texts, and the notes in the latter edition (by Cristina Carletti) are very full and helpful.

Many thanks, as usual, to Cristina Carletti and Nicolau Sevcenko for their hospitality in São Paulo, and to Elmar Pereira de Mello and Hilda White Rössle de Mello in Rio de Janeiro. Thanks, too, to Antônio Dimas and Elias Thomé Saliba for the loan of material for the writing of the introduction.

PREFACE

WHAT LIES BEHIND THE VIGOR of the novels of Machado de Assis's mature phase? Is there any relation between the originality of their form and situations peculiar to Brazilian society in the nineteenth century? What are we to make of the enormous shift in quality between *The Posthumous Memoirs of Brás Cubas* and earlier Brazilian fiction, including Machado de Assis's first works? To put it another way, what kinds of changes allowed a provincial cultural universe, completely lacking in credibility, tangibly secondhand, to be raised to the highest level of contemporary literature? These are the questions I have tried to answer in this book.

In a famous formulation, which represented for him a kind of aim to work toward, Machado said that the writer could be "a man of his time and his country, even when he deals with subjects remote in time and space." The critic was trying to secure for Brazilians the right to deal with every kind of subject matter, as opposed to the point of view "that only recognizes national qualities in works that deal with local topics." One could also say that he laid claim to the best portion of the Romantic legacy — the sense of historicity — as against the fashionable conjunction of the picturesque and the patriotic, which at that time was already turning out to be a straitjacket for the intelligence. That said, the Brazilianness that Machado had in mind, and would bring into being in the second phase of his work — an "interior" Brazilianness, "different and better than if it were purely superficial" — is not easy to demonstrate in detailed, concrete terms.[1]

The existence of this Brazilian quality did not pass unnoticed by contemporaries, as is proved in a comment by José Veríssimo,* published thirty days after Machado's death: "After reading *Brás Cubas* I began to understand that one could be a great Brazilian writer, without talking about Indians, hillbillies, and the outback."[2] However, if we don't want to enter the realms of the ineffable, how can we explain this Brazilianness, which dispenses with external signs of its own existence? To solve the problem, Veríssimo would say that Machado, the only universal Brazilian author, was also the most national of our writers. This idea has often been taken up again, and has become one of those commonplaces that, although not untrue, impede serious thinking rather than encouraging it.

Nevertheless, we must persevere. For the writer, remaining steeped in his own time and place even when he deals with distant topics is a worthy aim, and one of special interest for the reader of the *Posthumous Memoirs,* where this aim is realized — even though it is unrecognizable. True, we will see that there is nothing, in the past, in the future, in the beyond, or in Timbuktu, that the narrator of the *Memoirs* doesn't take delight in talking about, and always like a Brazilian of his time. It is easy to register this widening of the range of subjects discussed, but the national flavor in the manner of treating them is less obvious and needs to be characterized. On one hand, as something constant and relatively indifferent to content, this national flavor must be described as a form. On the other hand, no description that limits itself to this level, in the manner of formalist studies, can be adequate. This is because this form of treatment is assumed to carry within itself the parameters of Brazilian reality, and if these are not identified and analyzed by the critic, the essential aim of his undertaking will remain unrealized.

Later, we will show that Machado's narrative formula consists of a certain systematic alternation between perspectives, in which a play of points of view is perfected, produced by the workings of Brazilian society itself. This literary form captures and dramatizes the structure of the country, which becomes, so to speak, the musical staff, the order beneath the writing. And it is true that Machado's narrative prose is one of the very few that, simply in their movement, constitute a complex sociohistorical spectacle, of the greatest interest, and in which the surface subject is of little moment. In this respect, comparisons could be made with the prose of Chateaubriand, Henry James, Marcel Proust, or Thomas Mann.

Writing about the difficulties inherent in the reading of Baudelaire, Walter Benjamin observes that his is a poetry that has absolutely not aged — not because it was young when it was written but because the circumstances that it does not speak of, but against which the poet composed his voice and his character, are still in place and make *Les fleurs du mal* no less virulent and difficult today than the day they were born. Almost a century had passed—Benjamin's notes are from 1938—and the calm of historical distance had still not been established.[3] I hope to convince the reader that something similar holds true of Machado de Assis. The daring of his literary form, where a social lucidity, an insolence, and a penchant for misleading the reader go hand in hand, can be defined by the drastic terms of class domination in Brazil: through a calculated artistic ploy, the author adopts an unsustainable position, *which, however, is commonly accepted.* Nowadays, a hundred and ten years after the novel's publication, in spite of all the changes that have taken place, a substantial part of those terms of domination still remains in place, with its accompanying sense of being the accepted norm, all of which might explain the fact that his readers have been collectively hoodwinked, and that they are still defeated by Machado's novels, which are themselves more up-to-date and oblique than ever.

The first half of this study was published separately, in 1977, with the title *Ao vencedor as batatas* [The Winner Gets the Potatoes]. Although this book is a continuation of the earlier one, I have tried to write them so as to make them independent of one another. Even so, if it's not asking too much, I am sure that both benefit from being read together.[4]

The possible correspondence between Machado's style and the particularities of Brazilian society, slave-owning and bourgeois at the same time, occurred to me a little before 1964. The idea carries within it the concern with dialectics prevalent at the time, and added on top of that came the swift reversal of the following period.[5] As far as the social interpretation is concerned, the reasoning depends on arguments developed at the University of São Paulo by my teachers' generation, and especially by a group that used to meet to study *Capital* with a view to understanding Brazil.[6] The group had reached the daring conclusion that the classic marks of Brazilian backwardness should be studied not as an archaic leftover but as an integral part of the way modern society reproduces itself, or in other words, as evidence of a perverse form of progress. For the historian of culture and the critic of the arts in countries like ours, ex-colonies, this thesis has an enormous power to stimulate and deprovincialize, for it allows us to inscribe on the present-day international situation, in polemical form, much of what seemed to distance us from it and confine us to irrelevance.

Over the years, practically everything written here has been discussed with friends and students, and I thank them most sincerely. I owe a special note of gratitude to Antonio Candido,* whose books and points of view have had a pervasive influence on me that the footnotes cannot reflect. My work would also be unthinkable without the — contradictory — tradition formed by Lukács, Benjamin, Brecht, and Adorno, and without the inspiration of Marx.

I had the good fortune to obtain a scholarship from the Guggenheim Memorial Foundation in 1977–78, and to be invited to the Institute for Advanced Study in Princeton in 1980–81, which permitted two years of full-time dedication to Machado de Assis. At the Unicamp (Universidade Estadual de Campinas, São Paulo) my colleagues in the Department of Literary Theory had the camaraderie to grant me a semester's leave on two occasions, without which this book would not have been completed. My thanks to all.

I

TOP-CLASS EFFRONTERY

I

INITIAL OBSERVATIONS

A STRIDENT NOTE, NUMEROUS STYLISTIC TRICKS, and the urge to call attention to oneself dominate the beginning of *The Posthumous Memoirs of Brás Cubas* (1880). The tone is one of deliberate abusiveness, beginning with the nonsense of the title itself — for the dead don't write. The affectionate dedication "To the worm that first gnawed at the cold flesh of my dead body," set out like an epitaph, is another impertinence.[1] The same goes for the intimate way in which the reader is challenged at the beginning, if he doesn't like the book: "I reward you with a snap of the fingers, and goodbye" ("To the Reader"). And what is one to say of the comparison between the *Memoirs* and the Pentateuch, subtly biased in favor of the former, praised for their originality? Summing things up, it is a real firework display of impudence, in which one provocation follows hard on the heels of another, on a scale ranging from harmless little jokes to profanation.

This persistent recourse to effrontery, without which the *Memoirs* would be deprived of their peculiar rhythm, works as a technical necessity. To obey it, the narrator repeatedly invades the scene and "perturbs" the course of the novel. These interruptions, which always infringe some rule or other, are Machado's most obvious and famous device. Criticism on the novel has treated them as the result of the author's psychological makeup, as a deficiency in the narrative, as a witness of superior intelligence, as something borrowed from English literature, and as metalanguage: none of these ideas is mistaken. In this essay they will be seen as form, a term that will have two meanings: (a) a rule for the composition of the narrative and (b) the stylization of a kind of conduct characteristic of the Brazilian ruling class.

In Machado's novels there is hardly a phrase that doesn't have a second meaning or witty intention. His prose pays extreme attention to detail, and is always on the lookout for immediate effects: this ties the reader down to the minutiae and makes it difficult to picture the wider panorama. As a consequence, and also as a result of the narrator's campaign to call attention to himself, the composition of the whole is less apparent. But it does exist, and if we keep a certain distance, we can begin to see the outlines of a social structure. These outlines are what give a third dimension, or novelistic integrity, to the somewhat effortless brilliance of the witticisms in the foreground. Though difficult to define, this underlying unity is one of the secrets of Machado's work. After pinning it down, we will try to interpret it, a process that will lead us to its Brazilian circumstances.

Chapter One   *The Author's Demise*

I hesitated for some time as to whether I should open these memoirs at the beginning or the end, that is, whether I should put my birth or my death in first place. Granted, the common usage is to start with one's birth, but two considerations led me to adopt a different method: the first is that I am not exactly a writer who has died, but a dead man who has become a writer, and for whom the grave was a second cradle; the second is that my writing would thus be more elegant and novel. Moses, who also recounted his own death, didn't put it in the introduction, but at the conclusion: a radical difference between this book and the Pentateuch.

This much said, I died at two o'clock on a Friday afternoon in the month of August 1869, in my lovely little house in the suburbs, in Catumbi. I was some sixty-four years old, robust and prosperous, a bachelor; I was worth about three hundred *contos*,[2] and I was accompanied to the cemetery by eleven friends. Eleven friends! It is true that there were no letters sent out or notices in the paper. I should add that it was raining.[3]

The bumptious affectation of this opening, in which the impossible is said in the first-person singular, is very great. It seems clear that the situation of the "dead man who has become a writer," contrasting with that of the "writer who had died," with its deliberately *cheap* wit, does not destroy the realistic effect, even if it mocks it. On the contrary, it bolsters it, because without that realism it would be neither original nor funny. Instead of affirming the existence of another world, Brás wants to heap abuse on ours, which is his too, and to inflict his impertinence on us. It is a "cheap" and methodical humor, something like a practical joke, tiresome at first sight but still a vital find, as we shall see.

In other words, we have a *narrator who is deliberately impertinent and lacking in credibility*. And what is one to think of the literary doubts ("I hesitated for some time"), logical considerations, and choices between different methods paraded by the dead man? In the abstract, in their subject and tone, they would pass for the concerns of an enlightened gentleman. In the context, they are no less false than the status of the false dead man itself, something that makes them all the more insulting. They are posturings that are not intended to delude, nor do they hide anything. It is not a question, then, of believing them, or of looking for their truth or logical coherence, but of admiring their cheek and the virtuosity with which they are handled. At every turn Brás puts on the airs of a modern gentleman, only to disparage them the next moment, then take them up again, setting up a system of inconsequentiality that in the course of the novel will become the norm. It is as if enlightened conduct were equally deserving of respectful consideration and mockery, functioning at one moment as an indispensable norm, at another as an obstacle. These pendulum swings provide the outline of a mode of existence.

There is also something of a falsetto about the prose. The intonation of the first lines is prim and proper: "I hesitated for some time," "Granted, the common usage," "to adopt a different method." The same thing goes for the rhetorical tricks of the dead man, which sound as if they were in italics, with their starched syntax, and above all their antithetical constructions: *beginning* and *end, birth* and *death, common* and *different, grave* and *cradle,* and so on. The aim of showing off one's superiority is obvious, even if it is inseparable from the absurd narrative situation. Thus, prestige and its opposite are joined together in the novel's diction. They are there together at every moment, and behind the combination the narrator always wins out, always triumphs twice over, first when he points out the merits of his own rhetoric, and then when he laughs at its absurdity. It is true that the discourse and the ambiguities in this case are the dead man's, and that they characterize him as an individual — if one can call him that — but their import does not end there, for the eloquence is all set out in order to point to social prerogatives and give a dimension or an aftertaste of class to the writing.[4]

The satire at this point is bland, for the reader will easily concede that the affected use of official culture and the educated trappings (*hesitations, suppositions, considerations, method*) is amusing. And it contains no surprises, since the voice from beyond the grave automatically puts parody into everything it says. In the final sentence of the paragraph, however, in a break with this — in the end somewhat tepid — humor, comes a real bombshell, out of the blue: "Moses, who also recounted his own death, didn't put it in the introduction, but at the conclusion: a radical difference between this book and the Pentateuch." Distinguishing between his work and the Bible on one precise point, as if they were comparable in other respects, Brás Cubas shows that his mocking disposition is not going to be limited to metaphysical literary banter, or to games with verisimilitude and literary conventions. His courage doesn't fail him when it comes to a clear case of "bad taste," and it reaches its true fulfillment in outrage and blasphemy.

Far from being presumptuous, the parallel with the Scriptures is the product of another feeling, much less easily avowed: there is a malicious satisfaction in humiliating and insulting, in letting it be known that the narrator's insolence will stop at nothing, that not a stone will be left standing — all of which represents something superior or inferior for him, we don't know which. The contrast between this provocation and the previous ones is marked, since it is one thing to belittle literary good sense, counting on the reader's complicity — itself malevolent, since Brás Cubas himself is the object of laughter — and quite another to trivialize Holy Writ in the space of a short sentence. In this second case, the intention is to overstep the bounds. Of course, the literary effect is neither in the little jokes nor in the profanity taken separately, but in the sudden intimacy established between the two, as they follow one on the heels of the other. Ignoring the difference between them, the narrator unveils what was only hinted at in the first affronts to the reader: that is, the desire to provoke and destroy, which is either attenuated or accentuated by the frivolity of the diction. This unexpected shift from humor to open aggression, the first of a long series, is a key maneuver in the *Memoirs,* where it appears at every level, as subject matter, as narrative rhythm, as a quirk of diction, and so on. We will find it again in more developed forms, when we will attempt to interpret it. For the time being, we repeat that it is the culmination, the unveiling of what is latent and implicit in the liberties the narrator takes with the norms, whether literary or not. The exercise of abuse for its own sake, the basic material worked with in the *Memoirs* — and which will be described later on — has one of its moments of truth in these sudden shifts to something more serious, when the narrator's subjective excesses are given full play.

The reader will have felt, in the paragraph we have quoted, that the impression Brás makes changes with every proposition. The character that in the first line hesitates as to the best way to compose one's memoirs is not the same one who, straight away, promises — just like that — to enlighten us about death itself. In turn, this is not the same one who takes pleasure in the paradox of the dead man who has become an author, who again is not the same one concerned about the elegance and novelty of his style (and so about fashion), who is not the same one who makes the joke about the Pentateuch. There are no transitions in this rotation of different poses: it is an exercise in volubility, and the literary effect depends on the vivacity and frequency of the contrasts. To round it off, the cultivated prose — itself a pose — lends a varnish of respectability to the narrator's leaps, maneuvers, and transformations. This veneer in turn disguises the crude aspect of the insolence, at the same time as it gives depth to his social characterization, as well, of course, as producing a comic disproportion. In any event, this is a rhythm that presupposes calculated effects at every turn, and a prose written as if one were watching oneself in the mirror. The personifications have to be created and completed in the space of a sentence, with one eye on the sentence before, another on the one just coming, and a third on the reader, without all of which the element of the unforeseen, essential to the liveliness of this rhythm, cannot be guaranteed. It is true that its manipulative, exhibitionist dimension makes for unease, and leads to a reading enlivened by reservations and mistrust. In their turn, these will be brought to the surface and manipulated ("don't be turning your nose up at me" [ch. 4]), bringing right home to the reader the relationship that the novel is examining.

Which of Brás's faces is the real one? None in particular, of course. The more so as the narrative situation (the dead man who has become a writer) is a self-evident joke that plays havoc with the parameters of fictional reality. In other words, since the narrator lacks credibility, the features that he constantly puts on and takes off have an uncertain truth status and become an element of provocation: this latter, on the other hand, there can be no mistaking. The same goes for the lack of definition, or for the jokes, which destabilize the book's literary status: as they create doubts about genre, they allow the threat that a stab in the back might come at any moment to hover above the text. These are shifting sands, and the reader has to find his way as he can, without the guidance of agreed reference points, with only the narrator's words to point the way — words that are said right to his face, with the undisguised intention of causing confusion. A kind of "anything goes" in which, in the absence of a conventional framework, the narrative voice is important in every single line forces the reader into a state of continuous alert, or maximum attention, that is characteristic of great literature.

Paradoxically, the rhetorical artifice and blatant insincerity make for an effect of the most indiscreet kind of nakedness, because they reveal such an obvious desire to manipulate appearances. By means of an inversion that lies at the basis of modern literature, the mistrust in the artist's power of representation — whose innocence is placed in doubt — does not abolish reality but displaces it into the very act of representing, which becomes its ultimate foundation and is never disinterested. In these circumstances, it's not a question of knowing if Brás is a conscientious writer of his memoirs, a straight-faced comic, a snob, or a cultivator of profanities, but rather of accompanying the movements of the will going on behind this procession of different embodiments, somewhat at our expense. In place of the convention of veracity, which is prevented from taking shape by the narrator's continual transgressions, there is created between reader and author a de facto relationship, a struggle to fix meanings, and an attempt to label one another — what kind of wise guy is this narrator? what kind of wretch is this reader? — in which the one tries to bring the other down. And so, the representation flows along quite openly in the element of will, or better, of arbitrariness, and objectivity is at most an appearance that Brás likes to make use of from time to time.

In analogous fashion, we can see that the liveliness of the sentences depends, without exception, on the presence of some peccadillo or other that gives them their piquancy. To recount absurdities as if they were the truth, to show no respect for the common man, to sacrifice eternal verities to novelty, to affront religion, and so on are modes of conduct generally thought of as wrong, and that Brás flaunts for their own sake. How can we fail to judge him, even if it's to let him off? Not even the ill-humored, somewhat cynical kind of reader, who perhaps sympathizes with the character's excesses, forgets the norm being flouted. It is Brás who obliges one to make moral judgments, at the same time as he pays no attention to them, setting up a situation that at once has no rules and is normative, that is permanently morally out-of-court and characterized by the unpunished abuse of power. It may be added that the picture here is purely of the narrator's subjective character, constructed on the basis of provocations and stylistic exercises. It so happens that the only given of external reality — the narrator's status as a dead man — is unrealistic, which removes its factual nature and makes it nothing more than a witty fraud. So, in the absence of an undeniable material reality that would establish the illusion of objectivity and commit the narrator to not countering his own words, the reader has nowhere to grasp him and is delivered up to him, tied hand and foot. The narrative relationship is one of disloyalty, and the last word, though it has no authority, always belongs to the narrator.

This much said, when we move on to the second paragraph, the reader will have noticed a different climate. In the space of two sentences, we learn the time, day, and place of Brás's death, as well as his age, wealth, marriage status, and state of health. The sense of relief brought about by a few facts is remarkable. Instead of the disembodied and disturbing voice of the previous lines, we meet a character with a visible outline, placed in context, whom we can label. The narration is now simply figurative and at least in appearance shorn of other aims, something quite different from the memoir writer's expounding of his motives in the first paragraph. We are in the stylistic realm of realism, whose postulation of an objective reality shared by author and reader has nothing to do with the importunate narrator we have been describing. This explains the interval of tranquillity that accompanies this step, during which for one moment the reader escapes, or seems to escape, the machinations of the author-character. The contrast could hardly be more striking, but the cease-fire doesn't last long. Suppose we say that the eleven friends who take Brás to the cemetery are a *fact* and nothing more, at least the first time they appear. In the following sentence, however, they are turned into *resentment,* for eleven at a funeral is not enough — but this resentment itself is aimed, in its turn, at amusing the gallery. "Eleven friends!": the tone is bitter, the intention comic, and we are back to the skirmishes with the public, where reality and the past have no value in themselves but are pretexts for immediate, self-centered satisfactions, whose nature still has to be defined. Like everything else, the realist style was a means to an end, another literary register among many, subordinate to the arbitrary inconstancy of the narrator.

From another angle, this is a good example of the permanent *breathing* of the text, its alternation between contraction and dilation. After the hand-to-hand combat with the reader, the feints and blows below the belt, comes indifference — which also has its own specific kind of pleasure. Throughout the novel, it will appear in several forms, more pronounced even than realist impartiality. See, for example, the point of view of Sirius, infinitely distant, or sexual satiation, or the immeasurable "contempt of the dead," or again distance in the memory, "when time has run its course and the spasm is over." However, nothing is more relative than these absolutes: far from being final positions, they are always moments of passage back to the previous disquiet, which, along with them, makes up one of the essential rhythms of the *Memoirs*.

The music in the first paragraph is syntactic, and its humor lies in the tension between the elegant grammatical shapes and the absurdity of what is being said. I would be grateful if the interested reader wouldn't mind rereading the passage, paying attention to its movement. Its rhythm is strictly binary, marked by alternatives, parallelisms, antitheses, symmetries, disparities. Thus, at the beginning the narrator hesitates between two ways of opening his memoirs, at the beginning or at the end, a disjunction formulated a second time in the same sentence, in a parallel form (my birth or my death), only this time as an absurdity, heightened by the repetition. Even terms that appear to be isolated have an implicit pair that makes them members of this order of duality: if Brás hesitated "for some time," it's because he no longer hesitates; and the doubt about the "first place" leads to another, about the second. The hesitation in the first sentence is followed by decision in the next; a choice is made against "common usage" and in favor of another "method," itself determined by "considerations" (two of them, again), which underlines the narrator's pretensions to enlightenment. The first of these "considerations" takes up the nonsense of the opening sentence and amplifies it as a conceptual opposition ("I am not exactly a writer who has just died, but a dead man who has become a writer")[5] duplicated in its turn in the antithesis between the "grave" and the "cradle." On pain of breaking the parallelism, the second consideration should also contain figures of language and thought, and above all should have a binary rhythm. Not so: without rhetoric, and in simple fashion, it announces its desire to please. The pairing of adjectives (the "elegant" and the "novel") continues. Its relative lack of articulation, however — there is no symmetry with the previous sentence, and no antithesis or marked contrast between the adjectives — only accentuates the anticlimax, which is comic in intention. It is as if the organization of the sentence were saying that, when the chips are down, the method and the opinions of the author don't complement one another and are nothing but modishness. At this point in comes Moses, from the Bible, who "also" (that is to say, like his Brazilian counterpart) recounted his own death: he comes in on the pretext of being something old, in contrast to the new voice, which we're already familiar with.

On another level, by dividing and subdividing his subject matter, by enumerating the terms that constitute it, by underlining their opposition and contrast, all this being embraced in a single phrase or a single movement—this whole manner of exposition *logicizes* reality, so to speak. It presents reality as a field conquered by the mind, which disposes or pseudo-disposes of it as a whole, no less, and as a whole articulated and reduced to its essence, over which intelligence has triumphed. It is a procedure that presupposes breadth of vision, analytical capacity, fluency and concision in exposition, and more, none of which prevents all these acquisitions being present in a ridiculous, clownish version. All this extends the area of the mockery to little-known regions: for instance, to the sphere of the faculties of knowledge as such. And in fact, either because they involve impalpable, remote questions or because they are a serious topic, reserved for philosophy, these faculties never seemed to be of any use as fictional subject matter. Machado, however, perceived in them a strategic base for the study and exercise of arbitrary power, so much so that, as we will see, the comedy of interests implied in the activity of classification, schematization, and abstraction is one of the original aspects of his work. It is evident that this order of problems was taboo to the realist novel, with its belief in objectivity and the power of illusion, all of which put Machado's writing into an advanced position in the nineteenth century. On the other hand, the contrasts between the carefully constructed syntactic framework and the rough edges of reality are a type of humor of eighteenth-century English extraction, making one critic note that Machado used archaic means to gain modern effects.[6] Finally, the mixture of classical and realist registers, to which other dictions will be added, is part of the stylistic bazaar created in the nineteenth century by historicism.

2

A Formal Principle

He made a rule of composition out of his caprice . . .
Augusto Meyer, "Underground Man"[1]

WHAT CAN WE CONCLUDE FROM OUR OBSERVATIONS up to now? They show — I hope — the profusion and crucial nature of the relationships implied in the rhythm of Machado's prose, and the extraordinary contrasts between the voices orchestrated in its truly complex music. Yet, despite their diversity, these observations converge on two linked themes: the extreme volubility of the narrator and the constant disrespect for some norm or other.

We have seen that within the space of a few lines Brás feigns being dead, methodical, paradoxical, and elegant, among other things. Immediately after, in equally quick succession, he will be cynical, making a link between his will and the eulogy preferred to him at the graveside; indiscreet, insinuating that one of the ladies present at the funeral "though she was not a relative, suffered more than the relatives"; and a charlatan, setting out a plan to make money and achieve fame with the invention of the "Brás Cubas Plaster." The same is true if we go back to the prologue ("To the Reader"), where cajolery, insults, and appeals to the reader's snobbery alternate, everything governed by the urge to recruit readers, characterized too by a slight bow in the direction of a civilization of market forces. Summing up, if we try to generalize, we can say that the narrator never stays the same for more than a short paragraph, or, better, changes subjects, opinions, or styles with almost every phrase. With a varying rhythm, this mobility continues from the first line of the *Memoirs* to the last. Instead of accompanying it step by step, which, taken to its limits, would add up to a complete paraphrase of the novel, let us try to understand its logic.

There is an element of self-congratulation in this tendency to mutability, as there is in the rhetorical virtuosity on which it depends for its realization. There are endless somersaults, invariably accompanied by self-centered satisfaction on the narrator's part, for they are, so to speak, the proof of his superiority. Brás, like his little childhood friend who would only play at being king, minister, or general, aspires to "some kind of supremacy, any will do" (ch. 13): the expression is a good description of the experience that the narrative rhythm tries to catch and renew at every turn. The means it uses are the sudden changes we have referred to, in which, by definition and in case after case, something is broken, in either form or content, and the despotic caprice of the narrator-character is imposed. At each switch this same character takes back what he has said, admonishes his readers, and for the nth time declares himself witty and the winner. The forced character of this humor is very in-your-face, and will certainly have irritated many readers. However, the course of the book not only justifies it — it sets great store by it: for it is the deliberate — almost didactic — accentuation of perverse, authoritarian aspects of the volubility we have been trying to characterize.

This movement is completed at the level of the form, in the Babel of literary mannerisms: styles, schools, techniques, genres, typographical devices are changed, all this being determined by the same urge to achieve "some" kind of superiority — any kind. Thus, the narrative moves from the trivial to the metaphysical or vice versa, from the linear to the digressive, from the word to the sign (in the chapter [55] in the Shandyan mode, made up of dots, exclamation marks, and question marks), from chronological progression to time reversal, from the commercial to the biblical, from the epic to the intimate, from science to a riddle, from neoclassical to naturalist to banal cliché, and so forth. The contrasts are innumerable, between phrases, between paragraphs, between chapters, but only one effect is aimed at, the satisfaction of the same constant capriciousness. More than a bass drone, this is the general medium that gives the raw materials of the novel their pertinence, via the magic touch of absurdity. *We can say then that in the course of affirming itself, the narrator's versatility demotes all the contents and forms that appear in the* Memoirs, *and subordinates them to itself, so providing the narrator with a kind of fruition or enjoyment. In this sense, volubility is, as was suggested at the beginning of this book, the formal principle of the novel.*

How wide is its sphere of action? So as to stretch it as far as he can, the narrator adopts an encyclopedic range, itself disproportionate to the humble context of the anecdotes he tells and that make up the plot. This dissonance is important, and we will return to it. For now, we might note that the initial pages contain the names of more than thirty illustrious men, literary characters, famous monuments, important dates. Biblical, Homeric, and Roman times are mentioned, the Middle Ages, the Renaissance and the Reformation, the French classical century, the English Commonwealth, and Italian and German unification.[2] Just so there is no doubt about the area of jurisdiction that this volubility lays claim to, the delirium chapter (7) — itself another kind of mental extravagance — goes from the origins of time to its consummation, first forward, then again backward. In a more discreet key, there is also the tacitly encyclopedic quality of the cultural references, dissolved into the various different points of view. Thus, in the extraordinary chapter 2, which deals with the invention of the Brás Cubas Plaster, this latter is presented successively as a "grandiose and useful idea"; as an idée fixe, which swings around on its own account on a trapeze in the brain; as a panacea for hypochondria, destined to "relieve our melancholy humanity"; as the object of a request to the government for a patent, on a charitable pretext and with the real aim of making money; and as an opportunity "of seeing printed in the papers, shop displays, pamphlets, street corners, and, finally, on the little boxes of pills themselves, these three words: *Brás Cubas Plaster.*" Respectively, the references are to liberal-bourgeois ideology; the philosophy of the unconscious (in a comic guise); the contrast between traditional cures and modern medicine; government patronage; Christian aims; capitalist aims, and finally, the synthesis of old-style vanity and the new commercial spirit, in the mania for advertising. Can one imagine a more completely universalized plaster? To finish off, not even time and space, those final defenses of common sense, are safe: volubility squeezes them, stretches them, and explores them in every direction, in any way it pleases. In other words, we have a firework display of a caricatured universal culture, a kind of down-market universality, in the best Brazilian tradition, in which Brás Cubas's caprice takes as its province the total experience of humanity and makes itself absolute. *It is no longer a passing tendency, psychological or stylistic, but a rigorous principle, placed above everything else, and that therefore is exposed, and can be appreciated all along the line.* This universalization establishes the axis that gives ideological power to the *Memoirs.*

Thus, from its opening the novel presents us with a narrator-character who makes use of the whole Western tradition with spectacular insouciance. His superiority consists in never letting himself be caught unawares, either by others or by himself, and it is reaffirmed by the systematic deidentification of himself. The counterpart of this is the constant assumption of new roles: no sooner is one adopted that it is cast off. All through this process, one after another, all the ideas and forms at the disposal of the cultured man of his time are taken up and then dropped, and so relativized (and stereotyped and cheapened). These substitutions, with the simplified contrasts between them and the background of indifference they assume, certainly don't add up to a critique, though they borrow the irreverence and taste for demolition that such a critique might imply. If I can put it this way, it is an acritical or nonspecific irreverence. The same can be said for the insouciance with which Brás moves among areas separated by tradition, reducing them all to props for his ebullience. His endless agility, expressed in the sprightliness of the narrative, which has eighteenth-century, "philosophical" connections, depends on presuppositions that in the end he doesn't share. It is unimaginable without the analytical and expressive achievements of Enlightenment thought, and without the groundwork of secularization and unification of human experience that the Enlightenment carried through, a struggle whose spirit Brás does not share, even though he makes use of its results, always stamping it with a note of derision. The universalization of caprice, in this case, means the incorporation of the *results* of the Enlightenment, but without the corresponding creative *process,* and under the guidance of a principle — still to be identified — opposed to it.

In sum, this is a narrative technique that is not restricted in range and not short on implications. Separated from its critical, reforming impulse, the Enlightenment switches tracks and becomes a kind of license; what is left is the stock of human experiences, all equivalent in their laughable way of operating, and which are banalized and offered up for the dissipated enjoyment of a cultured man, whose characteristics as a member of a peculiarly Brazilian class — Machado de Assis's literary specialty — we will examine later on.

3

THE PRACTICAL MATRIX

WHAT IS THE REFERENT — IF THERE IS ONE — captured and imitated in this prose form? The practice of arbitrary whim in the narration, an insult to common sense, would seem to take us to the erratic fluctuations of a single individual, and so to locating the *Memoirs* outside the field of realism. In an analogous fashion, the spectacular presence of metaphysical topics, "exotic" literary procedures and celebrities from all the corners of the globe (Lucretia Borgia, the battle of Salamis, Bismarck, Aristotle, etc.) would seem to imply an imaginary space whose boundaries are not determined by Brazilian matters. The thesis we are advancing, and that we will try to convince the reader is well founded, goes in the opposite direction. Without prejudice to the unlimited and, in that sense, universal boundaries of its sphere of action, the narrator's volubility and the series of abuses implicit in it retain the specific features, or, to use Antonio Candido's terms, are the "structural reduction," of a motion or course imposed on the Brazilian ruling class by historical circumstances — or, if one prefers, that those circumstances allowed it to have.[1] The explanation of this step requires a moment of extraliterary reflection, whose relevance, impossible to prove on the model of $2 + 2 = 4$, can be substantiated in the increased understanding that it hopefully allows.[2]

It is well known that Brazil's political emancipation, even though it included the transition toward a new phase of capitalism, had a conservative character.[3] The liberal conquests of Independence altered the political process in the upper echelons and redefined Brazil's foreign relations, but they did not reach the socioeconomic complex generated by colonial exploitation, which remained intact, as if it were owed a revolution. In other words, the master and the slave, the plantation and its dependent workers, the slave trade and export monoculture stayed the same, in a local and world context that was transformed. As far as ideas were concerned, the justifications that colonization and absolutism had created for themselves had fallen into discredit and were now replaced by the nineteenth-century horizons of the nation-state, free labor, freedom of expression, equality before the law, and so forth, all of these incompatible with those earlier justifications, and in particular with the direct personal domination of one person over another. On the politico-economic level, the international system centered on capitalist — especially British — industrialization was being consolidated, and its liberal side was the model to be copied, in the mind of the century.[4] What was the significance, in these circumstances, of the persistence of a system of production set up in the previous period?

To begin with, the new coordinates, themselves the expression of the historical change in the world's economy, brought with them a widespread switching of signals: what had been positive before became negative and above all retrograde. Moreover, the local, Brazilian course of events produced bewilderment, that is, when it did not produce dissenting opinions. The African slave trade, for example, continued to be big business, "the most lucrative on earth" (Alencastro, 409), until its final suppression in 1850. The same thing goes for the ascendancy of coffee in Brazil, decisive and long-lasting: the prosperity it brought was based on slavery and, later, on semiforced labor, a system that has lasted down to our own times. Thus, the country's links to the revolutionized order of capital and of civil liberties not only didn't change the *backward* means of production; it actually reinforced and promoted them in practice, and on these foundations laid a process of evolution based on *modern* premises, all of which naturally showed up an unexpected side of progress. The colonial labor dispensation, which gave the worker no rights, now began to operate for the profit of the newly established Brazilian ruling class, which had vital interests in its continuance, for the sake of its own advancement. The culturally segregated labor force, with no access to the freedoms that had become the standard, was thus no longer an ephemeral survival and became a structural part of the independent country, along with parliament, the constitution, revolutionary patriotism, and so on, all of them equally indispensable. From the practical perspective, slavery was a *contemporary* necessity; from the emotional perspective, a *traditional* presence; and from the ideological perspective, an *archaic* disgrace — all of them contradictory attributes, but real in the light of the historical experience of the ruling class.

As far as liberal ideas are concerned, we find a similarly contrasting set of evaluations. Since they are necessary to the organization and identity of the new state and of the elite, they represent progress. On the other hand, they express *nothing* of the reality of actual labor relationships, which these liberal ideas either reject or fail to recognize *in principle,* not that this prevents the elite from living with them quite congenially. From this stems a special kind of modus operandi that has no obligations to the cognitive and critical duties of liberalism, all of which undermines the latter's credibility and gives it, along with its enlightened side, an aura of the *gratuitous,* the *incongruous,* and the *iniquitous.* This complementarity between bourgeois and colonial institutions was present at the nation's origins and still has not completely disappeared. Because of its key position, and also because it has its picturesque side, when one considers its *deviation* with respect to the Anglo-French canonic norm,[5] this articulation — disjointed by its very nature — has been at the center of theoretical and literary reflection about Brazil, and indeed has become almost its distinctive mark. However, one has only to look at the new international division of labor, in which it was the ex-colonies' lot to be the consumers of manufactured goods and the providers of tropical products, to understand that the modern development of backwardness was only in the first instance a Brazilian (or Latin American) aberration. Its real basis lay in what Marxist tradition identifies as the "unequal and combined development of capitalism,"[6] an expression that points up the unruffled sociological calm peculiar to this mode of production, which achieves its economic aim — *profit* — either on the ruins of earlier forms of oppression or by reproducing and aggravating them.[7] Quite the contrary to what the appearance of backwardness makes one suppose, the ultimate cause of Brazil's absurd social formation is in the advances of capital and in the planetary order created by these advances; the absurd conduct of our ruling class is as legitimate an expression of its *up-to-dateness* as is Victorian decorum. That said, we can say that Brazil was being opened up to the commerce of the nations, and virtually to the totality of contemporary culture, by expanding modes of social organization that were becoming anathema to the civilized world (Alencastro, 414).

The most drastic aspect of this situation was to be found in the Atlantic slave trade, forbidden as "piracy" in international law, condemned from a religious, moral, political, and economic point of view, shorn of the government sponsorship it had once enjoyed, in a word, transformed into an immense illegal undertaking — and yet to which the normal operation of Brazilian commerce was tied, structurally associated as it was with this violation of the law (Alencastro, 408, 417). An observation of Luiz Felipe de Alencastro's, according to which the new government, when it was negotiating the diplomatic recognition of Independence, obtained legitimacy abroad by promises of abolition, and at home by guarantees of the continuity of slavery, gives the measure of the dissonance (401–2). In short, independent Brazil had been set up in a manner that was sui generis, with its own practical and moral-ideological issues, of enormous general relevance, in which the present state of the world revealed some of its secrets and could, in its turn, be problematized.[8] We are not, of course, trying to write a history of Brazil here, only attempting to set out succinctly the contradictory framework of experience that would be figured forth and investigated by the literature of a great author.

Taking up the thread of our argument about the prose of *Brás Cubas,* we can see that its form reproduces structural implications of the historical picture set out here. A vital part of the volubility, as we have described it, is the accelerated and perfunctory consumption of attitudes, ideas, convictions, literary manners, and more, soon abandoned for others and thus discredited. This movement has recourse to the stock of enlightened appearances, and in this way, when it is taken to its final consequences, mocks the *totality* of contemporary thinking, which is subordinated to a principle contrary to it and thus deprived of credibility. This is the course or trajectory that history allowed, or imposed on, the Brazilian ruling class taken as a whole. This class, too, had to inspect and absorb the relevant culture of its time, so that it could, in patriotic fashion, acclimatize it to the country, that is, associate it to the institution of slavery, whose kernel of discretionary personal domination, however, mocked pretensions to civilization and was no longer publicly sustainable. Now, a legitimacy based on contrary *raisons d'être* is a matter for disquiet, making for permanent internal and external dislocation, and lack of self-identity. Thus, leaving aside for a moment the historical conditions, these are the consequences, the traits everyone shared. An example is the unusual combination of eagerness for and, at bottom, indifference to intellectual novelties, and the rapidity and wide embrace of these twists and turns, as well as an effect of generalized demoralization. From another angle, we can see that volubility always contains some kind of *disrespect,* and an equivalent *self-satisfaction,* so that the tones of the *inadmissible* and of *affront* become omnipresent in the narrative. The same terms and the same heterodox ordering of priorities had been set up, in the practical world, by the advantageous slave-based situation of our liberal elite, with its corollary of respectable, *bien-pensant* illegality. Finally, we suggested that the dizzy changes in the narrator's attitude presupposed the intellectual and stylistic resources of the Enlightenment. In this sense they came *later* and placed themselves as if in a more *advanced* position. One by one Brás Cubas's transgressions — the documents of his "supremacy" — pointed to the powerlessness of the enlightened position and overtook it, leaving it behind. On the other hand, we have seen, equally clearly, that voluble conduct always comes *before,* denoting a *previous* stage, a primitivism ridiculous to advanced minds. In other words, the movement of volubility contains in itself opposing logical sequences, and contradictory evaluations of the historical position of reason, which is seen simultaneously as having been overtaken and as not yet having been reached. In the world outside art, the triumph and the promising future of social structures that were obsolete, and condemned to disappear, implied a perplexity of the same kind.

At the risk of repeating ourselves, we should underline this ideological ambivalence of the Brazilian elite, which is truly a part of their destiny. They wanted to be part of the progressive and cultured West, at that time already openly bourgeois (the norm), without that affecting their being, in practice, and with equal authenticity, members and beneficiaries of the last large slave-owning system in that same West (the infringement). Now, was there a problem in figuring simultaneously as a slave owner and an enlightened individual? For anyone concerned about moral coherence, the contradiction could be embarrassing. However, since reality didn't force one to choose, why forgo the obvious advantages? Might not moral coherence be another name for a failure to understand the way life really works? Giving credit to the norm and despising it at the same time were in the nature of the case. . . . Backed up by stable class interests and linked to the historical framework of society, the daily process of adjustment between accepted ways of social existence, which according to the then dominant European ideology would be called contradictory, engendered and diffused throughout the social fabric this oscillation between criteria that we are trying to capture.

Thus, Brazilian life imposed on the bourgeois conscience a series of acrobatic stunts that scandalized and irritated the critical sense. An example is provided by a famous parliamentary speech by Bernardo Pereira de Vasconcelos,* according to which, contrary to the usual way of thinking, it was Africa that would civilize Brazil. To the surprise of his colleagues in the Chamber of Deputies, the statesman explained: "Yes, Brazilian civilization came from there, because from that continent came the robust workman, the only one who under these skies . . . could have produced, as indeed he did produce, the wealth that provided our fathers with the means to send their sons to study in the academies and universities of Europe, and there to acquire knowledge of all branches of learning, the principles of the Philosophy of Law in general, and of Constitutional Public Law, which gave the impulse toward Independence and hastened it into being, presiding over the organization hallowed in the Constitution and in other laws arising from it, and strengthening liberty at the same time."[9]

In these circumstances, could the friends of progress and culture be the enemies of slavery? Shouldn't they support it? Mustn't the enemies of the shameful institution also be the enemies of law, the Constitution, and liberty? Or, rather, as well as being an infringement, the infringement is the norm, and the norm, as well as being a norm, is an infringement, *just as in Machado's prose*. In short, this progressive defense of the slave trade raised ideological problems that were difficult to solve, and embodied that portion of falsity and affront to common sense that accompanies the life of ideas in modern slave-owning societies. This ambivalence had foundations in reality, and Machado de Assis, as we will see, knew how to imagine its immediate and more distant implications.

Bernardo de Vasconcelos's speech pointed to the nonliberal foundations of Brazilian liberalism and invited the deputies to realize the interests that the classes who looked to the progress of civilization had in barbarism, another name the nineteenth century reserved for the slave system. This lucidity did not eliminate — but underlined — the contradiction, which could only be lived with thanks to the connivance of those the system favored. But this connivance was not limited to the rich: it could also be found among people of modest means, who depended on the rich via various forms of clientelism. In other words, and always keeping the nature of Machado's humor in mind: the Europeanizing sectors of Brazilian society did participate in bourgeois civilization, though in a peculiar fashion, at somewhat of a distance, which made them invoke the authority of that civilization and refuse to obey it, alternately and indefinitely.

The expansion of caprice in the *Posthumous Memoirs* has a kind of grandeur about it. Brás submits virtually the totality of subject matter and forms, no less, to this caprice: something that, it should be said, requires a varied literary invention, on a grand scale, for without it this subjection could not come into being. But it is also true that, despite his superiority, asserted at all times, the narrator always appears as an inferior figure; something about his triumphs doesn't ring true, and their sum adds up to a defeat. How can we explain this inversion, or better, this concomitant effect of superiority and belittlement? The volubility, in this case, is a relational value, whose conception and evolution are always thought of in relation to the bourgeois model of objectivity and constancy. It recognizes the primacy of this model, at the same time as it must show disrespect for it, in order to affirm its own primacy. Recognition of and disregard for this norm are what determine its movement, reflected in the play between superiority and inferiority. Thus, though in a negative manner, the bourgeois spirit is a constituent part of Machado's volubility, and the manifestations of that volubility depend on it, even down to their details. Despite its brilliant career, caprice carries within itself a perspective that makes it look like a deficiency, somewhat difficult to pin down but plainly visible. This failing can be understood in a metaphysical register (the precariousness of the human spirit "in general"), and in terms of contemporary history (as a peculiarity and sign of the backwardness of Brazilian society). The two readings are both unavoidable, and rather than preferring one to the other, one should interpret the fact that they coexist, a process that depends on an attentive appreciation of the overall movement of the novel.

Seen from the angle of literary composition, that simultaneous impression of mastery and inferiority has to do with the aftereffect of the life that is narrated on the voice that is doing the narrating. As the reading advances, we become familiar — in practice — with the rhythm and the breadth of Brás's imagination (the *superiority*). At the same time, at the level of the anecdotes that make up his world, there is one case after another of mental disarray, both in himself and in others. Already in the first pages appear the delirium, the idée fixe of fame, the fixation with the family tree, lies told with the greatest conviction, and more, all of which mark out an area of recognizable craziness, into which the memoir writer's volubility — itself an inordinate way of boasting and showing off — is integrated quite naturally, as just one more instance of the same thing (the *belittling*). Along the same lines, there is a kinship between Brás's sovereign freedom of spirit, metaphysics and all, and the humiliating atmosphere of genealogical faking, miraculous plasters, and self-seeking funerary orations that he lives and thrives in: a circumscribed, discredited atmosphere, with a great deal of local flavor, where the exhibitions of false culture and the facile taste of the narrator for pseudo philosophy and the genre of the apologue fit in perfectly.[10] The deep unity of the book depends on this kinship, which in turn explains the polyvalence, or doubt, that dogs the *Memoirs'* narrative gesticulations: are they a supreme elegance, an elementary failure of composition, or a provincial illusion?

Thus, the volubility is a general feature from which nothing is safe, which does not prevent it equally being an obvious form of foolishness, with a local, picturesque, and *backward* effect. At one moment it functions like the substratum and basic truth of human conduct (contemporary included), which only the mad fail to recognize; at the next as an example of a deluded form of conduct, somewhat primitive when judged against the background of the bourgeois norm and used as an element of local color and satire. This basic uncertainty, far from being a defect, is an artistic achievement of very great power, which gives the objectivity of form to an ideological ambivalence inherent to the Brazil of its time. The bourgeois, enlightened, and European criterion, according to which caprice is a weakness, is no more or less real or "Brazilian" than the criterion that emanates from our nonbourgeois social relations, in which the element of personal, arbitrary will is prominent; this latter in its turn detects and uncovers the presence of caprice everywhere, above all in the would-be objectivity of that other world that condemns it. Where is real superiority to be found, and which side should one take? Modeled on the practical interest of a single social class that is as linked to bourgeois precepts as to the discretionary, arbitrary aspect of slavery and clientelism, the two evaluations existed and were backed up by the guarantee of experience and necessity. In other words, more real than the conflict was the accommodation between them, incongruous but advantageous, one of the marks of Brazil's "monstrous" inscription in the contemporary scene. The form, in this respect reflecting the daily life of the ruling classes, does not attempt to dramatize the opposition between these two points of view and bring them to a crux—which would be unreal. But it goes beyond this, to the extent that it makes them coexist and switch places in an extremely restricted space, with a systematic intent, underlining and drawing out the incongruous effects of their coexistence. The result is an alternation with a great deal of satirical, Brazilian scope, where the inconsistency of the criteria, or better, the duality of the standards applied figures as a permanent, inexorable reality, the simultaneous proof of inferiority and superiority, which provides the subject matter of the novel with a total context. To complicate matters, it may be noted that Machado's stylization of the Brazilian preeminence of caprice is carried out according to the model of English *whimsicality*.[11]

In other words, Brás Cubas's volubility is a narrative mechanism in which a set of problems of great importance in Brazilian terms is implicated. These problems accompany the stages of the novel, which in turn are given their immediate context by them, even when they are not made explicit or even alluded to. An effect of tacit complexity is created, present at every instant, even at moments of apparent simplicity, which is a fact of composition and, naturally, a trump card in Machado's prose fiction. *They are the properties, one could say the automatic properties, of a literary organization, which speaks its own language and can be studied, so to speak, in the abstract.* Or, to say the same thing another way, these are the contents of the prose form itself, ubiquitous, nonthematic presences, to a certain extent independent of the vicissitudes of the action, to which they nevertheless respond, composing with them a harmony with a profound Brazilian and historical resonance. When in the famous essay "The Instinct for Nationality" (1873) Machado preferred the "intimate feeling of his time and country" over local picturesqueness, I presume that he had in mind something of this more impalpable situation, as he formulated the problem to which, seven years later, the prose of *Brás Cubas* would provide the solution (*OC* 3:817). Let us look in detail at some of the results of this narrative pattern, whose inner articulation can be read as the transcription and exposure of a historical destiny.

4

SOME IMPLICATIONS OF THE PROSE

THE SUDDEN AND REPEATED CHANGES in the narrator's character form the elementary cells of the literary device — volubility — that we are studying. For the narrator, the jump from one personification to another brings three kinds of satisfaction or "supremacy" with it. The first is linked to the taste for novelty; another to the offhand abandonment of a previous manner; and the third to the putting-down of the reader, who is disoriented and inevitably tuned in to the "old" character, the previous one, who has just fallen by the wayside. With the repetition of the cycle, each promising novelty ceases to be one and goes to join the other abandoned positions: their relative weight then grows and this in its turn lowers the value of future novelties that, although unexpected, will, when they make their appearance, already seem ripe for rejection. Discredited, the prestige of novelty will become just as sterile as the other two pleasures, and the movement itself is thus deprived of any justification outside the instants of unacceptable and subjective superiority that it provides. Even so, insofar as it lies within its power to do so, its movement engulfs the whole universe.

The relation of content between Brás's satisfactions and the appearances he adopts and then puts aside is minimal. His mocking indifference in this respect is the essential thing about the superiority itself. Thus, to each satisfaction there corresponds, at the level of the figures the narrator takes up, only to free himself from them at the next moment, the cessation and frustration of a dynamic. For instance, how would conflict X continue, if it were elegantly laid out in analytic prose? Allegorical prose comes onstage and can't provide the answer, all to good comic effect. In the same spirit of inconsequentiality, concerned only with immediate effects, the spontaneous aims that keep the narrator going don't advance the situations in which they are inscribed, nor do they deepen them: they don't have the time, their horizons are too narrow, their substance is too simple. The disproportionate side of this makes one laugh, because it challenges reality and implies irresponsible conduct on the part of the narrator. In the end, all it is is a subjective urge to reconfirm one's own power, and its substance lies in a lack of commitment to anything. The solution, monotonously the same throughout, is standardized as a mechanical operation: the arbitrary abandonment of one position for another. The substance of this movement is provided for the novel by contemporary history, on which caprice is superimposed, or, again, on which caprice imposes its limited, primitive dynamic. The effect is violently *reductive*. Insufficiency and dissatisfaction are part of the very idea contained in this rhythm.

Generalizing therefore, the witty, clever moment, the one the narrative tries to produce and reproduce over and over again, lies in the interruptions. It is through them that the narrator seeks recognition, and it is by means of interruptions — as if they were a kind of victory — that its subjective movement is carried to fruition. In other words, subjective satisfaction and objective frustration are systematically linked in the rhythm of the form. The short segments and the strong contrasts, in which discontinuity is highlighted, are the formal rule and an artistic necessity.

This discontinuity is extended without disfunction to the subjective and objective spheres: since the narrator's superiority lies in cutting his obligations, continuity cannot seem any more tolerable to him in his personal existence than at the level of subject matter. The innumerable and extremely varied interruptions and self-interruptions that populate the *Memoirs* are the expression of this necessity, and in fact they make this process of segmentation all-pervasive.

Apparent exceptions are the anecdotes, comic theorizing, and short semiallegorical tales scattered through the novel. However, since they are intercalated passages, their presence constitutes an interruption in itself. And if we examine their tone, we will see that they illustrate precisely the triumph of whim, of an unfitness for reality — as well as being short, having no direct continuation, and brilliantly serving Brás's need to be brilliant. Whether it is on the level of the form, through the interruptions, or on that of the content, through the anecdotes and apologues about the vanity of human affairs, there is no change in the experience that the prose aims at capturing. Finally, we can observe that apologues, anecdotes, vignettes, puzzles, caricatures, unforgettable human portraits, and so forth — all short forms, in which Machado shows his consummate mastery — are forms closed off in themselves, and in this sense second-class novelistic material, foreign to the demand for overall, global movement proper to the nineteenth-century novel. It is true that they are given new meaning by their harmony with the narrator's motives, which ensures that they have their function within the *Memoirs* as a whole, but that does not mean that they lose their other aspect, that of an easy, showy genre, with something commercial about it, linked to the exhibition of a simple kind of virtuosity. Curiously, the absolute rigor with which Machado bent the form of the realist novel to the demands of volubility, a rigor that carries within it a large dose of bitterness and disbelief in relation to contemporary society, allowed him to make good use of amiable, accessible, well-accepted ways of mirroring society, in a spirit not that different from Macedo's *A moreninha,** or the newspaper *crônica** of the day, all of which must have facilitated the success of such a strange writer.

Taking up the thread again, we can say that in the *Memoirs* the representation of contingent reality, characteristic of the novel as a form, has no continuity, or, better, never fulfills itself. At every turn the narrative interrupts it and transforms it into a jumping-off point for a move toward self-satisfaction, whether it be for the narrator, the characters, or the reader, and this happens therefore *at the expense of reality*. The regular repetition of this move can easily be observed through the various differing circumstances: it dominates them, in fact, and takes on a metaphysical air, in which the realistic details find that their historical or psychological import is defused, and that they come to serve as the allegory of a higher truth or of some worn-out abstraction: what stands out clearly is the *universal* figure of the human spirit, eternally incapable of limiting itself to reality and reason, always ready for a flight into the realms of the imaginary.

This setup is reflected in many ways. If human beings are unchangeably disposed to be capricious, the multiplication of episodes and the very variable ways of conveying them are superfluous. This conclusion, moreover, finds support in the novel itself, which at times seems to say "the same thing over and over . . . the same thing . . . the same thing" (ch. 8). Yet, because it is unnecessary, all this abundant empirical reality is itself marked as gratuitous or capricious; it is not merely the portrait of this caprice but its effective presence. In this sense, the redundancy is irritatingly functional: this, however, does not cancel out earlier reservations about its lack of continuity. What is more, while it is true that the narrator's versatility, once it is clear that it is universally applied, can dispense with the multitude of situations, ideas, and styles that add nothing to our conception of it, an inverse process also takes place: the profusion of circumstances discredits volubility's claims to universality, making it operate as an absurd, laughable rationalization of individual social and psychological interests.

One constant emerges from these many changes, and its relation to them is that of an essence to an illusion. It so happens that among Brás's various attitudes there is one — one of the commonest — that says just this, and, for good or ill, seems to formulate the real meaning of this device. It is a philosophical, or philosophizing, attitude, which proffers generalities about things human in a sententious or aphoristic form. Its topics are the constancy of inconstancy and the universality of self-centeredness. Nevertheless, though unified by this reflective stance, this attitude is not homogeneous either: it is fed by Ecclesiastes, French moralists, eighteenth-century materialism, liberal universalism, nineteenth-century faith in science, and the philosophy of the unconscious. These are mutually incompatible intellectual horizons, whose plurality is basic in the construction of the book's problematic and farcical atmosphere, as we will see later. For now, let us grasp the fact that universalism is brought to the surface in actual fact and, frequently, by the narrative movement, as well as being glossed at regular if sporadic intervals in a "philosophical" register: this accounts for its solid presence, which is in acute contrast with the variety and suggestive power of the empirical realities present in the novel.

The opposite ends of this discord are literary and ideological attitudes that remain stable, as well as being comic. They are, respectively, the detail from everyday existence that has no realist function, that is, that lacks continuity at the level of the plot; and a universalism without a critical function, or with a false one. Each one in its way — that is, the trivial daily presence and the flat generalities — ensures the primacy of innocuousness. The whole designates, however, in depth, a real historical experience. Machado was well aware of the narrow, conservative nature of this position, as well as its Brazilian dimension, so much so that in "Education of a Stuffed Shirt," the key to his mature satirical style, an aspirant to success on the national stage listens to a complete lecture on the topic.[1] According to the father/teacher in this story, the surefire way of saying nothing and avoiding controversy is to limit oneself, on one hand, to "minutiae" and, on the other, to "metaphysics," which are complementary extremes, each as empty as the other. And in fact, in Machado's prose, small talk and great abstractions form an inseparable comic duo, like Laurel and Hardy, pointing up the bad fit between familiar reality and more ambitious thinking — a fatal tendency in Brazilian thought still operative today. However, we can still note an inversion of roles, which is interesting from the point of view of literary evolution: the observed empirical reality exchanges its realistic potential for an allegorical function, working toward a generic picture of the human spirit, while abstraction, uncharacteristically, is examined from the several angles of its insertion in a practical context and acquires social dimensions. The local material is the basis for a universalistic perspective, while universalism, permeated by circumstantial interests, which it thus begins to express, takes on the shape of a historic dynamic and functions as an ideology.

By definition, the victory of caprice means the defeat of subjectivity in its demanding bourgeois meaning, which weighs on that subjectivity like remorse. In search of immediate satisfaction for the imagination, the narrator, the character, or the reader gives up on the external or internal relationship that at any given moment they *really are in*. As we see, when it is transformed into a rule, volubility makes any consistency in ideas or in actions impossible, and without this, the power of the subject-narrator, which lies in the effort to transform reality, and himself, does not exist: nor does the dialectic between individual and society, since the individual consciousness does not reach the point of giving shape to itself as an effective force. Right in the middle of the era of individualism, that is an important kind of abdication, ideologically crucial. The series of effects it brings about, in literary terms — it is no exaggeration to say that they are powerful and profound — gives some idea of the sheer extent of its implications.

Let us begin with the discrepancy between the idea that the volubility has of itself, and the picture that emerges from an overall appreciation of its dynamics. Step by step, we accompany a spectacle in which caprice sets the imprint of its own freedom, or will, on what seems to be necessity: the accent is on the primacy of the mind over the circumstances. The impression made by the whole, however, is totally different. The movement of volubility conforms to a simple, repetitive principle, which is even — what a humiliation for the conscious mind! — open to explanation in mechanical terms (Brás Cubas ventures various theories to that effect). Where caprice seems to reign, causality is in fact in charge; the diversity doesn't manage to hide the monotony, and the key to interior existence turns out to be a simple mechanism — what is more, of a grotesquely (pseudo)scientific type. The rejection of the kind of conditionings postulated by positivism, naturalism, and so on is no more than a vain boast and only gives further depth to the triumph of determinism. In the same line of argument, it can be noted that, since the narrator's motion is produced not by the clash between two positions but by the pressing need to substitute one for another, it is infinite — in other words, interminable. You can't say it advances, much less that it ends; it repeats itself, and the most one could say is that it is gradually worn down. In appearance it is as free as one could wish; in fact it is compulsive, and exhaustion is its only true result, the real lesson it has to teach. Taken singly, the exchanges that make it up are witty moments, because of the contrasts of style and position they imply, but the process seen as a whole is dreary and depressing. What is this picture, in which superiority, cunning, constant initiatives, clarity in aims and movements produce such an impression of inferiority, impotence, inertia, meaninglessness, and more?

From another angle, putting together all these inverted or clashing effects, we can say that there is movement and the sense of a final aim on the subjective side, where repetition and, as a consequence, stasis are the rule (the *perpetuum mobile* of Brás's caprices, which are always identical to one another), whereas on the social side there is no logic or coherent tendency to be noted. Here, the impression is of haphazardness and little articulation, though this does not affect the fact that substance lies on this, the social side, in opposition to the frivolity of the subjective element. What is secondary is in motion, though it is going nowhere, whereas what is essential is motionless, giving an acute feeling of a meaningless life.

Something parallel happens in the texture of the prose. From the artistic point of view, the volubility stands out more, and is the more dizzying, as the various patterns it makes are shorter and more defined. That is the reason for the stylistic search for values that may contrast and even conflict in the level of the demands they make, but that can be brought together by means of clever formulas — values such as the essential, the sophisticated, the facile, the famous, the topical, which can only cohabit in the context of a cheapened aesthetic norm such as this. The proximity to the epigram, the commonplace, and the anthology set piece is yet another provocation — that is, when it's not a cue for applause. This is above all a showy style of writing, which presupposes varying and contrasting ways of proceeding, such as a daring, analytical exploration of different subjects, the gathering of set phrases and famous quotations (whether or not they are relevant), the coining of pithy expressions with a classical or official look, the mocking invention of aesthetic, moral, and intellectual solecisms — though appearances are always kept up. In short, this may be an ingenious process of construction, but absurdity is one of its essential ingredients. The results act as fixed supports and give the prose an accelerated mobility, with the corresponding pretense of control. Thus, as well as inhibiting any possibility of movement in the materials he uses, by means of the dividing, segmenting tendency of the prose, the narrator brings these same materials into our purview in finished form, free of the clash between thought and experience, with none of the marks of the process in which they originated. This is a "perfection," however, which is produced according to a debased criterion, and the continuous note of futility, which puts it in its rightful place, acts as a commentary on it.

The scandal of the *Memoirs* lies in the way it subjects modern civilization to volubility. The subjects under discussion can be as varied as one likes, but this does not prevent the fact that this is the effect of the prose. We have already insisted on the oscillation between contrasting evaluations that results from this, above all in the way superiority turns into belittlement. It is as well to remember the twist in the opposite direction. For example, if the voluble prose makes the reader laugh, because it suggests that the narrator is incapable of sustained effort or of putting off immediate satisfaction, it also makes one laugh at those same sustained efforts, since, in contrast to them, volubility at least searches for and gets satisfaction at every moment, even if that satisfaction is imaginary. We are laughing here at nothing less than the achievements of the modern Western world.

The motivations for this volubility are immediate and limited to the individual. Its dominance prevents the bourgeois norm from operating, even though it doesn't remove the latter's prestige. This prestige is indispensable for the civilized notion that the volubility of Machado's style has of itself, and for showing off to others. A strange combination — prestige, yes please, but no real validity — which rules in the domain of ideas in the *Memoirs,* is the immediate effect of the narrative form. Earlier on, I tried to suggest that Brazilian ideological life obeyed a comparable law, determined by the country's social structure. Unless I am mistaken, Machado was elaborating a literary procedure whose objective makeup put the life of the mind into parameters compatible with Brazilian reality, quite independently of one's convictions about this or that doctrine. The foundation of its historical accuracy, of its being a "good fit," lies not in this or that opinion but in the technical solutions in the prose that forms their context. Mimetic accuracy has become the effect of the rigor of the construction.[2]

Volubility, in the abstract, is the opposite of constancy. On this trite level it is neither good nor bad, for people can be happy or unhappy being either voluble or constant, and they are never a single thing. The voluble Brás

Cubas, however, from the first line of the novel goes and sits in the dock, though it is true that he does it for comic effect. He doesn't want to defend his own volubility, where the true blame lies, but, rather, to show up the powerlessness of his adversaries and rejoice in his own impunity. What is the nature of this impunity? To reply properly to this question, we must leave the sphere of the prose-in-itself, to which we have limited ourselves until now, and look at the character-narrator in the context of his relationships: that is, we must go to the domain of the novel's situations, of their sequence, of the plot, and so to the second part of the novel. Not, of course, that it is divided between chapters of writing without subject matter and others with a story, even though this separation has some foundation, as we shall see.

In the conventional sense, the plot begins in chapter 10, with the birth of the protagonist, and goes on, in more or less linear fashion, until his death, which happens in the chapter after the last, that is, in the first: another prank. The observations we have been making until now describe above all the opening section (chapters 1–9), an interregnum in which Brás, pushing paradox to its limits, is already dead, has not been born, and speaks to the reader from the heights of eternity. Here, arbitrariness and affronts to verisimilitude rule without rival, and the universe is totally subjected to the sudden movements of the consciousness of the dead man, who does not suffer the chronological and causal constraints that to some degree the biographical form will impose on him. Moreover, from this point of view, this entire first part can be taken as an extended joke in bad taste, with the object of delaying the beginning of the novel proper ("Don't sit there turning your nose up at me, just because we haven't got the narrative part of these memoirs" [ch. 14]). The volubility is operating at full tilt, since above all it is a formal principle; whereas in the following parts it will be found mostly in the motivation of the characters, or in the content. This does not mean that it disappears, but there is a very obvious difference, which echoes the stylistic discontinuity between the two opening paragraphs that we commented on many pages back. At the level of the composition, musically so to speak, the confusion of marches and countermarches in terms of time, space, and subject matter — the barrage of digressions at the beginning of the novel — will be followed by a thin narrative line, which even then winds around and from time to time is broken. And it can't be denied that delaying the start of the action is one way of introducing it and making the reader wait for it. What does this sequence mean?

A lover of paradoxes, Brás Cubas begins his *Memoirs* with the end, a fact that in his view can be accounted for, since the "grave" of the man was the "cradle" of the novelist. The hypothesis of the "dead author" has been taken seriously by some critics, who have deduced the structure of the novel from it. We will have a look at these arguments shortly. For those who don't believe them, the question still remains: what is the object of nine wayward, actionless chapters, in which volubility puts its most disruptive effects on show? We can say, very much in the abstract, that they establish the debased spiritual atmosphere — types of power, real motives, contradictions — without which the life of the hero and the anecdotes of Brazilian life, which are the substance of the events related, would lack artistic dignity, or would be "having the wool pulled over your eyes," to use a notion dear to the novelist ("Anything! my friend, anything! except to have the wool pulled all the time!").[3] In this sense, these chapters are an indispensable preamble. Monotony, degradation, truncated arguments, wasted material, dissonance, sterility, and so on are not accidental presences but important, basic effects of the movement of the prose, as we have tried to show. They are the result of the riot of capriciousness that occupies the foreground, or, to put it another way, they establish the minimum criteria of consistency and realism necessary to situate the figures and situations that will populate the novel, and along with which they compose Machado's equivalent of reality. The figures and situations were not new, since they were already present in the fiction of Martins Pena,* Macedo, Manuel Antônio de Almeida* and Alencar,* as well as in the humorous journalism of the time. But now, by means of these exercises in mocking futility, they reach the status of great art.

The irreverent spirit of the *Memoirs* and above all its delight in provoking havoc still cause confusion today. Brás Cubas himself comments on this tone of his and attributes it to the sense of detachment appropriate to the dead. "But in death, what a difference! What a relief! What freedom! . . . Gentlemen living, there is nothing as immeasurable as the contempt of the dead" (ch. 24). This suggestion has been accepted by the critics, with the result that the freest and most daring formulations belong to the dead man, who no longer has anything to fear, while the pettiness belongs to the living characters, involved in the constraints of real life.

Despite the authority of the narrator/guarantor (which is precisely nil), this perspective does not take us very far: (a) it ignores the element of farce in the situation, and in the place of its insolence, which is part of a worldly, skeptical relationship, it puts the uncharacteristic, "serious" contrast between life and death, one of those metaphysical generalities recommended in "Education of a Stuffed Shirt"; (b) it fails to see that the living, too, have "absolute" moments of ennui, disillusionment, cruelty, and more, and that in this, they cannot be distinguished from the dead narrator; (c) it hides the most important thing, to wit — that the Brás Cubas "freed from the brevity of this life" (ch. 4) is as petty and pursued by social vanities as the most deplorable of his characters, something that is clear from the very first page, where he finds it hard to resign himself to the tiny number of people present at his funeral. The comedy is to be found precisely in the earthly passions of this dead man, who is very much alive.

In other words, the switching back and forth and the mutual contamination of the metaphysics and the gossipy backchat characterize not only the narrator but *all* the characters in the story. The book's unity is founded on this generalized similarity, in spite of the differences in tone, which do exist. The identity is no less meticulously prepared than the contrast. Already in the second paragraph we hear Brás's funeral oration: the work of a friend, which, however, could be his own, with its sardonic display of rhetorical ingenuity. A little further on, in chapter 3, the genealogical passion of Cubas Senior is a piece of "show-off" — "but who in this world isn't a bit of a show-off?" — and is not substantially different from the son's various whims. A little earlier, for instance, he had prided himself, already as a dead man, on the amorous preferences of a married lady. Here we find, quite palpably, the universalization of volubility, which gives no privileges to the narrative voice. We can say, then, that there are in the novel two literary registers, one of great intellectual import, the other humbler, *which are both manifestations of the same order of experience, of the same search for primacy,* and that the superiority of the first is attributed by Brás Cubas to the frankness of the dead. The distance and proximity between the two, their alternation, the "breathing" (cf. 13), and the modus vivendi that they set up — daring conjunctions, whose ring of truth, however, is quite striking — are notable achievements of narrative orchestration and architecture. It is criticism's role to interpret these rhythms. To attribute the duality to the distinction between life and death is not a solution but a ruse, which, moreover, is why it's funny.

Volubility appeared to us first of all as the narrator's most notable feature; was it merely a subjective trait, a passing tendency, soon to be corrected? We have seen that it is not: it is everyone's permanent propensity. Perhpas, then, it denotes a metaphysical failing in human nature. Yet it has no lack of connotations of local color, more generic, then, than the tendency of any Tom, Dick, or Harry, but not universal, for all that; in this meaning, volubility would be the distinguishing mark of one society among others. When we accompany its rhythm, the prose sanctions these three perspectives: volubility is the human condition, it is a feature of individuals, and it is a Brazilian characteristic. According to which of these three dominates, the tone is absolute, as suits ultimate truths; funny, when portraying an individual defect; and satirical, if it denotes a Brazilian attitude. This involves a logical problem, for the same attribute both individualizes and universalizes: is volubility Brás Cubas? Is it everybody? Is it Brazil? Artistically, this lack of definition hardly gets in the way. Rather, it is an element of humor and diversity in the tones of the language, which contrast but for some reason do not undermine one another. Perhaps this is because the real opposition is a different one, and can be brought into play by any one of them or by all three alternately; in this sense they function as *ideology*. As I will try to show, there is also a fourth reference in the novel, discreet but crucial, expressed (but not made explicit) in the aggressive, wicked attitude of the prose. To understand it, it is necessary to examine the problems of the action, that is to say, of the plot and the system of social relations that dictates its motifs. Class antagonism, in a form peculiar to Brazil, is the key to the style we are in the process of studying.

5

The Social Aspect of the

Narrator and the Plot

ALTHOUGH IT IS VERY LOOSE, the form of the novel is biographical, interspersed with digressions and episodes of life in Rio de Janeiro. The stages of the life of a rich, idle Brazilian pass in front of us: his birth, the atmosphere of his early childhood, law studies at Coimbra University in Portugal, love affairs of different sorts, flirtations literary, political, philosophical, and scientific, and finally his death. Absent from this course of existence are work and any kind of consistent project. The passages from one stage to another take place via boredom, which stamps the mark of class privilege on this movement. Relationships with others are *antisocial* in the literal meaning of the word: that is, they are not guided by equality in the modern sense, while at the same time the existence of that equality is postulated. Brás's volubility appears, in other words, as the reverse side of the omission of any kind of work or real perseverance, and as the extension of social injustice.

Subordinated to caprice, the conventional list of the ultimate aims of bourgeois life takes on a cheapened aspect, with something of operetta about it. So, instead of study we have a few years of high jinks in Portugal (ch. 20); instead of poetry, the literary flourishes of a very recent widower (ch. 19); and instead of politics, a parliamentary speech on the advisability of reducing the size of the shakos of the National Guard by two inches, to make them lighter and easier to handle (ch. 137). Philosophy is represented by social reflections inspired by dogfights, while the invention of the Brás Cubas Plaster stands in for science and free enterprise. An exception can be made for love, which doesn't come out of the novel any the worse for wear, since caprice does not impede its natural progress: the amorous performance of the protagonist is vigorous and complex, even though, from a romantic point of view, it may seem wretched. It is as if, in Brazilian circumstances, characterized as they are by the preeminence of volubility, love were the only possible form of fulfillment, while other manifestations of the spirit are condemned to a mean and paltry existence.

The satirical accent suggests in this context that science, politics, philosophy, and so on are nothing more than affectations. This does not prevent their being active presences, indispensable to the makeup of the character, who would not be himself if he didn't aspire to fame, fortune, learning, and a job in the government. The absurdity of these pretensions is an expression of their historical dislocation, but only in part, since Brás perfectly incarnates the principle of modern subjectivity, which has no respect for limitations and knows it has a right to all the latest things the world has to offer (in this, the protagonist differs from a slave, or from a dependent). With its limitless expansionism, volubility brings to the novel a nontraditional dynamic, peculiar to modern society. Overstating the case a little, we could say that Brás adapts a Faustian anxiety to local conditions. Why should a Brazilian bourgeois not want *everything*? As it happens, even though it is no respecter of restrictions, the negating spirit does not attack iniquities sanctioned by history; but, to judge by the narrator's conduct, it does free the ruling class from any obligation to those it rules, and gives free rein to its irresponsibility.

What is Brás's future? "Perhaps a naturalist, a man of letters, an archaeologist, a banker, a politician, or even a bishop — even a bishop — so long as it was a post, a preeminent place, a great reputation, a superior position" (ch. 20). The form of the Romantic novel, linked to the self-realization of a young man and the vicissitudes in his way, is present, but emptied out; the sameness of the appetite for such varied supremacies, and the readiness to get them all without any effort, discredits them all. The comic distance between the plaster and science, between the shako and politics, is the same distance that separates the wandering, tensionless plot from one with an energetic, enterprising central character.[1] These are all versions of the — humiliating — contrast between Rio society, given shape in the first term of these comparisons, and a "model" bourgeois society, that is, a European one, in which these "professional" specialisms require an appropriate career and discipline, and are not mere ornament. However, Brás's "deficiencies" do not express just inferiority (though they are inferior, from a European point of view) but also the right to have contact with contemporary civilization (this from a Brazilian point of view, whether that of the classes excluded from that contact or that of those who enjoy it).

When we commented on the prose of the *Memoirs,* we observed that its dynamism lies in its versatility, associated with the search for "any kind of supremacy," where the "any" discredits each particular supremacy that might be chosen. In the same way, at the level of the story we encounter something similar, apparent in the central character's conduct; his social position and its logic should allow our analysis to go one step further. In other words, the rough handling of the repertoire of Western values, values necessary to the configuration of the superiority aimed at, is an *immediate* effect of the narrative procedure, and the *indirect* consequence of Brás Cubas's mode of existence, developed in the biographical sphere, which by its very nature is spacious. The result in the first case is aggressively short; in the second there is more explanation, with a great deal of observation of reality, and some real miniature profiles of Brazil's cultural style. *We can say then that the plot repeats on another scale and in slow motion the movement that the prose goes through at speed, and at every instant.* This redundancy, or mutual confirmation of prose style and plot, is crucial. The events of the plot are immersed in their spiritual equivalent long before they produce their own effects. This explains such a complete impression of impasse, of repeated relapses, of conscious evildoing.

More than a suggestive parallelism, this is an achieved *result,* in which creative processes of very distinct kinds come together, such as the development of a model of prose — a struggle in its own right, which takes place on many fronts — and the in-depth study of at least one social type. The biographical career of this type (the narrator) allows one to glimpse a rhythmic constant, which will be fixed, abstracted, and improvised on. What then becomes obvious is its affinity with the cadence of the narrative procedure, which assures the novel its cohesion (a structural fact) and verisimilitude (a mimetic fact), as well as its formal originality in the proper sense of these words: that is to say, an artistic design produced on the basis of peculiar historical circumstances, which find in it their logical (though not at all obvious) form and causal sequence.

The succession of the episodes is directed by volubility and lacks internal necessity. There is no lack of desires, which indeed have plenty of life, but there exists no continuity of aims, something that chimes in very well with the central character and is easily explained, since the end of caprice is boredom. That is the reason for the erratic, loose story line, very original in its way, and the plot that lacks the tension provided by conflicts, since these latter require some kind of constancy. The complexity is tied not to the unfolding of contradictions—they are deactivated by the inconstancy of desire—but to the subtleties and rhythms of unconscious change, of tedium, of the drift from one stage of life to another. These are topics, moreover, that place the *Posthumous Memoirs* among the modern anatomies of the will and the experience of time, and at the margins of bourgeois territory properly so-called, which is characterized by the dilemmas in the projects of individuals. In short, this is a rhythm without a dramatic nucleus but still full of temporary necessities, since *all* its moments, the characters' as much as the narrators', are ruled over by caprice. A strange conjunction, in which life is full of satisfactions but empty of meaning; in which the logic of the separate moments, short and monotonous like caprice itself, and repeated over and over, underlines the aleatory character of the whole; in which the vital energy of mediocrity is considerable. Areas of experience that poetic justice cannot allow to be seen together and whose disharmony, aggressively grating, lies at the heart of modern art are combined. Suddenly we are exposed to the dissonant—and atheistic—hypothesis that life may have no sense. *The beauty of these effects is essentially anticonventional.*

However, despite the discontinuity of the plot and the absence of dramatic trajectory, the novel has its progression. This is something like a movement made up of other movements, but that does make sense: a rhythm in which the interest of the narrator and the characters, like that of the reader, goes through ever-renewed cycles of animation and boredom, though the whole slips from liveliness to surfeit and death, all of this taking place without a durable aim in sight. The *Memoirs,* like the other novels of Machado's maturity, end in *nothing.* This can be understood metaphysically, or, in my view, more usefully as a final destination and conclusion, in which case analysis has to take into account the experiences that that "nothing" claims to sum up. (In passing it can be said that some of the best Brazilian books, notably *Macunaíma,** with the extraordinary sadness of its final pages, discovered a comparable rhythm.)

The episodes are linked by means of a common denominator, very much emphasized, that the reader soon notices, and that produces laughter: instead of the continuity or unfolding of an action, we have the regular repetition, in various forms, of a single, unchanging insufficiency or failure, typical of the human condition. This insufficiency soon superimposes itself on the episodes, as being their essence, and not only theirs, but of any others that might occur. This conclusion seems critical, for behind the illusory diversity of daily life it points to a constant truth, a bitter pill to swallow. In the conventional reading, this is the essence of the book, and of the author's pessimism. However, this conclusion is too assertive and easy for the final destination of a novel that is, above all, slippery. This conclusion itself, abundantly commented on in theories, maxims, and apologues, which try to interpret it in quite discrepant ways, is also subject to ironic comment. Far from allowing safe conclusions, the absolute turns out to be as diverse and controversial as the empirical facts, at the same time as it is illusory, which is naturally an element of comedy. If we were to believe in these various miniexplanations, the key to the volubility would at one moment be psychological, at another mechanical, at yet another Christian, or Naturalist, and so forth. Incompatible doctrines these may be, but they function in the same way, which makes of them so many ideologies, or differences that make no difference. In a literary sense, that is, taking the movement of the work as a whole into account, their divergences matter less than what they have in common, which lies in the *universality* of their formulation and in what it postulates: abstract man, or man "in general." This latter *is* in fact a decisive ideology, on whose properties the construction of the book depends.

It so happens that the "human condition" functions differently, depending on what social relations it is inscribed on. The variations have enormous importance: something on which, as we will see, the realist richness of the novel depends. Taken as a universal key, the explanation by volubility belongs to the sphere of abstract universality and contains a sociological a priori that is atomistic. That is the reason for the unvarying character of its conclusions, which make the particular nature of any given social formation and, more specifically, any antagonism between classes irrelevant. Seen in context, however, this explanation works in the opposite direction and takes on the role of showing up asymmetries. Faced by social inequality, the universalizing argument is itself put to the test and begins to seem like a shameless avoidance of the real subject, all the more interesting in that its spirit is enlightened. And it is true that the activity of explanation in the *Memoirs* is never disinterested: the satisfaction it provides the explainer always provokes a *smile,* whereas its specious role in relation to class matters is always *demeaning.* The decisive and tacit dimension, and the one more difficult to make explicit, is the second of these two, though this does not prevent the fact that the two form a single musical chord.

The social links that give specific outline to Brás's character and by means of which he is defined arise as the episodes come and go. Despite its discontinuous, apparently aimless form, the collection of portraits is complete in its way and allows one to realize that there is a discipline, dictated by the content — those relationships that must be present if there is to be internal and external verisimilitude. So, as far as the *slaves* he mistreats are concerned, Brás appears as a *little devil*. An *old dependent woman,* who hasn't even a place to drop down dead, will find in him a *protector,* ready with sarcastic thoughts about her. To the *poor girl, the illegitimate child,* there corresponds the *well-born young man, happy to take advantage of her.* A *brother-in-law into shady deals, and ex–slave trader,* will find in him an *understanding relation,* capable of justifying him and even of acting as an intermediary in selling supplies to the navy (a scam of the period). For the *marriageable girl,* whose father has *political influence,* Brás represents in a single person the *bridegroom chosen by the family* and the *future member of parliament.* And so on.

Seen as a whole, these are situations (and advantages) founded on slavery and clientelism, accompanied, however, by the — determining — shadow of the nineteenth-century bourgeois norm. It is this that marks them negatively, as something wrong, and causes the intimate combination of social satisfaction and moral dead end that Machado's readers are so familiar with. In other words, the ideological impasse of the Brazilian elite, which we discussed some pages back, finds an equivalent in the framework of characters and episodes in the *Memoirs.* Inside the book as outside it, the peculiar form taken by the life of the mind expressed the discomfort and delight at participating in modern life without relinquishing the benefits of injustice, that is, without paying tribute to the principle of formal equality among human beings.

It can further be noted that, in spite of their differences, all the situations in our selection come with the stamp of approval of family feelings. These latter mitigate and justify them, naturally with a comic result. When he cuts open the head of a slave woman, little Brás is his mother's and father's *little darling;* when he gives out cynical pronouncements about the social function of the poor, the heir to the family wealth does it as the *protector* of a dependent; when he flees from the modest Eugênia, the only person in his life for whom he has genuine feelings, it is in his role as the *young man from an important family,* with duties to his career and the like. Along with the liberal norm, and with a presence just as systematic, we have here an ideology of the family, based on the Brazilian-type extended family, with its system of filial and paternal obligations, taking in slaves, dependents, *compadres,*[2] godchildren, and allies, along with the blood relations themselves. This ideology lends familiarity and patriarchal decorum to the difficult marriage between bourgeois, clientelist, and slave-owning relationships. To the liberal *condemnation* of Brazilian society, strident and harmless, is added the *justification* of that same society by the pious virtues of family bonds, whose hypocrisy is another of Machado's specialties. The condemnation and justification contribute equally to the chorus of unacceptable voices of which this novel consists.

It is plain, then, that there is an intention to encapsulate a representative type of the Brazilian ruling class, through relationships peculiar to him. It is the plot's job to make these relationships concrete by means of appropriate personifications and anecdotes. This is the reason for the presence of a varied cast of social characters, necessary to give reality to Brás. From another angle, this spectrum of characters represents a system of positions whose links with the political and economic organization of property in the country are palpable. Thus, the in-depth portrait of any given type obliges one to sketch out the corresponding historical structure. To give life to the protagonist, it was necessary to bring onstage a cast of characters who, on a certain level, would provide a résumé of Brazilian society. Reciprocally, we can say that Brás is the expression of this society, which fact, given the metaphysical and universalizing atmosphere he moves in, is in need of some explanation. These are observations that it would not be worth making for a realist novel of the usual pattern, since they would be obvious. In our case, they are more relevant, since the foreground narrative technique, centered on discontinuity, monopolizes the attention and puts the social structure in the shade. This latter, however, as we have tried to show, does exist and surely does make its determining power felt, even at a distance.

Brás Cubas's volubility shows its full colors only when it is considered in the framework of the "unacceptable" (because antisocial) relations that condition it. See, for example, the mocking pleasure with which the narrator destroys the expectations he creates at the moment they come into existence: he recounts his death before his birth, satiety before love, failure before the attempt, and so on. Contraventions of this type are numerous and deliberately sterilize the plot. In the abstract, they would be ways of disturbing and challenging the conventional order. In context, however, they say more, and to a certain extent they say the opposite. They are something like narrative precautions to assure — whom? — of *the nonproductiveness of time,* which passes in vain and leaves everything as it was. The aim is to deprive the conflicts of their potential in the eyes of the reader. The inversion of these sequences disarms the devices intended to produce curiosity, and exposes their mechanics, with an antiillusionary, or critical, effect at the level of the form. The other side of the coin, however, is anticritical, since the disrespect for the narrative order naturally aligns itself with the antisocial or "unacceptable" relations mentioned above, to which it gives prestige and aesthetic dignity. The turning of lucidity into disrespect for the norm and a stimulus to the barefaced exercise of power is constant in the *Memoirs*. The overt target of this power is literary convention, which functions, however — as will become clear later — as the substitute for the true victims, who are the poor and the unprotected.

Along the same lines, it can be seen that there is no shortage in the plot, or in Brás's life of moments when the romantic option — always present as an ideological horizon — seems a possibility that might suddenly turn the tables. One has only to remember his enthusiasm for academic glory, the spellbinding effect of a poor, lame girl, or finally the desire to snatch the lovely Virgília away from her marriage and go live with her in some far corner of Europe. None of these three urges will be put into practice: soon, the rich kid's fun and games take the place of study; cynical thoughts about the uselessness of the poor drive away any spontaneous feelings; and comfortable installation in a fashionable adulterous affair takes the place of the mirage of anonymous happiness on another continent. In no case is the accent on the defeat of individual potential or on its costs, as Romanticism would demand. Quite the contrary, it is on the benefits that accrue, on the satisfactions that would have to be forgone if these whims were obeyed and that Brás's social position and inconsistency allow him to enjoy. The interests that make the well-heeled Brazilian not want to give up on any of his advantages push him both to project from and to disbelieve in liberalism and Romanticism, depending on the circumstances. That is why there is a certain somewhat cynical pleasure in destroying illusions: this is an exercise that the *Memoirs* draws out and refines, in its affronts to formal convention. We have seen how these affronts are systematic: in them, the indifference of the Brazilian ruling class toward its dependents, and also to the bourgeois norm itself, is dramatized, radically exposed, and taken to its final consequences, without avoiding extreme forms of abject behavior.

Analogously, in terms of the plot, we can say that the nature and position of the crises are unusual: they have no dramatic character, nor do they depend on a moment of ideological or moral choice. The value of such things has depreciated; it will appear later, in the vague form of tedium, linked precisely to the *absence of any need to choose*. The theme of individual self-realization, with the tensions and definitions that go with it, is relegated to the position of a daydream. In its place the plot gives us, as its law of movement, an alternation between agitation and melancholy, impatience and indifference, opposites that carry no tension and are unconcerned with the final aims of the concrete action: the individual is released from his normative function, that of being the vehicle of the sense of history. The novel does not seek to grasp the contradiction, much less the transformation; rather, it accompanies the progressive wearing-down of the process whereby a parasite devours his portion of the advantages to be had by social injustice, whose limits remain beyond our ken. However, Brás would cease to be himself if he could give up on his role as a modern personage, and a leading figure in science, philosophy, politics, and so forth. The oscillation between this latter character and the other, the full member of an unjustifiable system of domination, with rights to all its perks, is the core of his volubility. Thus, the lively rhythm of the narrative sets up the same pattern that we identified in the basic situations of the plot, which swing between antisocial and progressive — but it distances itself from that pattern's provincialism or "backwardness" by its elegant airs and the breadth of its references. What are we to think of this supremacy? And what if the infinite freedom of the "dead man who is now an author" does not hover above the vicissitudes of the living, as it claims to do, but, on the contrary, is an ideology in which this freedom has found the most favorable expression it can hope for? We come back in the end to the Brazilian ideological comedy, in which Romanticism and liberalism, and, in the final analysis, the totality of modern ideas, were available and gravitated according to the laws imposed on them by the slave-owning and clientelist basis of society.

The plot of the *Memoirs* attempts to anchor itself in Brazilian history and to bring out its meanings, by means of references that are sometimes explicit, sometimes hidden. Something has already been said about structural correspondences. However, relationships of a more direct nature are not lacking. Here, we are following the discoveries of John Gledson, who is in the process of showing the role that some salient political episodes, like Independence, the Abdication of Dom Pedro I, the Majority, the Conciliation Ministry and the marquis of Paraná, the Law of the Free Womb, Abolition, and the Republic have in Machado's fiction.[3] According to Gledson, these dates, rather than being simple time markers, point up historical questions, and it is from these latter that the fictional incidents and the composition of the characters draw their substance.[4] At one extreme, this reading turns the novel into a political allegory. Without going that far, we will see that there is no lack of correspondences, which do inject allegorical possibilities into the characters and try to lift them above the irrelevant or simply domestic measure of their conflicts.

In passing, Gledson raises an interesting question. What if Brás were Brazil, since his name is the first syllable of the country's name? (*Ficção e história,* 71) The chronology of the *Memoirs* is intricate, but not confused, and at times suggests this type of parallel. Seeing that Gledson has practically not written at all about *Brás Cubas,* and his perspective helps our analysis, we will try a few steps on our own. And in fact, one has only to look at the dates for the inferences to come thick and fast. Thus, the protagonist is born in 1805, in the last years of the colonial period. His education, when he learns not to recognize norms but only to obey his own caprices, falls in the "good old times" of King João VI's presence in Rio de Janeiro [1808–21] (chs. 9–13). His first *captivity* — a "libidinous" passion for a *Spanish* woman of easy virtue — coincides with the celebrations of *Independence,* a paradox that is not accidental. "We were two young lads, the people and I: we had come from our childhood, with all the enthusiasms of youth." The parallel between the "dawning in the public soul" and Brás's "first gleams of light," these last due to this same lady of doubtful reputation, has a great deal of poetry in it, and the intention to shock (ch. 14). It is not the only profanation in this episode, and anyone inclined to do some sums will find others. It's enough to recall that Brás spent "thirty days to go from the Rossio Grande [where the celebrations and their first encounter took place] to Marcela's heart," which takes us to October 1822, since Independence was in September. Let us also remember the famous sentence "Marcela loved me for fifteen months and eleven *contos de réis*" (ch. 15), and we come to March 1823, when in the outside world Dom Pedro I granted his Constitution, ending the liberal adventure of the Constituent Assembly, whose most discussed model was the *Spanish* charter.[5] But then, what if the Constitution and the frolics with Marcela . . . ? The risk of making arbitrary comparisons in this kind of deciphering is of course great. There is also the temptation to abandon formal analysis for the chase after historical allusions, or, from another angle, the risk of preferring the author's *intentions* to the real, effective artistic result, that is, the result that has been transfigured by the organization of the fiction. However much this approximation might be suggested, how much do Marcela and the Constitution have to say to one another? Not much. Even so, questions of literary effectiveness to one side, historical puzzles are an important presence in Machado's work, as Gledson's studies are showing us, and it is essential to take it into account, on pain of not understanding the reason for a large number of details. There is no doubt that it does reveal the desire to comment on Brazilian history in an unconventional key, even though it is prudently coded and reserved to a small number of readers, whether attentive or initiated.

When his affair with Marcela has been forcibly terminated, Brás goes to Europe, to soak in the culture of the time. These are the years of the "practical Romanticism and theoretical Liberalism," lived "in the pure faith in a pair of flashing eyes and in written constitutions" (ch. 20), during which Brás takes "from everything their phraseology, their shell, their ornamentation" (ch. 24). It is not forbidden — nor is it obligatory — to see an allusion to the First Reign, to the emperor and to the way in which Brazil, having just emerged from colonial restrictions, embraced modern ideas. However this may be, the parallelism with historical periods continues: the European phase ends with Brás's hurried return, when his mother is at death's door; since he hasn't seen her for eight years (ch. 22) we are in 1832. His father dies soon after, and Brás becomes an *orphan,* as it was said Brazil had become an orphan with Dom Pedro I's abdication in 1831 (ch. 44). The next stage of a wasted, dissolute, and semireclusive life coincides with the years of the Regency and is covered in the short chapter 47. With the Majority (1840), Brás comes to grace the life of the capital, in his role as beau and "half-secret and half-public" lover of one of the fashionable women of the time. The year 1855 finds him a deputy and aspiring to be a minister, when he proffers his speech about the shakos of the National Guard — a possible allusion to the political conjuncture of the Conciliation (1853–57), when the futility of parliamentary battles had begun to look like a deliberate policy (chs. 137). From this same period on, Brás begins to give ears to a philosophy composed of monism and social Darwinism, which reveals him as a precursor, since the Recife school* comes at the end of the 1860s. Even his death, in 1869, chimes in with the country's evolution, since the decline of the Second Reign [that of the emperor Pedro II, 1840–89] dates from those years. In the immediately previous period, Brás had begun to interest himself in colonization, the exchange rate, the expansion of the railways, and sensational inventions (the plaster), an allusion to the new outbreaks of speculative fever and to "Yankee"-style enthusiasms.

Politico-social innuendos constitute one method giving extra meaning to the text therefore. In an analogous spirit, the references to Brazilian literature point, more or less covertly, to a heterodox view of national life. Let us look, for example, at the Marcela episode, which, without informing the reader of this, takes up a situation from José de Alencar's *Lucíola* (1862), itself modeled on *The Lady of the Camellias* (1848). Paulo Silva meets Lúcia at a festival of the Assumption, "one of the few popular festivals in the capital" (*Lucíola*, ch. 2). A little later, he encounters her again at a binge organized at the suburban house of Dr. Sá, a childhood friend. Among others are present a "pretty young Spanish woman" (!) and Sr. Rochinha, "a precocious libertine, bowed down by consumption" (ch. 2). With much moral suffering, Lúcia on this occasion steps up onto the banqueting table and reproduces, live, the erotic pictures hanging on the wall (ch. 2). Later on, Paulo will find out that she is pure, and that the young men who accuse her of being grasping are wrong. Not only did the heroine not keep her admirers' presents for herself; she used them, all of them, for her sister's education. Paulo, too, is a young man with honest feelings: very susceptible in questions of honor and unable to resign himself to the lack of virtue of the fallen women he frequents.

Despite the different atmosphere, the parallel with the *Memoirs* is undeniable. Brás meets Marcela "in the night, blazing with lights, as soon as the news of the declaration of independence arrived, a spring festival, a dawning in the public soul" (ch. 14). A little later, he finds her again at a "dinner with girls, in Cajueiros." The banquet is presided over by Xavier, "with all his tubercles" (ch. 14). This said, it can be observed that in the episode rewritten by Machado the girl really is grasping and specialized in fleecing young men. The first encounter coincides with the foundation of Brazilian nationality, which gives it a wicked, if not allegorical, echo; to get to the "imperial" phase (of exclusive possession), Brás passes through a "consular phase" in which "the government of Rome" is shared with Xavier (ch. 15). As for the living pictures, Marcela quite happily poses in the way her lover asks her to, "You're a Sheik of Araby, she would say" (ch. 15). The general spirit of the parody is deidealizing, which doesn't say much, however. Brás takes up Paulo's situation again, to give it a more realistic social and psychological setting: his performance is the true version of what Paulo would be and do, making explicit the arrogance and hypocrisy of the cultured young man, faced by a woman with no family to protect her, who is not idealized either. It is as if Machado were saying that Paulo at bottom is Brás, or that the virtuous young man is in fact pretty despicable. In this sense, it is not really a case of parody, but of the identification of a social type behind the Romantic commonplace, which is treated with magisterial distance and concision. The literary model, ideologically and socially prestigious, enters as a *negative* ingredient into the composition of a prototype of the Brazilian ruling class. It is a considerable turnaround, and depends on the realist capacity to see in artistic representations a valid moment of the historical process. Nothing could be more characteristic of Machado's literary independence than this silent and self-confident use of the intellectual limitations of his mentor, the highly esteemed José de Alencar. Is this a desire to outdo or to demystify an illustrious predecessor? To increase the allusive density of his own work? To amuse a small circle of initiates?

The search for extraliterary energies borrowed from the world of history is constant and takes advantage of the most varied resources, from the straightforward reference to the whispered hint. As we have seen, Brás Cubas's biography runs parallel to the stages of national life; the set of social relations within the novel is indicative of the Brazilian social structure in its particular aspects; there is a reuse and rectification of situations defined in the earlier Brazilian novel. Thus, the amount of historical material assimilated into the plot of the *Memoirs* is large, and it would be natural if the dynamic movements corresponding to them were to weigh in the interpretation: what do the evolutions of Brás and Brazil have to say about one another? What, for instance, is the meaning of the progress of brother-in-law Cotrim, who goes from being a slave smuggler (before the end of the transatlantic trade, in 1850) to being the beneficiary of obscure transactions with the Naval Arsenal (possibly during the Paraguayan War, 1865–70, a period of large, corrupt deals, and, for Machado, a moment when his patriotic feelings underwent a process of relativization)? Might it tell us that the illegal trading in slaves was replaced by other forms of commerce, equally immoral? What are we to think of the destiny of the good Eugênia, born out of wedlock in 1815, almost raised to wealth by one of Brás's caprices in 1832, and begging for alms in a slum in the early 1860s? Left to itself, that is, separate from its formal connectedness — which is always an artifice — the novel's material invites this kind of understanding, *which, however, is restrained by the rapid, brief cycles of the volubility.* This cycle cuts short the material characteristic of the realist novel, marked by history and the practical dimension of life, and turns it into its opposite, signifying the presence of an unavoidable human condition. In other words, the raw material and the formal principle seem to diverge drastically: whereas the first postulates a sociohistorical dimension, the second affirms a metaphysical condition, or, at least, one of great generality, whose processes are more abstract than those implied in the social material — and they provide this material with no continuity. The break with the past could not, at first sight, be more obvious. Paradoxically, considered as a whole, this is a rule of composition and of unity possessed of the very greatest interest.

To propose a formula, whose real operation is embodied in its variants, we can say that the narrative pattern of the *Memoirs* is the following: (a) An episode of action proper, that is, taken from the life of Brás Cubas or from his sphere, in a realist vein. This is a world of neighbors, *compadres*, relatives, and dependents, as well as the slaves. Here, the relationships of dependency and the liberties of familiarity, both gentle and brutal, have sway, as do, in contradiction with them, the ideals of nineteenth-century bourgeois civilization, linked to the autonomy of the individual. Machado's specialty lies in the inconsistencies typical of this mixture, and in particular in the mental juggling that allows people to reconcile these irreconcilables, all to the good of the self-esteem of the narrator, who wants to be a modern man.

(b) An intercalated episode that differs — in topic and genre — from the first, and whose movement it interrupts. It can be an apologue, a puzzle, an anecdote, a reflection, or whatever, as long as, at its core, imagination has precedence over reality. Because of what it signifies in terms of conscious disrespect on the part of the narrator, the interruption carries with it a slight taste of power, as well as playing over again the discrepancy between social and antisocial relations mentioned under (a). Thus, when the thread of the action has been cut, there is formed between the realist episode, the interpolated anecdote, and the narrative gesture, the link of the common denominator, which the reader gradually begins to divine. It is our old friend, the search for "some kind of supremacy, any will do" and for the consequent versatility, which appears as the fixed point in the middle of diversity, the essence at the core of contingency. Its form is "philosophical," or universalizing, that is to say, obtained via the decontextualization of behavior. Or, to put it another way, it is the point the mind arrives at once the practical circumstances in their modern — that is, their historico-social — sense have been removed. The explicit form of the narrative reduces the realist ingredient to the level of a picturesque detail, leaving its dynamic in a formless, merely potential state.

(c) Another episode in a realist vein. As it ties up with the previous one, it underlines the arbitrary character of the intercalation. However, as it does not tighten up or discipline the plot, this continuation in its turn is gratuitous. It too is integrated into the narrative by means of the reiteration of volubility — the abstract common denominator — and helps establish its primacy. The practical conditioners of the action, which give a realistic character to the episode, are demoted and remain unused, that is to say, they do not flow forward, in clear continuity of movement. However, with the repetition of the cycle, the relation between what is essential and what is not is inverted, without one being able to point to the precise moment of the inversion. The common denominator stays the same, while the "circumstantial" dimension of the anecdotes increases in volume until it forms the sociohistorical atmosphere of that same common denominator — an atmosphere according to which this latter will be seen, interpreted, and judged. Thus, the ostensible form of the *Memoirs* is outlined by the movement, or, better, by the frivolity of the narrator; on the latent level, the sorcery turns against the sorcerer, and the mass of circumstances — however devalued — takes over the determining role. Their relevance, by definition, escapes the narrative voice, which, for this reason, becomes discredited. That is the reason for the powerful and diffuse presence of the social material, which lacks a clear outline, a manifestation that weighs and exerts influence but is not reflected in any definite formulation. *In other words, this is a novel written against its pseudo author.* The structure is the same as that of *Dom Casmurro:* the indictment of a prototype and paladin of the ruling classes is undertaken in the perverse form of an "involuntary" self-exposure, that is, of the first-person singular used with a distanced, hostile intention (normally reserved for the third person). The key to this procedure lies in the calculated inadequacy of the narrator's attitudes toward the material he himself presents. The effect is the more insidious in that Machado uses with absolute mastery the ideological and literary resources most prized by his victim. Yet this leads to a similarity between ferocious criticism and an apologia, which can lead to confusion.[6]

There is noting more opposed to volubility than planning. However, we have seen the encyclopedic breadth adopted by the narrator: we have seen the quasi system of enlightened activities — art, science, philosophy, love, politics — that he devotes his attention to; and we have seen the cast of figures and episodes especially chosen so that Brás can show his true colors, or, better, so that the spiritual and historical consequences of his volubility, in Brazilian circumstances, can come to light. This, then, is a plot that serves to methodically expose a way of existence, rather than to develop the action, and that makes one assume that there is a narrator behind the narrator, a narrator interested in consequences and thus the opposite of the voluble narrator. The object is to make the narration go through a chosen group of relationships, which presupposes the distance and vision of a whole, proper to the realist novel. Of course, it is true that Brás hampers the crucial relationships as if by accident, without spoiling their immediate effect, which gains in importance precisely thanks to the way the whole trajectory has been studied in advance. Is this a structural inconsistency? At the final reckoning, is the narrator voluble or not? We will return to the question and try to interpret it. For now, it is enough to note that volubility is not alone as a rule of composition, even it takes up the whole foreground. At its side, almost invisible, but with the necessary background to throw it into relief, lies the novelist's sociohistorical perspicacity.

6

The Fate of the Poor

Eugênia

A lad saw the rose
Saw the rose in the meadow
— Goethe, "Heidenröslein"

He is poor . . . and so must be sensitive.
— José de Alencar, *Sonhos d'ouro*

The flower of the bushes, with a charm that is the consequence neither of artifice nor of noble birth, is an image dear to the Enlightenment, to Romanticism, and to democratic feelings. It's an expression used as a chapter title at an important moment in the *Memoirs,* where, however, it has a second meaning, opposite to this first one. It contemptuously designates the girl born out of wedlock, conceived behind the bushes, in the undergrowth, so to speak. The conflict between these two meanings sums up the ideological tone of this episode, while the coarseness of the play on "bushes" gives a foretaste of the extremes the narrative will go to.

Eugênia and Brás live out a short rural idyll: she is the illegitimate daughter of Dona Eusébia, a spinster who frequented the Cubas household in a menial role, he the wealthy, well-born young man we are already familiar with. The episode takes place in Tijuca,[1] where the lad has retreated in search of repose. The circumstances, the protagonists, and the social obstacles between them lead one to expect romantic complications, and these do make an appearance, but the conclusion has another character altogether.

When she receives the young man, the girl takes off the ornaments she usually wears, and appears without earrings, brooch, or bracelet. It is a poetic, demanding move, dictated by her own sensitivity. By underlining the material differences between them, Eugênia cuts short any fantasies about social equality and shows she knows her place; yet, it's plain that the gesture has another meaning, since doing without these superficial baubles is also a way of recalling the essential equality among individuals and of forbidding the young man to treat her as an inferior. These are careful calculations, though even then there is a thought of seduction present: for an enlightened sensibility, the unadorned truth and natural charms are the most attractive of ornaments, superior as they are to the external accidents of fortune.

Dr. Cubas, a veteran of some years of "practical romanticism and theoretical liberalism" in the Old World, is not insensitive to this. He approves of the girl's dignity, which is above her irregular parentage and precarious situation, and runs the risk of "really" falling in love, that is, as equals, and marrying. At the same time, he feels the itch to have an illegitimate child by the lowborn girl. If the first were to happen, love would lead him to overcome the prejudices of family and class and recognize the equal rights of individuals (at least of free individuals). If the second hypothesis were to be played out — its sordid atmosphere already determined by the fact that the girl's dignity has already been acknowledged — this would mean disrespecting this equality and enjoying the advantages of his own wealth and position, plainly complementary to Eugênia's poverty and lack of status.

When commenting on the girl's reserve, we observed a related pendulum swing, for not only does she accept the lowliness of her situation (thus leaving the young man in a superior position), she also affirms, though more discreetly, her absolute personal dignity (which demands respect, and doesn't exclude love and a socially accepted marriage). Thus, there is a strict correspondence between Brás's conduct and Eugênia's situation, and the doubts on either side mesh with and feed on one another as parts of a practical situation, which has real weight in historical terms as well as in the fiction. The relationship implies a gamut of objective possibilities, explored by Brás, whose character, in turn, they also fit. This character is, finally, formalized in the book's language: as we will see, the narrator's insulting volubility, which time after time postulates and violates a norm, literary or otherwise, creates a movement that has similar ideological referents. It is this that makes up the complete unity and coherence among the social observation, the dramatic schema, the character types, and the pattern — as well as the class viewpoint — of the prose.

Literary form and unjust social relations rigorously fit one another, so that investigating one of these poles implies fixing the dimensions of the other. Any critical appreciation, then, requires that the material be defined and treated historically. The vital thing is to delineate the differences as much as possible, and not to dissolve the sociological particularities of the idyll into the archetype of the poor girl and the rich young man.

Eugênia, moreover, is not precisely poor. Educated close to the world of the wealthy, she could even make a good marriage and become a lady. But she might also end up, as in fact she does, begging for alms in an overcrowded tenement. On what does the conclusion depend? — on the sympathy of a young man, or of a family with money. In other words, it depends on a caprice of the dominant class. This is the crux of the matter for anyone who had heard — as most people had — of the Rights of Man, and made more crucial yet by the extreme terms of the choice between lady and beggar. Since there was no practical foundation to the autonomy of an individual who lacked means — because of slavery, the labor market was embryonic — the value of the person depended on arbitrary (and humiliating, if the pendulum should happen to swing) recognition by some member of the owner class. In this sense, I don't think I am going too far if I say that Eugênia, among other figures of similar type, embodies the generality of the situation of the free, poor person in slave-owning Brazil.

Being neither owners nor slaves, these people are not classed among the basic structural elements of society, something that has prepared a disconcerting ideological situation for them. Their access to the benefits of civilization, given the marginal importance of free labor, happens only via the possible, discretionary benevolence of individuals of the respectable class. Thus, if they don't manage to get any kind of protection, the poor live at the whim of chance, cut off above all from the material and institutional sphere of the contemporary world. This latter, in its turn, modeled on the classic countries of the bourgeois Revolution, is, by its own principles, opposed to that same protection that, in Brazil, is the ticket providing entry to its precincts. In other words, the participation of the poor person in modern culture was granted only at the price of a sizable moral-ideological concession, which he might deal with in various ways but could not escape from.

It is, then, no exaggeration to say that personal favor, with its inevitable and already in those days unforgivable element of caprice, is placed in the foreground by the social structure of the country itself. It was natural that the singular tangle of humiliations and hopes linked to this situation should become central subject matter in the Brazilian novel, which to a great degree can be studied as an introduction to and investigation of the dilemmas it involves. However that may be, it is in relation to this specific form of misfortune that volubility takes on its full force, being perceived and perceiving itself as a social power that keeps, as the only real possibilities for others, the big prize of cooptation (i.e., the marriage of unequals), the humiliation of the dependent, or the modern indifference to the fellow citizen (who is not a real citizen, however, and lacks the means for survival). The range of available destinies, which has a dizzying and disastrous narrowness from the point of view of the poor, is, from that of the owners, a wide field of choices open to the exercise of caprice. Faced by such an imbalance, it is hardly surprising that the latter develop an exalted sense of themselves and their own importance, which makes them masters of all they survey. On the flip side, their exposure to the chaotic search for imaginary supremacies and the real power that goes with them gives the exact measure of the abandonment of the poor.[2]

Some days after plucking Eugênia's first kiss, the young man remembers his father, the obligations of his career, the constitution, his horse, and more, and resolves to come down from Tijuca to Rio. The sign is given by an inner voice, whispering words from Scripture ("Rise, and enter the city," Acts 9:7) (ch. 35). Brás understands the divine advice in his own way, taking it that the city referred to is Rio and that it's time to escape from the girl. Where the Paul of the Bible was converted from being the scourge of the Christians into their apostle, his Brazilian emulator is deconverted from enlightened temptation and comes down on the side of oligarchic iniquity. He remembers his father's advice: "you must continue our name, continue it and make it even more illustrious. . . . Fear obscurity, Brás, flee from what is low. For, look here, men achieve merit in various ways, and the surest way of all is to find merit in the opinion of other men. Don't throw away the advantages of your position, the means at your disposal" (ch. 28).

What is the meaning of this behavior? As far as the plot is concerned, the episode ends with no further consequences or revelations, and with the young man's departure. It's a perfectly banal ending, which couldn't be flatter, or more characteristic. The critical effect lies in the frustration of the reader's romantic desires (Eugênia, familiar with this story, stifles her feelings and silently leaves the stage). Given the asymmetry of these relationships in which, for the reasons already given, the poor count for nothing, everything is summed up in the owner's decision, to which there is nothing to be added. From this point of view, the reduced length of the narration is an expression of the relative power of the forces at work and reiterates the silent aspect of power. However, this does not mean that the Rights of Man and the nineteenth century don't exist. The possibilities that Brás in practice refuses, and so excludes from the plot, are still alive in his mind as a modern individual, where they are put together again as the situation demands it. All that is needed is to add to the episode the moral repercussions that logically correspond to it in the context of *an enlightened man* — the one who is on the dominant side of the relationship — and we will discover a social portrait with an expressiveness unparalleled in Brazilian literature.

The idyll takes place under the auspices of four butterflies. The first, a simile of the young man's idle imaginings, heralds the theme. The second, made out of gold and diamonds (and what does that suggest?), is put in Eugênia's thoughts by the rich young man's courtesies. The third is big and black, and comes onto the veranda where Dona Eusébia and the young couple are sitting. The good lady and her daughter are frightened, perhaps out of superstition, thus giving the recent graduate the pleasure of feeling that he is strong and philosophical, as he chases the insect away with a handkerchief. The same afternoon, as their paths cross, Brás notes that Eugênia greets him as an equal. He supposes that a few paces on, she will turn her head to look at him, which doesn't happen. His disappointment still irritates him and provides the context for understanding the fourth butterfly, big and black again, which appears in the young man's room the next day. At first it is well received, since it reminds him of the scene the previous morning, with the pretty gestures of the girl, trying to hide her fright, and above all the superior role taken by the gentleman. Later, the butterfly changes meaning, perhaps because it stays there and goes on gently moving its wings. For Brás, it now represents the girl's persistence in his memory and her lack of a subaltern gesture, which had already annoyed him the previous day. Brás feels "an attack of nerves" (ch. 31) — an acute form of volubility — and with a flick of a towel puts an end to the matter.

The brutality of this conclusion prefigures the denouement of the idyll, which at this time has barely begun. Applied to an inoffensive being, the mortal blow lays bare one aspect — methodically haphazard — of class domination. The content of the social relationship is extended to the relationship with nature: the *natural* (or civic) dignity of Eugênia, which does not bear the marks of subordination to the oligarchy, makes spontaneity on any level, even that of butterflies, seem odious. And as nature also exists inside us, it's plain that, beyond the insect and the girl, the flick was, in Brás's inner self, aimed at spontaneous respect for another person's value.

At this point, the reader of the *Memoirs* will not have failed to notice that we have omitted a decisive feature of the episode, the one on which Brás's principal reactions will be focused: Eugênia's physical defect. As well as being illegitimate and poor, the girl is lame. Notice, however, that the young man does not notice the defect until later, when the poor girl's dignity has already made him feel uncomfortable to the point of knocking her down in effigy. In other words, the logic and the conclusion of the episode have been fixed in terms of *social* inferiority, and the natural imperfection that is added to this does not affect the course of events. Nevertheless, it is this physical inferiority that will be the pivot of Brás's cogitation. He will unload on the natural deformity the disagreeable feelings inspired by the class difference, and, more importantly, he will see social injustice through the prism of the irremediable mistakes of nature, for which he cannot be blamed.

How are we to understand this substitution? In the normal way of things, the naturalization of historical relations serves conservative interests. It is obvious in this case that this is very convenient, since the girl's social situation is a problem for the young man's conscience, while the physical defect is something definitive and, in that sense, comforting. Things, however, are more complicated than that, because it is plain too that her defective leg would not prevent Eugênia from being a perfect wife. So, apart from not being the real reason, this alleged reason does not convince, and confirms the climate of threadbare excuses and avoidance of the subject, in the end of malice, which is central to the coarseness — evidenced in an extreme form — of these chapters. The mocking explanation, which doesn't aim at justifying anything, and rather points to the reality of brute force, is here one element of nastiness among others. In fact, the ten or so pages in which Eugênia, the only person with integrity in the book, figures, constitute a detailed exercise in defilement. The cruelty is so great, so deliberate and detailed, that it is hard for the reader to assimilate in its full extent. It is as if the extreme character of these passages prevented their strangeness from being perceived. Let's try not to reduce it to a question of psychology — the element of sadism is clear enough — and see in it a realistic unfolding of the social order that we are trying to characterize. It is the coordinates of the social conflict that provide the protagonist-narrator's excesses with transparency and artistic integrity.

We have already mentioned the demeaning interpretation given to an innocent phrase like "the flower of the bushes." A nearby chapter is called "Lame from Birth," another uncharitable phrase. When he swears "by Diana's thigh" (ch. 34)[3] that he meant no harm to Eugênia, Brás is obviously trying to go too far, indeed further than anyone could possibly dare to go. In all this, the girl's rights are in question, and so, in consequence, is the enlightened-romantic-liberal view of the individual, which the protagonist will insult with an exasperated deliberateness — not out of Satanism (though these pages do owe a debt to Baudelaire) but because he is a common or garden member of the Brazilian ruling class, for whom this view is an obligatory point of reference, even though Brás knows that it is unreal in local terms and experiences this contradiction as a destiny and a continual irritation. The impudence reaches paroxysm in the chapter addressed "To a Sensitive Soul," where Brás's cynicism is abruptly turned against the reader, and moves on to open aggression, as he tells him to clean his glasses — "because sometimes these things are down to your glasses" (ch. 34) — presumably misted up with useless tears shed over the fate of the innocent Eugênia. So, the exorcising of liberal sentimentality and the return to the reality of privilege culminate in this passage in direct insults to the reader, who is forced to feel in his own person the outrageous aspect of the narrator's volubility and of the nature of the power relations that makes it tick.

"I give you my word of honor that Eugênia's look wasn't lame, but straight, completely sound" (ch. 32). The malice here is in the swearing, which assumes a disreputable reader (*mon semblable, mon frère*), reluctant to think that a defect in a leg need not imply any lessening of the person. This assumption of complicity aims to be insulting, and in fact makes explicit the aggressive nature of the innumerable familiarities taken with the reader throughout the book. However, if we look again, we will see that the swearing is not merely aimed at convincing the audience. It is also said for internal consumption, and in this aspect is an expression of embarrassment rather than of surprise, and functions as an inner exclamation mark. Why should it be uncomfortable that Eugênia's spirit does not display an appropriate inferiority? The next paragraph begins with a similar explanation, developing the first one: "The worst of it was that she was lame." "Worst" designates a handicap greater than the others — enumerated straight away: "Such limpid eyes, such a fresh mouth, such a ladylike demeanor."[4] These features, which are what retain the young man's attention, have naturally become negative qualities because they belong to a poor girl and create a moral and sentimental impasse for the scion of a respectable family. Let us keep three points in mind: (a) the basis of the whole question is really one of class, and the physical defect is merely an addition, useful to him as an alibi; (b) in the context of class domination, the human advantages of inferiors are seen as so many misfortunes; (c) the temporary convenience of the voluble character is not ideologically sterile — on the contrary, it is itself inventive and engenders ways of seeing and speaking that give it precise expression, however nonsensical they may seem by enlightened criteria. This third point is exemplified one sentence later: "Why should she be pretty, if she was lame? Why lame, if pretty?" In other words, if the universe was sensibly ordered, lame (poor) girls would not be pretty, and pretty girls would not be lame (poor). What we have here is universal harmony, but seen from the point of view of the most immediate personal convenience, with all other viewpoints suppressed, and, above all, with class domination left in place.

What are we to think of this orgy of iniquities? It goes on at the level of the language, whose narrative, expositional aims from time to time give way to a primitive desire to humiliate. Here and there, with no precise raison d'être, just as a pure mocking contribution to the general climate, the word "foot" [*pé*] and others connected to it surface. Thus, Brás is "next to" [*ao pé de*] Eugênia, who is "next to" him in her turn, as well as there being a "Diana's thigh," a "lame Venus," and a large number of "feet" in the literal sense, *boots, cobblers, corns, legs* that *limp,* and, finally, a human tragedy that can be *"stamped on."*[5] Within only a few pages, there are more than thirty allusions of this kind, of questionable taste, seventeen of them concentrated in the short chapter 36, titled "Concerning Boots." The procedure itself is very coarse, despite the immense subtlety of the context: we could say that Machado was attempting a kind of sublime form of dirty joke. And, in fact, as a consequence of the repetition, the desire to gloat shows more and more aspects of itself. At the beginning it was a matter of burying the girl and all she signifies under a series of gibes. Yet, the ostentatious vulgarity of the allusions is also a way of embarrassing the reader and underlining the narrator's own impunity. Finally, the savage cruelty in which the process culminates, with taunts on almost every line, reveals Brás's need to crush the "sensitive soul" inside himself. Seen as a whole, the dominant trend is to trample on any forms of spontaneity that escape the oligarchic order: this in the characters, the reader, and the narrator himself, that is to say, everywhere.[6]

"Well, a flick of a towel put an end to the adventure" (ch. 31). With this cutting phrase, Brás remembers the episode of the black butterfly, whose social content we have tried to analyze. A little later, the chapter dedicated "To a Sensitive Soul" ends in a comparable fashion: "and let's be done with this flower of the bushes for good" (ch. 34). At other moments in the book, before this or after it, at points where the subject or atmosphere are quite different, we will find the same concluding gesture in innumerable forms, ending a paragraph or chapter, dismissing some kind of aspiration or fancy. Remembering the scruples of the impoverished Dona Plácida, overcome by a sum of money that he himself had obtained for her, Cubas ponders: "That was how her disgust ended" (ch. 70). To the leaves on the trees, which, like everything else in this world, are not eternal: "You will fall" (ch. 71). And here he is, concluding his reflections on his mother's death: "A sad chapter: let's go on to a happier one" (ch. 23). In all these endings there is an echo or a foretaste, more or less attenuated, of the blow aimed at Eugênia. The potentialities and rights of the individual, above all in the figure of spontaneity taking off like a bird in flight, were frequently evoked by the spirit of the time. To bring them down to earth requires a moment of malignant determination—the "attack of nerves" that allows the young suitor to destroy the insect. The subjective recurrence of barbarism is the price paid for the reassertion of the slave owner's or clientelistic patron's whim: this in the middle of the great century of liberalism. On the other hand, it is a reassertion that has nothing extraordinary about it, being simply a routine part of Brazilian life. The taste for the curtailment of individual rights and aspirations, seen as unnecessary trifles—and in the circumstances this view has an element of truth in it—is a recurrent constant in the prose, and is transformed into a linguistic habit, a tic of irritation and impatience in the face of fancies and desires that have no right to exist. This phenomenon can be found disseminated throughout the novel, generalized in the form of the narrative's atmosphere, and the ideological consequence of a social structure, which is also transposed into the dramatic plan of the episodes. This is another factor in the book's powerful unity, which cannot, however, unless with a sarcasm appropriate to Machado himself, be called a harmony.

When he finds Eugênia, Brás has completed a first cycle of his life and is summing up his profits and losses—which is the reason for this section's special prominence. The dominant note of his childhood and youth had been that of the exploits of the rich kid to whom nothing is denied. His stay in Europe, again under a frivolous star, made an educated man of him: "From everything I took the phraseology, the shell, the ornamentation" (ch. 24). His mother's death brings him back to Rio and, above all, to the "fragility of the things of this world" (ch. 26). The recent graduate takes refuge in Tijuca, to meditate on life, death, and the emptiness of his existence up to now. Faced with nothingness, what is left of his whims and desires, and of the — purely external — quest to assimilate the newest European trends? Against a background of crisis in his life, his feelings for Eugênia act as the possibility of a transformation. To appreciate this properly, we must detail the choices that precede it.

By the end of a week, Brás is fed up with "solitude" and impatient to return to the "hustle and bustle" (ch. 25). This moment alludes to passages in Pascal about the need men have to be distracted from themselves. In the Brazilian context, however, the terms of the dilemma are less Christian, and their real substance defines a possible alternative that lies within class privilege. On the side of the hustle and bustle lie all the visible social advantages that an important family provides access to: political distinction, the social whirl, a civilized life full of novelties. On the side of solitude, also based on wealth, "living like the bear that I am" (ch. 26): hunting, sleeping, reading and doing nothing, attended by a slave boy. In the first case, there is no real *merit,* in the second, no *work.* In both, the individual has no worth, which is the only justification for social differentiation (from the point of view of the bourgeois norm, whose relevance is attested to by the satirical character of the portrait).

Cubas Senior, a partisan of a splendid, showy existence, tries to attract his son to a good marriage and a place in the Chamber of Deputies, advantages that come together, given the future father-in-law's political influence. The frivolity of this arrangement is twice made plain: first, by the contrast with the death that has just happened (the metaphysical angle); second, by the emptying-out of the individual — that is, the modern — dimension of marriage and politics, which are here subordinated to the system of patronage and exchange of favors (the historical angle). Thus, life lacks meaning because nothingness lies on its horizon, or, also, because its horizon is Brazilian social organization. The two reasons are both present in Brás's tendency to misanthropy and are accompanied by a third. "I gripped my silent pain to my breast, with a unique sensation, something that can be called a voluptuousness in boredom" (ch. 25). A disbelief in and rejection of the world in this case contain an element of disdain for the ridiculous roles that society forced on an up-to-date young man. In a very audacious move, characteristic of his capacity for inventive adaptation, Machado was formulating, with the language of Baudelairean ennui, the melancholy and satisfaction of the Brazilian man of means as he faces the perspectives open to him: "Voluptuousness in boredom . . . is one of the subtlest sensations of this world and of that time" (ch. 25). It is plain, however, that the Cubas with *spleen* is no less arbitrary, and no less a member of the owner class than the Cubas who wants to be a minister. The to-ing and fro-ing between "hypochondria" and "love of fame," between apathy and the hustle and bustle (see chs. 28 and 44), complementary aspects of the same class experience, hints at the equivalent status of these two opposites and is one of the most important movements of the book. To participate or not to participate in the meaningless glitter of the capital, or, in a wider sense, of the Europeanizing section of society ("the phraseology, the shell"), that is the question, in which, naturally, the question whether to-be-or-not-to-be a member of the socially privileged classes does not enter. We can add that the relative retirement from the world and the rejection of the comedy of public life may signify not ideological scruples but more liberty to enjoy the advantages of property, free of the embarrassment of liberal ideas. Summing it up, in the father's words: "Don't just stay there, useless, obscure, and miserable; I haven't used money, effort, influence with people, not to see you shine, as you ought" (ch. 28). Thus, when he's not useless, Brás is frivolous, and when he's not frivolous, he's useless; he is pushed from one state to another by the drawbacks inherent in each.

The near proximity of death underlines the emptiness of these alternatives even more and functions as a call to regeneration. This is where the idyll with Eugênia comes in, with its promise of a complete transformation of the protagonist. Individual worth and spontaneity would be recognized, or, generalizing, a breach would be opened up in the blank wall of oligarchic injustice for equality between human beings, in particular between members of the owner class and poor people with education. We have seen, however, the furious belligerence with which the character refuses this route, in which limits would be placed on his caprices: a route whose national, Brazilian dimension we have tried to describe. Far from bringing about a change, then, the meeting with Eugênia consolidates the system of abuse, now in fact made worse by the transformation that didn't happen: a non–turn of events, if I can put it that way, after which everything goes back to square one, only worse. The abstract profile of the sequence provides us with the general outline of the narrative: the first anticlimax lays bare the practical ineffectualness of the fantasies of a willed liberalization and then exposes the insignificance, due to the same ineffectualness, of Brás's later life, which takes up the greater part of the book. The liberal norm is both a stupid thing to expect and an inexcusable absence. This inconsequence has a devastating effect and gives expression to the ideological blind alley that the thinking fraction of the country's population found itself in.

Years later, Brás is open to the possibility of marrying Nhã-Loló, another girl in a social situation inferior to his. How are we to explain the difference, since the protagonist himself has not changed? Trying to climb the social scale, Nhã-Loló studies and tries to understand fashionable life, and tries to "mask the inferiority of [her] family." At the opportune moment she disowns her father, whose affinities with the popular classes embarrass her. "This seemed to me to be a very noble feeling; it was one more affinity between us," remembers her fiancé, who has decided "to pluck this flower from this swamp" (ch. 112). The problem, then, was not in the unequal marriage, quite admissible so long as the power of the owner class is recognized. What cannot be allowed are the dignity and rights of the poor, which would limit the space available to the arbitrary actions of respectable people. We can also see that class prerogatives are energetically defended, but with no accompanying ideology or conviction of the defender's superiority. This absence of a consistent justification almost makes one like the man, because he comes close to being frank and open. From another angle, however, it is part of a crude, indiscriminate adherence to any kind of social privilege, which is very characteristic, and completely unburdened of the obligations that, for good or ill, a more complex self-image would bring with it.

When there is action, the Eugênia episode is a masterpiece of realist technique. The concise storytelling, with its economy of detail, both rigorously ordered by the social contradiction, produce the poetic rhythm of the great nineteenth-century novel. Still, it is a fact that the conflict has almost no continuation, or rather, it only has a continuation outside the ambit of the plot, in the moral outbursts of the male character and the narrator's cynical explanations. In this way, the subjective element and the act of narration grab the foreground and, quantitatively, outweigh the practical dimension of the conflicts. It's plain that this exuberance allows Machado to be seen as in the vanguard of postnaturalist literature. Without disagreeing, we should point out that the proliferation of subjectivity — volubility, in other words — here has its roots in a clearly social terrain, of which it is a crucial expression. From this point of view, the unconventional formal solutions can be read as ways of giving added depth to, and of radicalizing the picturing of, a practical state of affairs. For example, the lack of proportion between the brevity and the importance of the episode is a *fact about the composition* that is eloquent in itself. In truth, Eugênia is the only person in the book worthy of respect: she has a clear understanding of social relationships, an enjoyment of life, and moral rectitude — but her role takes little more than an instant. It's as if the way the narrative is organized were saying that in the context of Brazilian life, the best qualities of the poor will be cut short and wasted, all of which gives shape to and passes judgment on a historical tendency. We have also seen that the conflict develops hardly at all at the practical level, and a great deal in Brás's imagination — *and the last word, an insult what's more, is still his.* The one-sidedness of this procedure is scandalous, and is also expressive of the asymmetry of the social relationships, which has the added merit of displacing the moralist perspective. Instead of the injustice suffered by Eugênia, which would be focused on by an equitable narrator, we watch its reflections in the conscience of the person responsible, a conspicuous member of the ruling class, whose point of view the narrative adopts in a maliciously unconditional fashion. From the beginning, the partiality of the narrative puts moral feeling out of the reckoning: faced with open, acknowledged injustice, it does not disappear — it may even become more strident — but it loses the tacit assumption that it might have any practical effect and so appears as a restricted perspective. Once again we are in an area explored by Baudelaire, who also enjoys literary sharp practice and trickery, conceived as parts of a strategy of aggression. The poet enjoyed taking the part of the oppressor, but only to unmask it through his excessive enthusiasm, as he humiliates and scourges the oppressed for any passivity in the face of oppression.[7] Behind the one-sided narrator, who at first sight is repugnant but whose only possible substitute would come from another one-sided faction, is opened up the modern scenario of a generalized social struggle, from which even narrative procedures have no means of escape.

Dona Plácida

The schoolmaster to whom Brás owes his early education had taught children "for twenty-three years, silent, obscure, methodical, stuck in a small house on the Rua do Piolho."[8] When he dies, no one — "me neither," as the narrator himself says mockingly — sheds tears for him (ch. 13). A life of humble, honorable work, and he gets no recognition: that is the crux of this episode.

At another point, when Brás encounters a childhood friend in tatters and begging, he has an opposite reaction: what he now laments is that his erstwhile companion should disdain work and have no respect for himself. "I wanted to see some dignity in his misery" (ch. 60).

Thus, that same dignity that Brás will not grant to the worker, he demands from a wastrel. In each case, what matters to him is staying on top, or, more exactly, having no obligations where poverty is concerned. He owes nothing to someone who has worked, but someone who hasn't worked has no rights to anything (except moral disapproval). Whichever suits the case, it is either the bourgeois norm or contempt for it that prevails.

Here, too, the variation between criteria has its basis in class. The modern, European yardstick makes right-thinking people turn up their noses at lower-class idleness, whereas the slave-based foundations of the economy allow one, whenever convenient, to ignore the services given by poor people. The situations of these two groups are complementary, and what for the rich is a wide margin of choice — two weights, two standards — for the person with nothing to his name is a total *lack of guarantee*. Since they lack property, and slaves carry its burdens and most of its actual labor, these poor people are on slippery terrain: if they don't work, they are marginalized, and if they work, only by good fortune will they be paid or given recognition.[9]

A common complaint was that the close proximity of slavery demoralized free labor. As a consequence, the work ethos — one of the pillars of contemporary bourgeois ideology — was given little credit in Brazil.[10] In the twentieth century, in a process linked to signs of the general historical exhaustion of this ideology, this skepticism previously attributed to our "backwardness" was taken up again, with a positive connotation, and could be given universal status in the meditations on sloth by Mário de Andrade* and Raul Bopp,* and in Oswald de Andrade's* utopias.[11] Antonio Candido has shown how important the contribution of this skepticism was to the originality and scope of the Brazilian novel, in his essay "Dialectic of Malandroism," already mentioned. Possibly more modern than the modernists, whose euphoric tone does not stand up to serious reflection, Machado saw the other side of the coin: right in the middle of the bourgeois era, work without merit or value is the acme of historical frustration. As an example of this, we can take the portrait of Dona Plácida, one of the greatest and toughest moments in Brazilian literature.

Dona Plácida's life fits into a few lines, in which there alternate periods of overwork, misfortunes, illnesses, and frustrations, which in itself would not be remarkable or enough to explain the episode's terrible effect. The poor woman works as a seamstress, makes sweets to sell, teaches the neighborhood children, all alternately and with no rest, "so as to eat and not drop" (ch. 72). "Drop," here, is a euphemism for contingencies like begging or walking the street, degradations that there will be no way of avoiding, however, as the narrator notes with evident satisfaction. Later, forced to it by poverty, Dona Plácida ends up offering her services as a go-between, though she is a sincere devotee of marriage and family morals. In the same way, though she works tirelessly, there comes a moment when she is forced to look for the protection of a rich family, to whom she attaches herself, nothing of which stops her dying in utter poverty. In sum, an honest, independent life does not lie within the reach of a poor person, who in the eyes of the wealthy is presumptuous when he tries to achieve it and despicable when he gives up: in fact, this is a formula for the abject class humor practiced by Brás and exposed by Machado de Assis.

But let us return to Dona Plácida's troubles. Work undertaken with no regard to its concrete aim (sewing, cooking, teaching) and with no object beyond the salary belongs to the universe of capitalism, whereas the complete lack of appreciation for the effort involved belongs to the universe of slavery. In parallel fashion, it should be noted that the benefits that should compensate for these evils are absent: that is, the bourgeois dignification of work "in general" and the leisure that slavery can provide to nonslaves. In other words, Dona Plácida has got the worst of both worlds: abstract work, but with no rights to social recognition. Her efforts, the material payment for which is uncertain and minimal, also go unrewarded on the moral plane, which may explain the singular sadness of this character. The hardness of a life unredeemed by some sort of meaning is absolute.

From the point of view of Brazilian realism, Dona Plácida constitutes a type of capital importance, and we have already indicated the general scope of its class nature and the way it corresponds to the country's social structure. However, an accurate portrait has literary power only when it provides us with perspectives that are not obvious. In this sense, it can be seen that this poverty stripped even of consolations is not merely a portrait of destitution: it is also a critical outcome, and contains an element of reason indispensable for a more advanced conception of society. Without the precapitalist appreciation of the particular nature of different trades, and organization in guilds (which the realities of abstract work put an end to), and without the bourgeois valorization of that same work (which the institution of slavery gives the lie to), *what is left is a radically deideologized notion of toil,* which is stripped of intrinsic merit. This notion doesn't lend itself to mystification, and makes us breathe the rarefied air of great literature. With a different date, an analogous conversion of deprivation into lucidity gives strength to these lines by Carlos Drummond de Andrade*: "Heroes fill the city parks you drag yourself round, and recommend virtue, abnegation, sangfroid, conception."[12] On another level, we are close to one of Marx's formulations, who behind the illusions of modern wealth sees the muscular and cerebral effort expended by the workers, and nothing else.[13] In the end this is a materialist sense of work — enlightened and completely disillusioned — whose relevance moreover is not limited to the bourgeois order, since contemporary socialism is also, in its turn, *productionist*.

But it's not true to say that Dona Plácida's life has no meaning. If this sad lady were to ask why she had come into the world, Brás Cubas imagines that her parents would say this: "We've called you so that you can burn your fingers in the pans, ruin your eyes with sewing, eat badly, or not eat at all, rush from one place to another, hard at work, getting ill and getting better, so as to get ill and get better again, sad now, then desperate, tomorrow resigned, but always with your hands in the pans and your eyes on the sewing, until you end up one day in the gutter or the hospital; that was what we called you for, in a moment of mutual sympathy" (ch. 75).

The mockery of these lines operates in a complex manner. First, it pretends that the unacceptable realities of modern poverty have an aim in view ("that was what we called you for"). The condemnation is a two-way street: social reality is negative, because it lacks human meaning, just as the urge to find an aim for it at any price lacks meaning — in this context, the illusions of Divine Providence and its secularized substitutes are, in a Voltairean manner, exposed to ridicule. Neither the present order of things nor the justifications put forward for it satisfy the demands of reason, which points up their irrationality.

Furthermore, poverty is described in its regular, so to say functional, cycle, and there is method to its absurdity. In this sense it does have an end, even though a humanly unjustifiable one, which is to reproduce the social order that produces the self-same misery in which it exists. Where does that leave us?

The result is something like a mockery mocked, a kind of weeping without tears, to which is added the pleasure that so much inferiority gives to the social superiority of the narrator, who doesn't come out unscathed either. These, then, are raisons d'être that belong to the modern world, which have an affinity with scientific processes — such as the reproduction of the species, of society, and of injustice — and lack any transcendent justification. Seen as a whole, we witness a dizzying alternation of the perspectives of providentialism, the Enlightenment, and scientificism, according to the convenience of the Brazilian ruling class, whose indefensible mode of existence and manner of expressing it are universalized to the greatest degree possible by this literary form.

These are miseries with a recent date mark, which do not refer us to the Christian vale of tears, though the prose nevertheless takes its timbre from that universe, in the description of Dona Plácida's sufferings and labors.[14] For in a secularized context, the humble conformity in the terms used sounds like another taunt. This marriage of what artistic styles and the logic of the concepts should make one keep separate is one of Machado's great strengths. It can be noted, in the same fashion, that the explanation of the aim of Dona Plácida's life has the concise brevity of an eighteenth-century *conte philosophique* but also takes in the area of terrible fatalities contained in nineteenth-century Naturalism, without forgetting that its analytic coldness — universalist and classical in its style — has something jokey and crazed about it, which acts as *Brazilian local color* in the class characterization of Brás Cubas. In its turn, the nonchalance with which this multiplicity of prestigious registers is manipulated presages modern fiction.

As he contemplates his toe cap, Brás digresses on the fate of Dona Plácida, who has just left the room. The passage quoted earlier, where the unfortunate woman's portrait takes on generalized proportions, is part of these reflections. In his most intimate thoughts, the rich man has no difficulty in admitting the functional dimension of poverty, whose purpose on earth, if it has one, is to provide advantages for him: "A relative usefulness, I agree; but what the devil is absolute in this world?" (ch. 144). As in the Eugênia episode, the last word — in point of fact the second to last, since the last is left to the reader — rests with the party who benefits from the injustice, to the detriment of the poor, whose point of view remains unexpressed. The organization of the narration makes the accent fall on the ignominious side of the class relationship, with a result that is partly sadistic but also accusatory, keeping the fiction free of any role as cheap consolation.

Remembering previous observations, we can say that Dona Plácida's position is defined in the terms of this privilege, which can be understood as containing, as well as the material interests of Brás's class, his literary resources and repertoire of ideas. This procedure shocks by its "excessive" cynicism, which makes it self-denunciatory, a real class betrayal. Its merits, however, go further than this: through it, the form of poverty being discussed transcends the limited and intellectually isolated context that conditions it in the immediate sense, and is brought into the full daylight of contemporary conflicts and contemporary culture.

In other words, the mirroring of social positions in each other and in the diversity of historical styles does not undo the reality of classes, as purists of the popular point of view think.[15] On the contrary, it gives concrete form to their reciprocal mediation, and to the resultant complexity, which a more banal or doctrinaire notion of verisimilitude would fail to capture. It is this intensified realism that gives Dona Plácida an extraordinary fullness of reference, as well as her historical relevance, and rescues her from obscurity and apparent limitation. This is a breadth of scope in the understanding of poverty that only a cultured, sophisticated writer, at ease with a variety of styles, philosophies, and class experiences, could reach — and convey — which, from a dialectical point of view, is not a paradox.

Prudêncio

Look at the subtleties of the rascal!
Machado de Assis, *Posthumous Memoirs of Brás Cubas*

The episodes dealing with Eugênia and Dona Plácida stand out by the depth with which they invent (or observe?) the consequences that the Brazilian social structure brought for the underprivileged. This said, poor people are relatively numerous in the novel, where they compose a diverse, representative, and even systematically arranged group. There are, for example, three pretty girls: one a woman of easy virtue, another perfectly honest, and a third anxious to rise up the social scale, all of them contrasting with each other, and, in the other camp, with a girl, later lady, belonging to the upper echelons. As far as economic relations are concerned, the scale goes from beggary to paid work, passing through various kinds of personal dependence. In spite of the impression of haphazardness caused by the narrator's capricious methods, the caste of social types functions architecturally. Its composition caters to the need for a complete, non-repetitive exposition of the material; this implies a discipline that, in its turn, links the system of imagined positions to society's real structure.

As I have tried to show, slavery's presence is determinant, although figures of slaves are rare. A few scattered anecdotes are enough to fix the essential perspectives. This parsimony of allusions, whose repercussion is quite calculated, is, in its own way, emphatic: this is an expedient dear to Machado's humor, more drawn to venomous insinuation than open denunciation.

Hoping to please the Portuguese royal family, who at the time (1814) were still living in refuge in Brazil, Cubas Senior celebrates the (first) fall of Napoleon with a splendiferous dinner party. Among the food, the speeches, and the flirting, there's news of a new group of blacks who have arrived, the deal having been done in Luanda, a hundred and twenty altogether, of which "forty heads" had already been paid for (ch. 12). The indiscriminate mixing of family life, public festivities, and the horrors of the slave trade is a savage feature of "local color," a feature in fact borrowed from Martins Pena, who in a more innocent tone had already noted the comic nature of this mixture, in which the barbarous and right-thinking notes alternate.[16] In another chapter, little Brás splits open the head of a slave who had refused him a spoonful of dessert, or mounts, with reins and a whip, the slave boy Prudêncio, who is obliged to get on all fours and act as his horse. The lad's complaints go no further than "Ouch, massa!" to which Brás replies with his famous "Shut your mouth, animal!" [Cala a boca, besta!] (ch. 11). Just as the snapshot of the slave trade had cast the society present at the banquet in an altered light, little Cubas's acts of cruelty (or pranks, according to one's point of view) expose the social meaning of his education, and of the volubility that permeates the whole book. Both times, the slave has the almost exclusive role of pointing up sinister aspects of the ruling class.

There is also an attempt to see the slave from the point of view of what motivates him. Many years later, walking down the street, Brás encounters "one black whipping another," and replying to his moans with the "Shut your mouth, animal!" we are already familiar with (ch. 68). Naturally, it is Prudêncio, who, after he had been freed, bought a slave in his turn, and took out on him the blows he received years ago. Despite the daring with which it contradicts the humanitarian cliché, the episode suffers from a universalizing banality that almost transforms it into a parable: pessimism and evil can be clichés too. This impression is undone in the next chapter, which at first sight has nothing to do with the matter. The character in question here is a madman called Romualdo: "I am the illustrious Tamberlaine, he would say. Long ago I was Romualdo, but I got ill, and took so much tartar, so much tartar, so much tartar, that I became a Tartar and even King of the Tartars. Tartar has the power to make Tartars." Once the surprise is over, the reader given to solving puzzles will understand that the Tartar's savagery is the result of the tartar he has swallowed, just as the cruelty of the freed black — shocking, in that it suggests that suffering teaches one nothing — is the product of the blows that his masters had given him.

In conclusion, the scenes in which slaves condemn the Brazilian social order, define pernicious character traits, make obvious the impregnation of the upper classes by the habits of slave-owning, and make one see the slave within a framework of universalizing psychology, strictly no different from those of humanity in general. To appreciate the critical worth of this universalism, it's enough to think that in its light, the brutal actions of a freed slave are no less complex and spiritual than the divine caprices of an elegant lady, conversely to what common prejudice or the scientific racism then in fashion might think.

7

THE RICH ON THEIR OWN

Cotrim, the Brother-in-law

The best thing about a Russian is the low opinion he has of himself.

Turgenev, *Fathers and Sons*

IN SKETCHING THE PROFILE of his brother-in-law, in chapter 123, Brás Cubas operates with incriminating eulogies and damning justifications. The truly marvelous perfidiousness of this portrait explores embarrassments typical of the Brazilian situation.

The figure of Cotrim gathers together the most striking aspects of local bourgeois existence, and especially those that, from the civilized point of view, ought not to coexist. Well-established businessman, slave-smuggler,[1] loving paterfamilias, member of several brotherhoods (charitable, religious associations, characteristic of the colonial past), and patriot, this character is getting rich by means of shady deals with the Naval Arsenal, arranged through his brother-in-law Brás, now a deputy in parliament. If this situation were set in its contemporary context and given shape in a plot that developed its contradictions, we would have the basis here for a realist novel. And, in fact, the large number of details pointing to historical and social conflicts does anchor the *Memoirs* in this terrain, generally thought of as being brutally frank. The overt movement of the chapter, however, goes in a different direction, though of course without removing the validity of the other point of view, which is still there in implied form. Instead of giving depth to these contradictions, Brás tries to normalize them, and free them from the accusation that they are aberrant (in relation to what?). This is the reason for the series of accolades (or dagger blows, depending on one's point of view), which transform this compendium of the evils of the time into a model of all the virtues. The procedure is not simply a matter of ambiguously formulated mockery and jokes — that is, of rhetorical skill: it also affirms, in opposition to the liberal yardstick, the real experience of the Brazilian ruling class. To grasp the substance of this conflict between interpretations, think how, from a European viewpoint, Cotrim's biography would be exotic and scandalous, whereas from a Brazilian viewpoint, it is quite normal. The shudder produced by this divergence still runs through, for example, Gilberto Freyre's* reflections on the first viscount of Rio Branco,* "the son of an urban businessman who had become rich as an importer of slaves at a time — it should be emphasized — when this kind of commerce had not become, in Brazil, a degrading activity for an entrepreneur engaged in it, nor for his family. . . . "[2] Cotrim's portrait must be later, and the moral justification of this figure is now made at the price of a kind of insolence, which Machado takes great pleasure in.

The focus, then, lies not on Cotrim's actions and the *immensely* delicate questions they involve, but on Brás's efforts to gloss the picture over and exculpate him. In other words, the foreground belongs to the ruling classes' complicity in the face of historically unsustainable aspects of its situation, with a malicious emphasis on its grotesque consequences. What is being done is to put into words, as explicitly as possible, the intellectual and moral abrogation of duty made necessary by complete connivance with one's class; none of this prevents the social system's being laid bare, as it perhaps seems it might, since the solidarity of the beneficiaries is itself a substantive part of social reality and not just a character defect. Refining the argument further, it can be noted that Brás Cubas and Cotrim are different types, one well born, living off unearned income and with intellectual and political ambitions, while the other works tooth and nail to get rich in whatever way he can. In the novels of his edifying phase, Machado examined this difference from the point of view of traditional wealth and imputed most of the sordid actions to businessmen, or more generally to people capable of economic cunning. In the *Memoirs,* even though the sordidness of the business element is much greater and is given historical specificity, the contrasts that this causes among the well-off disappear, or are reduced to a question of style, with everything in the end being justified by Brás in the abject fashion we will see in a moment. His eulogy of Cotrim can be taken as a satire on the explanations that justify the alliance between these two sections of the ruling class.

"The Real Cotrim" — the chapter in question — is divided into two parts, the first in dialogue, the second a portrait. In the first, because Brás "loves family harmony," he goes to his brother-in-law to consult him on the suitability of the match with Nhã-Loló, Cotrim's niece. Cotrim refuses to reply, marriage being a personal matter, which should be kept separate from the interests of relatives. This position is as austere as it is comic, since the reader can easily see, and well knows from Cotrim's previous steps in this direction, that it is the uncle who is behind the maneuvers to marry the girl off. Moreover, the reader also knows that Brás doesn't give a toss for family harmony, and that he is motivated by weariness of a life of adultery, or, to put it another way, he wants to enjoy the privileges of conformity. On one side, then, promotion of family members' interests is done behind proclamations of respect for the individual's autonomy (the liberal, Romantic catchwords); on the other, the advantages of accommodation to the norm, which have nothing saintly about them, take on the mask of the quasi sanctity of the family. On both sides, the motives are completely transparent, even for the characters, which creates an atmosphere of hypocrisy that is sui generis, where veneration for and complete indifference to the norm go hand in hand. The aim of the dialogue is not to discover the secret motives of conduct, but to illustrate, in a colorful manner, the tone of collusion inherent to this comedy, and that everyone would be familiar with. Since apparently no one is harmed by this, the effect is especially amusing, all of which changes in the next stage, when the question of slavery surfaces.

Now the word is with Brás Cubas, who defends his brother-in-law in a compact paragraph with a brutal concision. Following on from the hypocrisy of the previous conversation, where the desire for accommodation was at its greatest, the direct prose, fed by a reflective, adult familiarity with the worst aspects of social life and their justifications (a register that, in Brazilian literature, only Machado has cultivated) brings a blast of cold air.[3] Now, the harmonized contrast between complacency and an incisive formulation of the facts tells us, among other things, that the wealthy are not softened by their lack of ideological rigidity, nor are they prevented by it from going to extremes to defend their interests.

It is one thing for Brás Cubas to attest to Cotrim's scrupulous respect for personal choice, which is obviously false but gives everybody extra dignity: common interest in reconciling clientelist practice and liberal appearances explains the reciprocal bonhomie. It would be something else to recognize the validity of the liberal-humanitarian view outside its function as flattery. The difference brings out a new tone, in which understanding is replaced by a determined indulgence in infamy. To the person to whom the savage part of this portrait is addressed, someone ideologically opposed to him, Brás does not reply with tolerance, but with every piece of sophistry at his command, and, above all, with the bleak reality, without avoiding the shameful truth. Why is Cotrim's manner very "dry" to the extent that many accuse him of being "barbarous" (the disproportion between these adjectives synthesizes — beautifully — the embarrassing way in which he is historically out of step)? "The only fact alleged in this respect was that he frequently sent slaves to the jail, whence they emerged dripping blood: but, apart from the fact that he sent only the perverse ones and repeated fugitives, it is also true that, having smuggled slaves for a long time, he had in a certain way got used to the somewhat harsher treatment that this line of business required, and one cannot honestly attribute to the basic nature of the man what is purely the effect of social relations." This politeness within the elite, making ostentatious use of the best of contemporary culture, nevertheless has as its obverse the brutality inflicted on the slaves. For the sheer daring of the adaptation, it's worth underlining the perverse use of sociological conditioning — "one cannot honestly attribute to the basic nature of the man what is purely the effect of social relations" — in favor of the slave trader and not against the institution of slavery.

The satirical mechanics of the passage lie in the excuses that in fact point the finger of blame, the arguments in mitigation that in fact aggravate the guilt, or, more generally, in the accusatory function of the defense, conducted in a manner distanced from itself, and with the complicity of the enlightened reader. This defense is, in truth, an indictment of the accused, and of the person pleading on his behalf. The duplicity in the exposition takes for granted the historical superiority of the *advanced* point of view over the *backward* one — a superiority guaranteed, in these circumstances, by *European* disapproval of slavery and colonial ways of life — so that the mere expression of the latter is, for the former, something one can joke about. Without denying the rhetorical ingenuity of this procedure, in which the act of formulating one point of view actually provides ammunition for its opponent, we can note its aggressively satirical spirit, designed to give strength to a victorious doctrine (even if it is one that is locally in opposition).

Seen in toto, however, the chapter doesn't stop here and points to more complex conclusions. Brás and Cotrim, the obscurantist duet, are made to look disreputable in the light of modern criteria. However, the same mixture of traits that defines them as backward and laughable also makes them respectable, not at all laughable members of the Brazilian ruling class. The inferiority that results from the modern principles we have mentioned, then, no longer goes uncontested. In other words, the dynamic of the episode is linked to the absurdity of the players *and to the vigor and reality of their positions,* which leave no space available for the moral demands that at the beginning had made us laugh a superior laugh. Taking up the previous argument, we can say then that Brás concedes and even details his brother-in-law's brutalities, but his desire is to explain them as part of the order of things, which is the only one we've got, end of story. Armed with learning and a facility for argument, naturally under Machado's auspices, the liberal of the slave-owning, clientelist type is made to pay down to the last cent the debt contracted by his social advantages, this in terms of an abjectness that becomes explicit in the light of a criterion that he himself gives credence to—and all this without preventing his moral ruination's appearing as a demonstration of his power.

To analyze this, let us look, one by one, at four perspectives that make up this ideological quid pro quo.

(a) *Cotrim's defense.* This consists in underlining the fact that he is strictly normal and fits perfectly into his social setting (a normal man can't be a monster). This procedure allows one to recognize virtues where there seemed to be weaknesses. Thus: why shouldn't a businessman be economical? How should a smuggler of African slaves not be hard? Don't perverse and runaway slaves deserve to be punished? A father who suffers so much when his daughter dies can't be lacking in feelings of pity! Impossible that the member of several charitable brotherhoods should be a skinflint! How can one criticize a merchant who doesn't owe anyone a red cent? The good sense of these reasonings respects a certain reality and its most obvious demands, and, according to the principle that the ruling classes are exemplary by nature, praises the brother-in-law as "a model." Coming from a character so fond of insulting others, this hyperconformity naturally takes on a cynical connotation and itself constitutes a kind of censure.[4]

(b) *The denunciation of Cotrim.* From the angle of a liberalism whose abstract principle functions as the frontier between civilization and barbarism, this defense is merely a condemnation: slavery is a deliberate infraction of the Rights of Man, physical punishment is an indignity, smuggling is illegal, while the exterior forms of religious belief denote backwardness. Fueled by each new phrase, the carefully built-up confusion between the viewpoints (or tones) of conformity, cynicism, and indignation is a great literary achievement in its capacity to sum up an insoluble historical grotesquerie. The farce is somewhat similar to — for example — what Mozart was trying to get in the opening scenes of *Don Giovanni,* where though in complete incompatibility, the voices of the libertine, of conjugal love, and of family honor are harmonized.

(c) *The indictment of the defense.* Cotrim's justification extends the barbarity of its project to the level of ideas, by giving it the context of contemporary culture, thanks to Machado's intellectual resources. Brás's argumentative ploys, perfected and given didactic form in a possibly Stendhalian spirit — today we would say Brechtian — are satirical documents giving witness of this nineteenth-century, liberal repositioning of slavery.[5] The routine use of the slave prison, for example, with whippings and bloodshed, serve to demonstrate . . . the lack of arguments on the opposing side, made indignant by this "single fact." The same torture then proves . . . Cotrim's humanity, since he "sent [to prison] only the perverse ones and the repeated fugitives." The very condition of being a slave smuggler occurs as an argument for the defense, since it makes these same barbarities explicable and thus natural. Nothing could be more humanitarian and modernizing, too, than to reflect on the historical conditioning of depraved conduct ("purely the effect of social relations"): a reformist notion, transformed, however, into a slave owner's alibi, and, above all, offering a splendid demonstration of an ultraconservative reuse of European intellectual innovations. Finally, the invocation of the religious and paternal feelings of the businessman serves only to make the picture more shameless. It underlines the limitation and partiality of his sympathy, and, since it is specious in that it defines the character by only one part of his existence — the presentable aspect, which excuses the other — it prompts the reader to the inverse consideration, where parental affection and pious sentiments are seen derisively, merely as elements that serve an immediate purpose, and are compatible with the most complete lack of humanity. Altogether, the defense makes use of considerations of good sense, moral reflections, information vouching for good character, sociological elucidations, sincere testimony, a battery of procedures linked to persuasion and the compromises involved in living in any society with one's fellows. The fact that slavery is in the near vicinity naturally destroys their credit, causing the familiar farcical effect, characteristic of the liberalism of the Second Reign. However, the irony of the *Memoirs* is not limited to denouncing this aspect of the question. The novel specializes in observing and conceiving sequences in which modern forms are twisted to serve the peculiar ensemble of local interests. The improper uses they are put to, or better, the fact that these improper uses fit in so well in this society, is the real blue-eyed boy of Machado's inventiveness, something in which he sees particular interest, and which is worthy of being put on show and questioned.

(d) *The overall result*. What can we call a man who is dry in his manner, economical, an exemplary head of the family, with no debts, inclined to philanthropy and actively religious? These are the attributes of a gentleman, perhaps an Englishman — and of Cotrim, if we are to believe his counsel for the defense. The subject of the portrait harbors the same certainty: one need only consider the respect — almost spectacular, one might say — with which he deals with his niece's marriage. However, in reply to his detractors, who have a less flattering view of the character, Brás gives us the details of the activities that this figure "modernizes" or "legitimates." Then there arises another Cotrim, the slave smuggler, adept at barbarous punishments, who practices backward forms of religion, eagerly lusts after cheap honors, and is as solvent as he is stingy. *The abyss between these two figures is the same as the one separating the Brazilian ruling class from itself — that is, from the paradigm of European progress.*

Why should a slave owner enjoying the advantages of his life with a full openness not be respectable and modern — as he was, in the local context? The impossibility of such a thing is a consequence of the standards established by the bourgeois revolutions, standards that were flouted everywhere, including the United States, Britain, and France, but that one could not *remain ignorant of,* on pain of being excluded from the civilized world.[6] Brás and Cotrim, moreover, cultivate this enlightened image precisely because they will not give up on the link with universal progress, of which they consider themselves to be the local representatives. It's true that they pay the price for this inconsistency on that moral front, but this has a more harmful effect on these moral standards themselves — mocked as being completely useless — than it does on them. Even so, the discrepancy cries out to heaven, and only some form of complicity will let it pass muster and escape protest — that same protest that will certainly be heard from those less well disposed to these characters, among whom the reader may well find himself.

As for the malice in the narrative, we should observe that the torture of the slaves appears on a secondary plane, as one detail among others in a formally very civilized argument, aimed at convincing us of Cotrim's Victorian virtues. That is the reason for its explosive effect, since slavery and the whip figure among the things most abominated by the ideology whose external signs the two brothers-in-law display and whose prestige they aspire to. The humor is the result of the concision of the account, which throws the baselessness, or barefacedness, of these ambitions into relief. So, removed from their routine contexts, smuggling slaves and physical punishment are suddenly, unexpectedly placed in the context of liberal ideas and attitudes, where they prompt rejection *on principle*. The strident tone of the sarcasm, abstract and moralistic — or aggressive, or even pseudoliberal — derives from this summary judgment of one historical experience according to the criteria of another, whose role is hegemonic and unquestioned. However, going back over our argument, it so happens that effective, public participation in nineteenth-century progress in fact takes on board the identity of those who profit from the Brazilian national system. So, the prose, which juxtaposes the incompatible dimensions of this class experience in the spirit of an accusatory montage, is not just the result of Brás's malice. In the total context of the novel, it gives objectivity to the moral scandal latent in the everyday life of the characters, who adopt and fail to adopt liberal criteria as they pass judgment on themselves. Thus, the narrator's tendency to be insulting can be seen as the external duplication of the awareness that the privileged section of society would have of itself if it wanted to be coherent.

We can see, on the rhetorical level, how ingeniously Brás's formulations give simultaneous support to two opposing points of view. The overt position sees no reason to object to the civilized reputation of a businessman with no debts and who fits in with local customs. The underlying position puts the emphasis on these same customs, pointing out the distance that separates them from the modern ideal. This second point of view could be made explicit if we said that, differently from Cotrim all along the line, the up-to-date individual does not own slaves, does not beat them or smuggle them; the philanthropy he practices does not serve to humiliate his fellowman or to achieve the honor of having his portrait done in oils for the brotherhood; the good deeds he performs are not published in the papers; his religious life has no need of accolades; and his scrupulous opposition to nepotism prevents his wanting to marry off his niece to strengthen family alliances. What are we to think of these forms of behavior, all of them unsuited to an enlightened person in the normative sense of the word but that are characteristic of Cotrim?

At first sight, they make their proud owner, his brother-in-law Brás, and, more generally, the society of the *Memoirs* seem *backward,* because they are either provincial or barbaric, and ridiculous above all in their claim to be *advanced*. Provincialism and barbarity in this case are seen as negative qualities, as deficiencies when confronted with rational, universalistic individualism, one of the ideals of bourgeois culture, and which lies tacitly in the background of the story. This negative characterization—reality as the negation of the model—discredits the façade of local progressivism. It functions as a killjoy and a stigma, with an undeniable though relative critical effect. This is because the satirical attack on slave-owning and clientelism, which do not conform to the modern norm and so are shameful, in its turn expresses a form of inferiority, insofar as it disowns its own social experience and is subordinated to the intellectual hegemony of the advanced countries, whose self-representation becomes an absolute criterion. To avoid this form of Bovarysm, itself an expression of backwardness, we can say that Brás's and Cotrim's presumptuous claims to civilization can be criticized or rejected as unjustified, but that this does not cancel out their existence, nor does it stop their having a real link, though a strange one, with progress. Instead of insisting on the absurdity of the morality involved, and so simply rejecting it, it is better to examine its reality and historical meaning, which changes the terms of the question.

Coming back to Cotrim's behavior, aside from the fact that it is inappropriate for an enlightened person, *it is typical of colonial society,* as is easy to see. Modern pretensions apart, labor relations, forms of sociability, religious style, the kinds of prestige, the crass disparity in the rules of behavior—some suitable for the colonizer's world, and others to the "somewhat harsher" relationship with those colonized—all of this has the mark of an earlier time, of the "Old Regime," which moreover gives a certain homogeneity to the atmosphere of the whole. At this point, it is worth reminding ourselves what was said many pages back about the conservative nature of Brazilian independence. In our case, the break with the metropolis and opening-up to the contemporary world were not accompanied by a social revolution, as we know, and were more of a deal done at the top. The immense complex formed by slave labor, the subjection of one person to another and by clientelism, developed through previous centuries, remained intact, while the local administration and local landowners, on the basis of this very continuation of a way of life, transformed themselves into the Brazilian ruling class and, what's more, into members of the world bourgeoisie then in the process of formation, as well as protagonists of modernity in the strong sense of the word.[7] This short digression shows, I hope, that the regular way in which modern and colonial traits appear concomitantly does not represent backwardness or absurdity, as analysis from a liberal point of view as well as liberal feelings on the matter might make one think, but is the logical and *emblematic* consequence of the form that progress took in Brazil. The privileged position held by characters whom the idea of civilization implied in this chapter would relegate to the position of relics of the past is indicative of this, on the literary level.

Right next to the Brás Cubas who is a fully paid-up member of his class we find his enlightened alter ego, who has a horror of this same class, winking at the reader and showing himself and his brother-in-law up as barbarians. There is, however, a third person who, without expressing himself directly, speaks through the composition. In silence, as befits his role, the architect of the narrative situations is telling us that enthusiasm for progress, of which liberal ideas are a part, is compatible with an iniquity that these same ideas condemn. Colonial barbarism's usefulness to the progress of the Brazilian elite is at the center of Machado's humor and his nihilism.[8]

The connivings of the rich have to do with the preservation of colonial connections in the context of the independent nation, in contradiction with the principle of liberal individualism. If our paraphrase is correct, the extraordinary apology and demolition of Cotrim, undertaken by his relative and ally, lays bare the ambivalence typical of this situation. At the level of synthesis that literature has privileged access to, the enjoyment of injustice, in the internal Brazilian setting, is conjoined with the shame of backwardness, on the international stage. We can say then that the irony of the prose takes its substance from a systematic reference to the transatlantic context. The definition of its area of operations cannot be local, any more than it can be universal, since the "anomalous" relationship between the bourgeois norm and the anecdotes lays out before us a *coloration* that is decidedly Brazilian. The rhythm of the writing, in other words, has to do with a precise historical situation, and with an external yardstick that is part of that situation.

On the other hand, it is plain that we are not in the presence of a confrontation of opposing social interests, in the manner of French realism. The great alliances that make up the contemporary scene are not considered in their total dynamic, but from the point of view of the moral problems set up by their coexistence. We can say that in the *Memoirs* the invention of the story line gives up part of its dynamic role to the narrative prose itself, which brings into the heart of a phrase, of a line of argument, of an ambiguity, and above all, into the heart of the moral conscience, the conflicting perspectives that, in its own interests, the Brazilian elite was trying to accommodate within itself. The continual changing of focus makes the anecdotes—trivial in themselves—feed a dizzying prose *whose historico-social movement lies in the twists and turns between the different trends in play*. Although these inconsistencies prolong and accentuate external realities, the scandalous atmosphere that surrounds them belongs to the moral sphere, and implies an inspiration to the very coherence that has just been flouted. Intensified by the narrative technique, the clash of these different points of view necessarily brings on a crisis, the substance of which lies in the incongruities of the Brazilian situation—when judged by enlightened criteria. The moral conscience questions them scrupulously, even if it is by means of a satirical form of approval, and, faced with their immorality, reaches the conclusion that it—the moral conscience—is powerless, which in this context is one further piece of information to go along with the rest.

Brás's Miseducation

How is Brás's character to be explained? The answer can be found in his childhood, in his domestic surroundings, in the temperament he inherits, and in the education he receives (chs. 10–12). His father, insensible to the demands of morality or reason, sees himself mirrored in the boy's pranks, with inexhaustible complacency and pleasure: "and if sometimes he told me off, in front of other people, it was a mere formality: in private, he would kiss me" (ch. 11). His mother "was a weak-willed lady, with not much brain and a great deal of heart, credulous enough, sincerely pious—homespun even though she was pretty, and modest, though she was wealthy: fearful of thunder and her husband" (ch. 11). Uncle João distinguishes himself by indecent exposure in the presence of slaves and women of easy virtue, while another uncle, Canon Ildefonso, irreproachable as regards purity, lives more for the ceremony of the church services than for the spirit of religion. In their turn, the slaves provide excellent opportunities for little Brás's caprices and brutalities, which are also directed as guests, whose indulgent attitude may well be due to the importance of the Cubas family. In all of these relationships, it is obvious that a certain ideal of reason, dignity, and inner integrity is offended. Seen as a whole, it is a milieu with nothing but defects, of which Brás's volubility—a failing in its own right—is in all likelihood the natural product. "From this soil and from this manure was this flower born" (ch. 11).

The chapter is inspired by Naturalism, though only to compete with it and outdo it. Here we have the search for causes, methodical observation, scientific ambitions, and even the argument about inherited features: his mother's melancholy disposition and his father's vanity are *transmitted* to their son (ch. 11). What can be seen too is that the legacy is a relatively fluid one, less drastic than the hereditary defects and racial fatalism of orthodox Naturalism. Nevertheless, this circumspection in the treatment of "natural" causes does not mean that there is any desire to attenuate or idealize the truth. Quite the contrary, Machado wants to beat Naturalism in the sphere of exact description, of explanatory rigor, of the perception of salacious details, though without breaking with decorum. Thus, he opposes to the clumsy determinism of climate and race the harmful effects of backward cultural habits, which he studies in tiny monographs of a few lines, each of great substance, in which the local reference and the analytic and critical spirit are combined. The result is a brilliant gallery of types, sketched in the manner of the universalizing moral portrait typical, for example, of seventeenth-century French writers like La Bruyère, but that targets sociohistorical realities: the wealthy individual who denies his son and heir nothing, the pious lady stuck in the house with her superstitions, Uncle João's antics with the slaves and the poor, the punctilious, obedient, and empty Catholicism of the canon. The whole thing forms a *social* environment, armed with causal efficacy that can be contrasted with the almost physical, and for that reason "scientific," causation proposed by Naturalism.

From another angle, we can say that Machado was setting against the vulgar materialism of some of the "advanced" thinking of his time, tailor-made for Brazilian racial dilemmas and the vastness of the tropics, an eighteenth-century rationalism of a Voltairean cut, with its humorous interest in the diversity and irrationality of human institutions. In this context, it is useful to bear in mind a classic objection to Voltaire's historiography, which despite its sprightly tone is in fact static: his repertoire of anecdotes gathered from here, there, and everywhere serves, according to this objection, to illustrate the superiority of bourgeois reason and human folly, two *absolutes* that for that very reason do not attain to a true sense of history.[9] This criticism seems to fit the narrative style of the *Memoirs* perfectly: in it, the comic distance between the anecdote and the norm is also constant. However, the fact that there is influence in the technique does not mean that the two have the same ideological horizon, nor does it exclude a different manner of operation. If we are to believe our conclusions above, Machado's opposition between life as he observes it and reason carries weight in modern terms, in spite of the older literary manner used to express it. In an unexpected way, this opposition captures the ambiguous relationship between Brazilian social structure and the ideology dominant in advanced countries, so much so that irony directed at rationalist dogma — no less than at local realities — is one of the recurrent forms it takes, and so expresses a specific historico-social configuration. Finally, the discipline imposed by brevity and the constant presence of the Ideal may look as if they are regressive, and incompatible with the movement toward deidealization and the raw subject matter, transgressive in terms of decency and the law, that made Naturalism so modern. But what happens is that the Ideal appears in a deidealized form in the *Memoirs,* while the brevity of these notations, whether because of or in spite of the spectacle they provide of an intelligence quick to adapt and react, extends to the realm of the spirit the lack of meaning that the naturalists base in the sphere of the instincts.

This much said, the exquisite quality of the observations and their literary expression does not prevent these passages from being weak moments at the level of the composition of the book as a whole. Although notable, the chapters centered on Brás Cubas's upbringing compare unfavorably with the other three-quarters of the novel, whose dominant tone, respectively, is the expansion of narrative caprice, the amorality of the adulterous affair with Virgília, and the extraordinary climate of tedium and breakup of the final pages. It is true that this faulty education plausibly explains the voluble character of the author-narrator. But it also clearly identifies him as inferior, something which, given the ambiguity with regard to values inherent to the form of the *Memoirs,* represents an artistic mistake and, consequently, a loss of tension. Despite its critical aim, the indictment of Brás's miseducation has something edifying about it, because it involves an implicit approval of bourgeois standards of discipline. For some few pages, we know where the truth lies, which harms the ideological complexity and formal integrity of the book.

Returning to relationships within the family, the father loves his own image in his son, above all in his misdeeds, which function as an amusing extension of his own impunity. Trampling on someone else's dignity and living according to the whims of caprice are ways of acting that seem to imply that he is above the law. However, the two Cubases conform strictly to the rules of the oligarchy, which are, according to the context, an arranged marriage, political nepotism, and a horror of the poor, as well as the aspiration to be advanced ("my father . . . applied to my education a system entirely superior to the one used at that time" [ch. 11]). Once more, disrespect for the law, conformity to the rules of the oligarchy, and pretension to modernity go together. As usual, the fact that this conjunction is untenable can only be ignored thanks to the conniving of other members of the same class. And in fact, the father's rapture at the abuses perpetrated by his little heir goes beyond the commonplace about love being blind: and this because it includes a social twist whose essence lies in the domineering of the rich, and in the historical situation of which it is part.

"'That's a clever lad you've got there,' exclaimed his audience. 'Very clever,' my father would agree, and his eyes were brimming over with pride; he would put his hand on my head, looking at me for a long time, lovingly, full of himself" (ch. 10). This contentment of the human soul with itself, thanks to the praises received by his son, corresponds to a particular interest of Machado's. It can be caused, indifferently, by a full stomach, by love, by someone else's envy, by a letter from a minister, by the cessation of some embarrassment, by eulogies lavished on some bad poetry. In these circumstances or others like them, the eyes turn delightedly inward—"He saw nothing, he saw himself" (ch. 12)—and the flux of life slows down. Episodes like this occur periodically and have a structural place in the matter of the *Memoirs*. They are the "good moments" to which Rubião will refer years later, in *Quincas Borba* (ch. 24), local variants of the plenitude that in Goethe's *Faust* suspends the restless movement of change and makes one wish for calm and a slowing-down of time. As with the cruelty of the chapter of the lame girl, or the connivance of the chapter about Cotrim, these states of rapture reveal one of the vital forms of the volubility we are studying. And here too the reference to an iniquitous social structure is the key to the underlying meaning: in this light, the understanding between accomplices or, at one extreme, the harmony of the soul with itself take on the demeaning connotation that, in this book, characterizes them. In the inner recesses of the conscience, or in the realm of class complicity, there is always the satisfaction of breaking the law and paying homage to it at the same time, which gives them the benefit of the applause due to both things.

Virgília

As a force for the individual's self-affirmation and definition, love in the *Memoirs* is weak and avoids confronting its adversaries. To a certain degree, social institutions, injustice, the prying eyes of third parties, and the inconstancy of the senses are even its allies. And, what's more, conformity doesn't spoil its plenitude, which at times is powerful, as well as being enigmatic.

There is nothing more mediocre or less romantic than the amorous triangle formed by Virgília, Brás Cubas, and Lobo Neves. Without investing too much effort, the lover tries to take the woman away from her husband, but soon settles for adultery, given extra savor by the tittle-tattle and envy of others—and all this without removing from the lovers the right to occasional tears and grand gestures. In his turn, the husband fails to notice the available evidence for as long as possible, and acts only when he is cornered by the buzz of anonymous gossip, which reveals itself for that very reason to be "a good solder for domestic institutions" (ch. 113). So the norm and its transgression exist, but work differently from the way one would expect. Between the two there is room for a variety of intermediate forms, which are more real than the conflict between them. The narrator himself is not romantic either, and his commentary, always mocking, doesn't polarize individual aspirations and marriage: he prefers to study the system of voluntary and involuntary compensations that make Brás and Lobo Neves live "pleased with each other," or almost (ch. 50). In other words, on the level of analytical curiosity, too, the satisfactions of settling for the lesser option win out over the demands of exclusive love. These are relationships at ground level, with nothing grand about them, which, however, will allow Machado to explore unknown territory.

The reduced stature of the male characters is due to the preponderance of chance and the opinion of others in decisions that are said—gravely and emphatically—to be taken independently. This discrepancy is not caused by the embarrassments of the adultery, does not disappear when they do, and is not limited to that sphere. Brás is romantic in the same perfunctory way that he is liberal, a scientist, a philosopher, a politician, or a poet: to keep up with the times, according to the prerogatives of his own position and without the discipline such things should demand. For Lobo Neves something similar is true. For this is a general mode of existence, whose foundations in class and whose ties with Brazilian reality we have already tried to point out. This naturally does not mean that in Brazil there were no elopements, or that husbands did not kill their rivals or unfaithful wives. It only means that Machado isolated a certain kind of relationship with the contemporary bourgeois norm as being characteristic of the country. The local color of the affair between Virgília and Brás is not the consequence of marital infidelity but of the peculiar way in which the norm of marriage is treated.

Virgília, unlike the gentlemen, does not have a reduced stature. She too wants the best of both worlds, which would give room for the audacities of the modern, elegant smart set, without excluding the advantages of her traditional position. Worldly splendor, a bit of agnosticism, romantic flirting, freedom in love — all without affecting a solid family life, public respect, a jacaranda-wood prie-dieu in her bedroom, an unstained reputation, and privilege. What happens is that the simultaneous quest for these contradictory advantages diminishes the men, since it removes any credit from their moral gravitas, which rests on a presumption of consistency. In the woman's case, in contrast, this same inconsistency is one more charming feature, and even an evidence of strength, since it indicates the possibility of satisfaction in every department, where masculine mania for coherence can see only impasses and the need to choose. Virgília, when she is faced by two alternatives, chooses both. Why should she elope with Brás? Wouldn't it be better to meet in a discreet little house? "I saw that it was impossible to split two things that were completely inseparable in her mind: our love and her reputation. Virgília was capable of great and equal sacrifices to keep both advantages, and flight left her with only one" (ch. 6).

In itself, the contrast between male and female psychology has nothing notable about it. However, on a different, displaced plane, it echoes the structural theme of the *Memoirs*. It alludes to the "indigenous" union of European progress and colonial archaism, and offers two ways of confronting it. Thus, in all conscience, an enlightened gentleman will say that this said union is an embarrassment, and some kind of unease will reveal itself, though this will have no practical consequences, since the situation is imposed by reality and there is no choice in the matter. Even the inner sanctum of the mind, that prestigious and universalizing place where the discrepancy makes itself felt, has something displaced about it; perhaps it too was a part of the equipment of the up-to-date citizen, in the same way as cigars or a frock coat. However this may be, contested as it is by the slavery and paternalism by which it is surrounded, the emphasis on principles gives a somewhat ridiculous imprint to male actions, something that goes beyond the psychology of the sexes and reveals the shape of one of the basic ways the Brazilian ruling class had of living with their problems. In the case of women, on the other hand, since they are alien to the universalizing rigor of bourgeois precepts, which would seem too harsh in their case, they choose not to choose: they don't see why they should forgo advantages within their reach and that only the superstitious belief in liberal appearances, or an idée fixe forcing one to justify one's actions all the time, make incompatible with one another. This antiformalistic attitude to the norm protects them from an illusion central to nineteenth-century Brazil. As a consequence, in Machado's universe, they are the figures who can reach a state of harmony, if this term is used in a nonmoral sense. The status of bourgeois rules in Brazil, which do and do not have currency there, is the distant referent of this relativization of scruples — charming or detestable, depending on the case at issue. When Virgília is disposed, as we have seen, to "great and equal sacrifices to keep both advantages," she is developing the unconstrained internal posture that allowed the ruling class to enjoy its mixed privileges of slavery, bullying clientelism, and modern life, without loss of face. In this context, the scene in which this same splendid lady is thwarted is suggestive: she bursts into tears and puts a handkerchief in her mouth, to stifle the sobs and not attract attention, a violent explosion in which there is no place for any sense of what is right or wrong.

Feminine psychology, novelistic structure, and the historical particularities of the country all intercommunicate and produce the kind of resonance befitting realist fiction. That said, the close proximity of women to nature and to instinct, which can work as an insult or a compliment, is a general idealization of the time, with nothing especially Brazilian about it. The contrasting term would be the artificiality of male existence, which at that time was being revolutionized by the systematic demands of capital — while mothers, wives, and daughters, so long as they were not poor, continued to be confined to family tasks and feelings, and were protected from, or deprived of, according to one's point of view, continuous direct contact with the new reality.[10] From this follows the set of differences that, from the middle of the century on, mixed in with Darwin and Schopenhauer, fed into yet another deepening of the myth of Eve, now seen as a pole antithetical to the prevailing order and even as a historical alternative to it. In this line of thinking, the feminine side came to represent an amalgam of unconscious, telluric forces and animal appetites, capable, according to its sympathizers, of regenerating decadent, masculine, Christian civilization. Analogous observations led misogynists to an opposite evaluation, highlighting the infantilism and amorality of women, always in need of patriarchal control.

A random set of examples will be enough to give an outline of this tendency, in which many of the themes of present-day feminism originate. Ibsen, for example, will look to women for an integrity capable of supplanting the conventionality and hypocrisy of the bourgeois world, represented by husbands and fathers bogged down in work. Rilke, in the *Letters to a Young Poet,* hoped that the concentration, the ability to wait, and the sense of mystery — all spiritual derivations of aspects of pregnancy — would found the new order of the future and liberate men from unhealthy, utilitarian dispersal of energy. Wedekind's *Lulu* shows sex as at last freed from family tutelage, as Karl Kraus looked for this same freedom in prostitutes. Otto Weininger, in his turn, sees female nature as the absolute enemy of normative, conscious life, and of culture in general, which, according to him, is masculine. Freud read *Sex and Character* with interest, and in fact, in the thirty-third introductory lecture on psychoanalysis, we again find, expressed in a perfectly polished form, this thesis of the comparatively amoral nature of women, which in his view is attributable to the girl's desire to marry her father, rather than kill him, as would be necessary if the superego were to be properly formed. Oswald de Andrade's speculations about matriarchy in Pindorama belong to the same tradition. Without giving too many examples, we can conclude that Virgília brought this intellectual strain to Brazil relatively early. Along with the other upper-class female characters in other works by Machado, she too disturbs in practice — rather than confronting openly — the bourgeois concept of reality, above all the contractualist concept of the self. When she proposes to Brás Cubas "a little house that will be just ours, tucked away, with a little garden, in some hidden street," Virgília speaks "with the naive and indolent tone of voice of someone not thinking she is doing anything wrong, and the smile that lowered the corners of her mouth had the same innocent expression" (ch. 64). No question of committing a crime, or of having rights, is involved, just of arranging matters in a satisfactory way, a naïveté that in Machado's world is at one and the same time divine and despicable. For the purposes of our argument, we can see that through the moral indifference of his female characters, Machado married new themes from the European philosophy of the unconscious with the historical position of the Brazilian elite, itself condemned by circumstances to play fast and loose with the rules.

In the prose of the *Memoirs,* everyday life in Rio de Janeiro lives side by side with baroque allegories of human insignificance, founding heroes of the modern age, biblical figures, and episodes from classical antiquity. This is a satirical method very much of its own century, which suits the impression of cheapening created by the reordering of society by private property. According to Marx's famous argument, the bourgeois revolution in its heroic phase had imagined itself dressed in a Roman toga, only to change it soon after for the clothes appropriate for the pursuit of profit, which was the real objective in modern times.[11] It was only natural that artists should put the emphasis on the toga, to highlight the contrast. In Machado's novels, however, literary forms linked to nonbourgeois universes have yet another function: indirectly, they point to real dimensions of local existence, also partly nonbourgeois, and that lie outside the individualist profile taken for granted in realist prose.

Virgília herself has a mouth "as fresh as the dawn and as insatiable as death." In her mature years, her beauty becomes "magnificent." Her figure is sculpted in Greek marble, "a noble creation, full and pure, quietly beautiful, like a statue." Her pupils "encapsulated love itself" (ch. 63). Later, she will look like "an imposing ruin" (ch. 5). The mythical echoes of her character (yet, she lives through the trivial complications of marriage, adultery, sick relations, disputes over inheritance, aristocratic pretensions, and more) are in line with the antiNaturalist reaction of the time. Leaving aside the question of literary models, let us look at the unexpected power of the social realism in these images. The stages of life, of each day in life, of desire, of the maturing and decadence of the body, are rhythms that, because of their generality and cyclical nature, do not fit into the framework of individualist and historical action in the modern sense. The same goes for the individual who is more than an individual, and who sums up in himself an entire aspect of human life, of which, in turn, he becomes the symbol. Of course, this vision of things was not excluded from realist fiction, which used it extensively, as a contrast capable of throwing new modes of existence into relief and problematizing them. In the *Memoirs,* however, its echoes appear in the heart of the plot, marked out, or, better, *disqualified* by the absence of any more forceful, defining form of individual action. In the absence of bourgeois virtues, which might give it substance through the characters' projects and contradictions, time flows in a manner that is not really defined, though it has substance, and its distinctive trait is the minor importance given to the deliberate, willed aspects of life. Conditioned by the fact that Brazil is historically out of phase, this narrative rhythm has a negative connotation (the inertia of those who take their profits from a slave-owning enterprise). The flip side of this diminution in stature, however, is the emergence of a peculiar kind of greatness, which Machado, with his extraordinary ideological and literary independence, allows us to see. It is a greatness compatible up to a point with the arsenal of images and formulas from classical literature — this time the connotations are positive — and can even support epic aspects, if we understand by the word the unity of the characters with the cycle of nature, and with themselves.

Virgília's beauty, for instance, peaks and reaches heroic dimensions quite apart from any biographical, moral, or social considerations, without asking their permission, so to speak. Also, Brás Cubas's clandestine love affairs after some time reach their zenith and stay there, all with no real aims in view — that is, without any real merit or remorse, no future perspectives, no exemplary qualities, and so on. This is a moral indifference that does not overcome guilt, does not assimilate it, nor, much less, is it innocent, and whose novelistic depth is the result of its affinity with the general relativization of the norm in the *Memoirs*. The poetic impact of these plot inventions is remarkable: in them, the way things happen in Brazil is condensed and questioned to the greatest possible degree — and tends to pass unnoticed. In this context, Virgília with her mouth like the dawn and like death is more than an allegory of the illusions of the flesh. In the analytical and unsentimental atmosphere of prose narrative, the classical, epigrammatic quality of the language means the suppression of complicating factors linked to the individual realization of the lovers — and this, paradoxically, works as a suggestion of their historical particularity. It is in the context of indolence and privilege — one could almost say of tropical indolence and privilege — set up in the plot that the novel's expression acquires its precise value.

Like a summer's day, unconnected with virtue, effort, or understanding, the plenitude of love is simply there. In the same spirit, when some time has passed, the only cause of love's decline will be boredom — it, too, free of other complications. Hardly connected with the norms and aims that preside over the individual's self-realization, desire follows a separate cycle, with its own seasons. Anxiety and satiety, curiosity and boredom, attraction and repugnance, with moments of plenitude along the way — these are the poles, with nothing Christian about them, between which love's appetite moves, in rapid and recurrent succession, each feeding the others and spurring them on: she-loves-me-she-loves-me-not, in both its splendor and emptiness.

This autonomous and differentiated reality of desire constitutes a critical feat in itself, and its literary presence brings other advances with it. In this sense, we can look at one fact about the novel's composition, one of those features of the plot in which the profundity of novels and novelists lies: the affair between Virgília and Brás is not just full, it is *long*, despite lacking the noble motives that in irregular liaisons also are usually the pledge of continuity. To the contrary of what the moralistic argument says, there are noncoercive reasons why human attraction lasts, and there are alternatives to contractually bound feelings other than chaos. . . .

The redefinition by the context of terms with traditional, consecrated meanings has analogous (and tacit) connotations: Virgília's mouth, "as fresh as the dawn and as insatiable as death," is baroque in its terminology but Darwinian in its real reference. It recalls that feminine personification of nature, the giantess that in the delirium chapter (7) had transformed motherhood, youth, hope, and death into something else, all of them modified in their essence by their subordination to the new concept of the preservation of the species. Thus, in the expression we're concerned with, dawn doesn't come at the beginning, or death at the end: the two of them are together in Virgília's glorious midday. We can see that the dawn here has nothing virginal about it: it's a freshness that, so to say, seems to become more intense with use. In its turn, death is greedy and not decrepit. The surprise of the whole formulation lies in the interpenetration of extremes that might seem to be opposed. So much so that the adjectives applied to one could qualify the other, or could be placed together. Fresh and insatiable, going — on the sexual level — beyond everything that a man can offer, the dawn is mortal, whereas death is always dawning. The terms and time itself are completely redefined, inside a process that has repetition itself as its aim — with its model in the reproduction of the species and having in view above all its indifference toward the morally sanctioned or bourgeois ordering of life.

Going back to previous arguments, we can say, then, that the clarity and specific movements of desire, which in this novel are so extraordinary, are due to a certain degree of indefinition in the characters — or weakness, if we want to use a moral criterion — that also does not fit with the accepted models of the time. In other words, Machado's fiction gives clear shape to the degradation caused by the imperfect functioning of the bourgeois model in Brazil, and at the same time makes palpable the room for maneuver and the fullness permitted by this same imperfection. From yet another angle, we can say that the incomplete embourgeoisement of Brazilian habits allowed Machado to study the unfettered dynamism of desire in terms similar to the — revolutionary — ones brought about by the emancipation of sexuality as an autonomous sphere of existence.

The pervasiveness of the note of pettiness and meanness in the novel is ensured by the narrator's procedures, which work as an a priori. Hardly has the love affair between Virgília and Brás begun, and already the dead narrator, cutting out any possible suspense, anticipates everything that will come later and sums it up: "a life of delights, of terrors, of remorse, of pleasures ending in pain, of sufferings flowering into happiness," and "the final residue, which is boredom and satiety" (ch. 53). In terms of the suspense, which is after all what gives a poetic dimension to individual life, the near proximity of beginnings and ends cancels the tension between these extremes and, with it, the interest of the passages in between. The same goes for the summary of the affair just quoted, which because of its degree of abstraction sterilizes the individuality of each incident, whose final end will, inevitably, be the same as all the others. "But the book . . . smells of the grave, has a certain cadaverous twitch about it" (ch. 71). On another level, the vanishing point defined by boredom and satiety has a similar flattening result. Having said this, there is a certain erotic aftertaste in the equivalence of everything to everything else, and to the will, which is purely and simply satiated. The insult offered to the individual dimension of life doesn't seem to weaken sex, quite the contrary. Nor does love seem any the less lively, just because it leads nowhere.

On the level of the action, too, the characters are weak from some points of view, and quite vigorous from others. Between two dances, while he is delivering Virgília to her next partner, Brás says to himself: "She's mine!" The mismatch between reality and imagination could not be better choreographed: the suitor embraces his fantasy just as the lady is moving away. Later, coming back home, he sees shining on the ground "something round and yellow. I bent down; it was a gold coin, a half-*dobra*. 'It's mine!' I repeated laughing, and put it in my pocket." The coin, of course, would have an owner, just like Virgília, for that matter. "[S]ome nudges from my conscience" make Brás give his find to the chief of police, asking him to give it back to the real owner: an admirable thing to do, with the aim of appeasing the scruples—of the dancer (ch. 51).

Reduced to their skeleton, these episodes provide us with an elementary diagram of human conduct in the *Memoirs*. Instead of being completed on the objective level, acts are concluded in the imagination, where real difficulties are immediately compensated for. In the second anecdote, the process is more complex. The satisfying of a secondary scruple serves to placate the first, principal one. The giving back of the money, accompanied by corresponding public applause, allows the character to turn a blind eye to the moral question of adultery. It should be noted that the substitution of one scruple for another transcends hypocrisy and the individual dimension of imaginary compensations. It is operated through the intermediary of real social approval, which in its turn takes the place of inner conviction, although it keeps the appearances of that same conviction. The structural interest that the Europeanized sectors of society have in avoiding certain subjects—in keeping up the civilized character of the country, in contrast to its brutal, uncivilized forms of domination—is the real ground of the universalization of this mechanism. The really crucial point where it applies is not adultery; just as adultery, although it lies at the center of the book, is not its real, deepest theme. Thanks to such movements, Brás can be in an irregular position and, at the same time, an irreproachable one (though in another area of existence). From a strictly enlightened point of view, these slippages demean the character, who fails to face his own reality, doesn't assimilate the problems it involves, and doesn't try to resolve them in a conscientious or universalizable way. But from the point of view of anyone prepared to connive with the narrator, the worthy nature of the substitute action ratifies our hero's *uprightness of character*. The social function of this kind of argument in the Brazilian case goes without saying.

The equivalence between things that are not comparable, determined by momentary convenience, seems to imply a not very well-integrated person: an object of satire, which puts (local) human weakness in the dock, and not the norm. However, sporadically and between the lines, this same material also allows development in an opposite sense, and disbelief in *uniqueness* and *insubstitutability* has a strategic place in the book. To this comedy of substitutions, whose characters live by infringing European standards of constancy and responsibility, is added another, more radical one that places identity itself in doubt — identity of the person, of love, of actions, of objects. And what if the unity of the individual and its correlates of private property, monogamy, and moral and intellectual autonomy are illusions, or, at best, a particular case engaged in a vain attempt at imposing itself on others?

An example of this is the bibliomaniac in chapter 72, for whom the content of books doesn't matter, so long as they are unique copies — which certainly insinuates that uniqueness is just another mania. "Unique!" In analogous fashion, at another moment Brás's father exclaims "A Cubas!" convinced of the singularity and nobility of his family, whose illustrious lineage he had taken it on himself to forge (ch. 44). These are idées fixes, or almost fixes, because fixity does not exist either, as the narrator himself reminds us, when he can't think of anything more fixed in this world than "the extinct Germanic Diet" (ch. 4). This said, if the unique is an illusion, that is not to say that diversity exists. When it comes down to it, human affairs form a "spectacle whose aim is to amuse the planet Saturn, who's very bored just at present" (ch. 135): all agitation is in vain, and everything, depending on the point of view, is the same, since in sameness there is neither uniqueness nor diversity (Saturn is the sign of melancholy). Along the lines of this general relativity, a wall that at the beginning of a love affair is nothing, some few years later, without having changed its height, figures as an obstacle it would be mad to try to climb (ch. 111). Toward the end, at Lobo Neves's funeral, Brás, the latter's rival and friend, is perplexed by his widow's tears: "Virgília had betrayed her husband sincerely, now she wept for him sincerely" (ch. 152). At this time, too, Brás's mind shows signs of cracking up, and comes and goes like a shuttlecock—one might note that earlier on things were no different. One can't even believe the lifeblood when it speaks: when Brás chides Virgília in the name of his rights as a future father, she turns her eyes away and smiles "in an incredulous fashion" (ch. 94), which makes one think that the "subtle fluid" (ch. 86), the "mysterious voice" (ch. 93), or the "secret voice" (ch. 90) can lie. Why shouldn't the legitimate husband be the father? And, in fact, two chapters later, Lobo Neves and Brás Cubas converse, each as inconsolable as the other, about Virgília's loss, which happened moreover "at the point where you can't distinguish Laplace from a turtle" (ch. 95), which, to the doubt about paternity, adds an uncertainty about the moment an individual becomes himself.

To get an idea of the upset caused by these points of view, which are generally cast in a comic vein, look at one of the violent sentences in the book. "A man's lip is not like the hoof of Attila's horse, which sterilized the earth on which it trod; it's just the opposite" (ch. 43). These words refer to the couple of kisses exchanged by Virgília and Brás, kisses that soon after do not prevent the girl from preferring another suitor—the same Lobo Neves who will later share her with the very same Brás. On one side the lip, the delicate and noble attribute of the most noble of beings; on the other, the hooves of the plague horse, ridden by the barbarian king. This comparison belongs to the list of the "enormities" whose periodic appearance destabilizes the detailed realism of the *Memoirs*, pulling it toward more drastic parameters, where routine and taboo sit cheek by jowl. Ostensibly, this comparison aims not to assimilate but to distinguish: a man's lip not only does not sterilize, it fecundates. In the context of broken oaths, however, with the emphasis on chains of exclusive possession, fecundation appears as a plague, and, since the opposite of *unique* is in this case *all*, it is a plague that has vast territories before it to barbarize, just like the chief of the barbarians himself. Moreover, when one listens to the intonation of the sentence, especially in its second part, one can hear that the disillusioned suitor *regrets* the difference, because if lips did tread the ground like hooves, faithfulness in love would be guaranteed, which, when all is said and done, throws light on a certain quality of savagery in the dispensation of monogamy. This stands out even more if we remember, along with Brás himself, that his interest in Virgília at that moment was nothing much. The tension of the passage is due to the moralistic horror that the enlightened position experiences when faced by its own conclusions: this, too, is the reason for the element of contempt to be found within its own tolerance. The fearless observer notes that one love brings others in its wake, and that desire, in its search for fulfillment, passes "sincerely" from one individual to another, or, to put it another way, that the circuit of imaginative energy is full of sub-stitutions, fusions, associations, montages, borrowings, and in fact is much more socialized and complex than the model of separate atoms characteris-tic of bourgeois mythology. With equal clarity, however, his normative alter ego invokes the stereotypes and bugaboos of strict morality: promis-cuity, barbarism, chaos. With no escape in sight, the categories of individu-alism are demolished as realities and reaffirmed as demands.

Thus, led by the unconvincing status of the norm in Brazil, Machado developed an extramoral analysis of human relationships, and, above all, of the functioning of the norm itself. This places him in the vanguard, and in the family of truly investigative writers, for whom reality certainly did not have the meaning it was proclaimed to have, if it had any meaning at all. Yet, that same unconvincing status was still a local defect, so that a clear view of this fact, while it produced skepticism, did not really produce a renewed level of existence — which today, if we think of the furious way in which ideologies operated at the time, might well seem like an extra form of superiority. At the highest level, with provincialism and bedazzlement both out of the way, we rediscover the limit of a civilization that is a reflection of another.

8

THE ROLE OF IDEAS

The new generation frequents scientific
writers: there's no poet worthy of the name
who isn't at least somewhat familiar with
modern naturalists and philosophers.
Machado de Assis, "A nova geração"
(The Present Generation) (*OC,* 3:836)

THE ABUNDANT PRESENCE OF SCIENTIFIC and philosophical theories in the *Memoirs* is a reflection of the concerns of the time. In Sílvio
Romero's picturesque words, the 1870s had witnessed the arrival of "a
swarm of new ideas" in the country.[1] Positivism, naturalism, and various
forms of evolutionism were competing for popularity with other schools of
thought. Their terminology, as prestigiously modern as it was foreign to
daily existence, held out hopes of a radical break with the past: it promised
to replace the backward mechanisms of oligarchic patronage with new
kinds of authority, based on science and intellectual merit.

It was natural that the enthusiasts for these new ideas should have
transformed the scientific spirit into a panacea, and into the opposite of
anything truly scientific. Machado, in contrast, perceived the ironies latent
in the situation and tried to explore them systematically. Where those
dazzled by these ideas saw future redemption, he took a step back and
noted the existence of a specific problem. In Brazil, reading and propaga-
tion of these new European teachings happened in a particular way, with
ridiculous aspects, which were also particular to the context.

Machado's essay on "The Present Generation," of 1879, emphasized precisely the inappropriate way in which poets were assimilating these recent European trends. Here and there, trying to bring out incongruities, he found formulas to express the objective comedy of this process. These annotations, seen as a whole, outline a set of problems whose implications are very far-reaching and give shape to, or draw out, literary material that will appear in the *Memoirs,* insofar as the novel concerns the functioning of intellectual life.

For example, these young writers "certainly manifest a desire to see something overturned," although they do not quite know what. Lacking a precise aim, this urge for demolition looks disproportionate to its objective, which, paradoxically does not stop its evincing an "optimism, not just quietly confident, but triumphant," since "the general order of the universe seems [to these novices] to be perfection itself." This is because "the theory of natural selection grants victory to those best adapted," just as "another law, which might be called social selection, will hand the palm to the pure in heart" (*OC,* 3:810–11).

This innocent progressivism might not have been exclusive to Brazil, nor even the predominant note at the time. Nevertheless, in conjunction with the surrounding backwardness, it takes on a pathetic aspect, with something local about it. And indeed, only if one were totally oblivious to reality, albeit in the name of a prestigious natural law, would the above-mentioned optimism and the corresponding self-satisfaction be possible. Machado had his doubts about this sudden new dawn by courtesy of science, nor did he believe in a sudden achievement of intellectual independence. "The present generation, whatever its talents may be, cannot escape being conditioned by its setting; it may assert itself by personal inspiration, or by the character of its product, but it is external influence that determines the direction the movement takes; there is not for the moment, in our milieu, the necessary vigor for the invention of new doctrines" (*OC,* 3:813).

In this context, it is interesting to read the digest that Machado makes of the review of the current scene undertaken by Sílvio Romero.* The latter "examines one by one the banners that have been raised, and soon demolishes them; none can satisfy our new aspirations. The revolution was short on ideas, Positivism is finished as a system, socialism hasn't even got the exalted philosophical meaning of Positivism, 'transforming Romanticism' is an empty formula, and finally metaphysical idealism is no more than a hysterical delusion; this is the résumé of three pages" (*OC,* 3:812). Here, modern ideas are everything — there is nothing beyond them — while at the same time they are nothing, as these summary beheadings indicate. The all-embracing ambition and the irresponsibility of the criticism, both of which are total, for good or ill give us the outline of a kind of intellectual and cultural situation. How can one qualify the immensity and the emptiness of such aspirations? Machado was discovering these modes of existence for literature, and was pinning them down to reflect on them. In the *Memoirs,* the same technique of ideological summary — "this is the résumé of three pages" — would allow him to give the immortal portrait of Damasceno, extreme nationalist, hater of the English, partisan of the reactivation of the transatlantic slave trade, and opera lover (ch. 92).

The second to last paragraph of "The New Generation" groups together some of the grosser defects of this provincial use of science. Contradicting its own most elementary precepts, this science served to humiliate any compatriots who were not sufficiently knowledgeable, and to give weight to the pedantry of the up-and-coming generation. "[T]hat is the reason why names still fresh in the memory, and terminology cursorily picked up, are immediately put on paper, and the crisper and fresher the names and the words, the better. I say to the young that true science is not added on for ornament, but assimilated as nutrition; and that the most effective way of showing that one has a scientific method is not to proclaim it at every move, but to apply it usefully. In this, the best examples are the luminaries of science; let the young reread their Spencer and their Darwin. They should flee, too, from another danger: the sectarian spirit" (*OC,* 3:836). The schoolmasterly tone is unattractive, but the quotation does document an observer at work, faced by a new phenomenon.

We can see that the opposition between invention and routine, or, on another level, between progressivism and reaction, does not account for Machado's position, which is founded on an acknowledgment: "there is not for the moment, in our milieu, the necessary vigor for the invention of new doctrines," which, moreover, "is simply a truism" (*OC,* 3:813). Although this is not a discovery, much less a theory, as the author himself reminds us, this opinion did incorporate a real aspect of the reality of the contemporary world. The truly defining innovations manifest a kind of vigor that is not present everywhere, or always. The international cultural scene is not homogeneous, and different problems correspond to its inequalities, according to the place and the time.

In the examples we have seen, it is the naive consumption of novelty that makes one laugh. It wasn't a question of rejecting this novelty or of not studying it — on the contrary. But the center of attention is directed at the manner in which it is used. In other words, the part played by adaptation, or of *judicious* imitation, is in the foreground in Machado's examination of cultural production. The adoption of this angle was a deliberate response to the problem of the new country, which willy-nilly incorporated some of the framework of contemporary society. Far from implying a passive acceptance, the recognition of a disadvantageous starting point created the true conditions for critical independence. This in turn transformed this ill fit between local reality and the borrowed form into an artistic tool and a means to knowledge, instead of simply bemoaning it or denying its existence. Let us remember yet again that the critical possibilities of this ill fit are not a one-way street: the mistaken uses of science, for example, even at their most preposterous, still tell us something about science and its historical role.[2]

However, let us return to the *Memoirs*. The profusion of theories in the book, very diverse in nature, and always in pocketsize versions, underlines the element of whim and contingency ever-present in the effort to think — and so, right at the start, we leave any illusions of objectivity behind. The book abounds with exposés of homemade doctrines, rectifications of other men's theories, records of unusual psychic states, psychological dissertations, moral parables, theses about the basis of human behavior, abstract analyses of some kinds of social relationships, and a chapter made up of maxims. The literary attitude in all this posturing goes from crazed buffoonery to analytic and descriptive prose of the most demanding nature. The quality of this latter can sometimes be a problem, when its power, however transitory, begins to dominate the weave of the fiction itself and unbalance the composition; the more so as good scientific prose is rare in Brazil, which makes it stand out all the more. Thus, the reader regrets that the excellent page dedicated to the character of Lobo Neves is just one rhetorical manner among others or — the same experience looked at from another point of view — feels that Machado has lost his touch and composed a few first-rate sentences, but which do not belong in the fiction. However that may be, the variety of registers could not be more marked, and their polished showiness conveys an impression somewhat like a bazaar, which possibly expresses the peculiar, somewhat inorganic position that Brazilian intellectuals held in nineteenth-century culture.

Caprice subjects philosophy, science, and other forms of intellectual superiority to its impulses; as a consequence, they are debased from the start, since things should be the other way round. The sphere of the mind in which impersonality and objectivity are the rule is present on a grand scale, but it is subordinated to individual fantasy, which changes its status, as well as defining Brazil's position in such matters in literary terms. The lack of seriousness is backed up by the subjects dealt with, which, within their own disparity, have one topic in common: the insubstantiality of the rational and responsible individual posited by bourgeois ideology. What is affirmed — and documented by their very presence — by such hoaxes as the theories of the opportune moment (ch. 56), of the advantages of wearing tight boots (ch. 36), of the successive reeditions of the individual (chs. 37 and 38), of the equivalence of the windows of the soul (chs. 51 and 105), or of the solidarity of human boredom (ch. 42)? In a caricatured form, they say that the same person is another, or several different people, according to the place and the moment; that psychic causation takes place by means of chances, compensations, and substitutions *that should not happen, according to normal rules,* and in which reason and morality have no part; that not even egoism, although it is a constant, can be seen as a rationalizing force: the ways to imaginary fulfillment are erratic and unpredictable. Formulated as they are by a past master of volubility, these doctrines of the essentially irresponsible individual work as a mocking alibi, since they present his *reprehensible* conduct as something *natural,* transmuting local bourgeois inferiority into philosophical anthropology. However, for all their clownish look, these theories hit their target, since the behavior of the narrator and the other characters, unstable to the greatest degree possible, confirms and illustrates them. Ridiculous but well-founded ideas, and vice versa: this is one of the disconcerting aspects of the book. The more so as these theories, once their anecdotal mask is left on one side, paraphrase the dismantling of the individual undertaken by the great writers, by Montaigne, La Rochefoucauld, Pascal, the British empiricists, and the philosophers of the unconscious. The reservations of the modern philosophical tradition when faced by the individual as a single entity are regrouped in the presence of the historical peculiarities of Brazilian experience, where the absolute valorization of the individual really could not be a credible notion.

The basic redundancy between these doctrines makes itself felt all the more in that their external aspects are diverse and showy. This accounts for the uncomfortable climate of pseudo originality, which itself is truly original. My own commentary thus runs the risk of itself saying "the same thing over and over . . . the same thing . . . the same" (ch. 8), though without the dividend, in terms of a critique, that the narrative gets from repetition. My analysis will, then, be restricted to some of the principal theories, taken in themselves and in their extraordinarily dense relation with the novel's universe.

Let us have a look, first, at the so-called philosophy of the tip of the nose (ch. 49). As he fixes his gaze on his own nose, which is a way of looking inside and out at the same time, the individual recomposes the world in such a way as to get his own back for any setbacks he has had, and to smooth down his vanity, ruffled by others' superiority: "this contemplation, whose effect is the subordination of the universe merely to a nose, constitutes social equilibrium." In this way, imaginary redress enables one to tolerate the inequalities of this world. Toward the beginning of the book, we suggested that the quest for "any kind of supremacy" determined the form and rhythm of the *Memoirs*. Now we have found a philosophy to fit it.

This is a general pattern ("Each man has the need and power to contemplate his own nose, so that he can see the celestial light"), and by its style it refers to the revolutionary declarations of the eighteenth century. We can say that the nose's universality points to an order in which all men are formally equal. Generalized rivalry and resentment, which would give a real basis to this psychological mechanism, also presuppose an abstract equality. In its turn, free and unlimited play with the facts of the social world — even if only in the context of a daydream — expresses the typically bourgeois alienation between individual and society. In this context, society is the object to be manipulated. On the flip side, however, there is complete harmony between individual and society, which leaves room for no "beyond": there is nothing so divine or "celestial" as imagining oneself to be the winner in competition with one's fellows. Summing this up, the amusing side of the argument doesn't cancel out the ideological premise on which it rests: a secularized society, in which everyone, without exception, competes with everyone else.

Combined with an aphoristic brevity, the ins and outs of self-love and the explanatory value of egoism are specialties of the French seventeenth century. So that this illustrious patronage should not go unrecognized, Brás Cubas makes explicit reference to La Rochefoucauld and Pascal: the mere presence of their names in the text, leaving aside their subject matter, can be guaranteed to improve anyone's self-esteem. Putting it very briefly, we can see that in these writers' reasoning, individual self-interest manifests itself as much in the quest for the approval of others and the display of noble motives as it does in simple greed, and is to be condemned in all cases — as opposed to unselfishness, which, however, is always an illusion. The aim of this kind of analysis is to lay bare the irremediably mean and petty nature of the self, which is the same in both cases.³ For the modern reader, in contrast, habituated by the nineteenth century to recognize the predominance of material reasons, the equal standing of the desires to *have* and to *impress* may seem like a cliché of the classical age, or an indication of the frivolity of certain human types who, being outdated, have not truly realized the inessential nature of appearances. At this point, vanity stops being a metaphysical attitude and becomes a psychological failing and proof of social obsolescence, the effect of a blindness toward the modern impersonality of value. This is a displacement that in Machado's prose is accompanied by yet further redefinitions, this time linked to Brazilian circumstances.

Given this national context, in which clientelism plays the key role we have discussed earlier, the effort to please and make a good show is a part of the real order, with nothing illusory or anachronistic about it, and its practical usefulness is palpable. That didn't stop our belonging to the bourgeois nineteenth century, with its demands for autonomy and reason, and, going along with that, a disdain for the art of currying favor. Thus, in spite of its seventeenth-century element, Machado's play with the futility of human beings as a species reflected two points of view with their basis in local, contemporary experience: on one hand, it was a manifestation of the irony of the Victorian gentleman when faced by behavior he would regard as deprived of genuine substance, on the other, the practical efficacy, and thus the reality, of the caprices of the imagination. The alternation between these points of view, founded on the particular historical conjuncture and determined by the formal structure of the novel, imposes ambiguity on the — very ingenious — arguments about the uses of illusion.

Given the universalizing form of the argument, what happens to the philosophy of the tip of the nose when faced with the slave? Although an expression of lack of commitment to one's fellow humans, and thus taking on some of the shape of an explicit contempt for anyone, it contributes to a flattering version of matters — in a relative sense. If imaginary redress "constitutes social equilibrium," the latter rests on the consent of individuals, even if they are resentful. The mordacity of this idea lies in the picturesque, generalized envy that it presupposes, and in the very bourgeois suggestion that fantasy is a substitute for weak performance in reality. Obviously, none of this has any validity in the case of slavery, whose stability does not depend on subjective assent but on brute force. Imaginary redress here, even if it exists, does not constitute the cement that keeps order in society. The argument according to which the imagination consoles the slave and makes slavery acceptable functions as an ideological rationalization. The pessimism of this theory, based on the universality of low, mean-minded motivations, serves as a screen for other, much more somber dimensions and aspects of society. The *justifying* and *excusing* role of points of view that at first sight would seem *critical* is one those ingenious complications in which Machado's sense of the real shines through.

At one moment, Brás Cubas recognizes that Luís Dutra's poetry is better than his, and for this reason would like to make him doubt his own talent, discourage and eliminate him—"all this looking at the tip of [his own] nose" (ch. 48). This attitude allows a man to fall short of human decency without any effect on his self-esteem, since sight, given over to contemplation, remains aloof from the dirty work undertaken by desire. "Nose, conscience without remorse" (ch. 49): this expression allows one to witness a caricature of moral reflection, in which consideration for one's fellow creature has a discreditable rather than a noble aim. Free from the pressures of the external world, conversing with himself, that is, retreating into his inner sanctum, the character thinks over the circumstances and chooses . . . an injustice that serves his interests. Thus, freedom and inner autonomy do not guarantee the person's morality. In the Brazilian case, moreover, despite the apparently individual scope of the phenomenon, the suspension of remorse has a function in terms of class. Furthermore, the collective nature of this intimate operation and the degradedly complicit feelings it provokes are the real, secret referent of the nasal philosophy in question. We can say that recourse to the tip of the nose and the blunting of moral feelings it facilitates point to a spiritual process peculiar to a slave-owning, modernistic elite: bourgeois fairness, represented by the libertarian dimension of Romanticism and liberalism, revives at every moment the remorse it was trying to stifle.

Anyone who has tried it knows that contemplation of one's own nose leaves the mind and the eyes with a squint. In other words, as well as functioning as a simile of human egocentricity, Machado's theory describes a possible form of behavior, to which there corresponds a particular subjective state, a possible object of scientific curiosity. The figurative language, which has a satirical intention, can equally be taken as a literal description, and the superimposing of allegory on Naturalist precision creates one more comic ambiguity. "As the reader knows, a fakir spends long hours looking at the tip of his nose, with the sole object of seeing the celestial light. When he fixes his eyes on the tip of his nose, he loses the sense of external things, is uplifted into the invisible, learns to grasp what is impalpable, becomes detached from the earth, dissolved, ethereal. This sublimation of one's being by means of the tip of the nose is the most exalted phenomenon of the spirit, and the capacity for attaining it does not belong exclusively to the fakir: it is universal" (ch. 49). This approximation of the fakir and an ordinary person opens simultaneous, opposing perspectives. In one of them exotic spirituality has its holiness removed and is revealed as a disguised version of the jealousies of this world; in an enlightened fashion, religion is brought down to earth and explained by familiar human defects. In the opposing perspective, the fanaticism with which the ordinary man devotes himself to competing with his fellows and beating them, even if only in his fantasy, appears in its turn as a kind of religious alienation, insinuating that modern individualism is far from being the comprehensible, rational, and sober form of life it is supposed to be. From this second point of view, our current form of behavior appears far off, placed at a distance, and no less strange than the exercises of a specialist in the denial of earthly happiness. There is a distance between the world "demythified" by bourgeois competition and a properly human and reasonable ordering of society, which the cult of the tip of the nose gives us some hint of.

It should be said that the transmutations carried out by Machado's narrator have a less unlimited repertoire than one might think. They are limited by a set of basic attitudes of his mind, which are constantly exchanged one for another: the contemplation of one's own nose is one of them. The whole forms a system, which is specific to a society, and has an extraordinary consistency. Here are some of its parts: periodic attacks on the rights of the poor; the delicious frisson caused by unjustified praise; the patriarch's rapture at his son's pranks; abject kinds of class connivance, tedium at the emptiness of the projects he has under way; and the strange plenitude of a long, routine adultery. The lowest common denominator of these features is caprice, which allowed critics to see in them a (redundant) illustration of the metaphysical inconsistency of human beings. However, if we give free rein to our sense of the particular, we will perceive subtler and less general relationships, a kind of complementarity, in which a definite historical structure reveals itself, stylized in the moral relationships that characterize it.

But let us go on to look at Humanitism, the most famous of Machado's philosophies. As its name suggests, it is a satire on the profusion of -isms in the nineteenth century, with an explicit allusion to the Comtian religion of humanity. The arguments make one think of other affiliations, since instead of positivist principles, they posit a universal struggle, in which everyone fights everyone else, in the manner of social Darwinism. This generalized state of war, however, is no more than an illusion, since its foundations lie in monism: Humanitas is the single principle of all things and resides equally in the winning and losing sides, in the victim and the executioner, so that nothing is lost, where there appeared to be a tragedy. Thus, pain does not exist, nor can it: "in substance, it is Humanitas that corrects in Humanitas any infringement of Humanitas's laws" (ch. 117).

Along with the theses concerning the "struggle for life,"[4] Humanitism also contains an encomium of a hierarchical, ritualized society, something difficult to reconcile with such notions. This inconsistency contributes to the general tone of absurdity, which does not prevent its admirably capturing the aspiration for "order and progress"[5] of several sociological theories of the time, which combined a conservative position with scientific and antitraditional aims, along with substitutes for providentialism and religious worship.

This said, perhaps the best part of the comedy of these chapters can be found in the relationships between the doctrines and the social context they encountered in Brazil. Commenting on the vogue for Herbert Spencer's philosophy in the United States after the Civil War, a historian points out the affinities between the historical conditions, modernized by the abolition of slavery, and that "product of British imperialism."[6] The speed of economic expansion, implacable competition, generalized exploitation, the loathing for those who had been defeated made of postbellum America "a vast caricature of the Darwinian struggle for existence and survival of the fittest. Successful business entrepreneurs apparently accepted almost by instinct the Darwinian terminology which seemed to portray the conditions of their existence" (Hofstadter, 44). Imported into a Brazilian context and mirrored in it, the same system had to change meaning.

See, for example, the classic "The winner gets the potatoes," the motto with which the crazed philosopher Quincas Borba sums up — in Machado's next novel, which bears this character's name — the essence of his "Humanitist" doctrine. It may be that the phrase is an acclimatized translation of the "survival of the fittest," a still more classic expression, invented by Spencer. The distance between the two formulas suggests something of the difference between the two situations. It is a fact that, before conceiving his theory, Quincas Borba had experienced ups and downs: from being a rich kid he had become a beggar, and then a wealthy man again. But there is no indication that these changes of status were caused by struggle or merit, the last twist in fact being due to the death of an uncle in Barbacena, Minas

Gerais. His disciple Brás Cubas, whose fortune was amassed by his great-grandfather, doesn't work either. Thus, since the society based on slavery is comparatively static, the principle of universal competition is deprived of dynamic meaning and now expresses something less portentous, something like everyone's indulging in envy and petty gibing. Not that Humanitist ideas were useless: they attested to the modern look, in philosophical and scientific terms, of two VIPs (Brás and Quincas); they gave an enlightened justification to the indifference of the rich toward their dependents, an indifference that in the light of more traditional precepts would seem to lack decorum; and, finally, they explained the necessary and legitimate character of colonial exploitation and its present-day consequences. "But I need no other testament to the sublimity of my system than this same chicken. It was fed on corn, planted, let's suppose, by an African, imported from Angola. This African was born, grew, and was sold; a ship brought him here, a ship built of wood cut in the jungle by ten or a dozen men, carried along by sails, which eight or ten men wove, not to mention the rigging and the rest of the ship's tackle. So, this chicken, which I've just had for lunch, is the result of a multitude of exertions and struggles, carried out with the single aim of satisfying my appetite. Between the dessert and the coffee, Quincas Borba showed me that his system meant the destruction of pain" (ch. 117).

The step forward represented by these fictional-philosophical exercises was a very great one. It brought to Brazilian literature, almost destitute in this regard, the conflict of modern ideas. Better than that, it did not bring it in the clumsy guise practiced by adepts and detractors: this clear, concise exposing of the inconsistencies of these ideas meant the appropriation of the essentials of the scientific spirit — at a level that in Brazilian terms was an achievement in its own right — and this without losing sight of their potentiality for use in a conservative or authoritarian manner, nor, above all, of the peculiar way they worked in local conditions. We can see, too, the critical value of this latter aspect, which contradicted the universal image with which science and progress were imbued at the time. In other words, the representation of the "act of theorizing" in the *Memoirs* meant a complex, highly demanding attitude, familiar with the innovations taking place in the main centers of culture but still free of the obfuscation arising from subaltern status, as well as being alert to the local Brazilian context and convinced of its importance. This balance is another name for the miraculous integrity of Machado's writing. Varying the angle of vision, and exchanging the national perspective for the sphere of contemporary history, we can finally say that the literary combining of recent theoretical tendencies and of social relationships typical of Brazil, explored in their intrinsically comic aspect, provided material that had far-reaching implications, capable of sustaining a great novel.

We have seen that the primacy systematically given to caprice removes authority from the constructions of reason. Deprived of the *responsible* context that makes their pretense to objectivity possible, philosophy and scientific theories take on an aspect that looks merely external, an emptied-out version of a process that happens seriously somewhere else. The affinities between this discrediting of abstract thought and the limitations of the Brazilian setting seem clear. Nevertheless, from the point of view of literary technique, Machado was close to the daring moves with which the modern novel responded to the latest developments of bourgeois society. We can point to the contemptuous way in which Stendhal reduced conservative discourse to a predictable contrivance, undeserving of the effort of complete exposition: thus the splendid "etc., etc."s that he uses to shorten it. In the systematic banalization of thinking carried out in Flaubert's writings, the ideas have the same solidity and visibility as things and are not distinguished from them; they slide with them, under the same conditions, over the famous, unflagging "trottoir roulant" [moving walkway] formed by the special use the author makes of the narrative preterit tense.[7] In both writers, these things are part of a modern perception of ideology, in which explanations of life are a functional part of the cement that provides social stability. Spontaneous thought is only apparently free and individual: this fact degrades it and transforms it into raw material for literature, with implications that are counterintuitive, requiring new kinds of treatment and pushing in the direction of the twentieth century. Something similar happens in Machado's fiction, where ideas are also thought of from without, with no innocence about them, as a social fact to be observed from outside, with a naturalist's objectivity. We have pointed out the Brazilian origins of this reification, and the literary resources with which it was recreated: nothing could be further away from Flaubert's world and style. Nevertheless, the technical precision with which both writers set up the mental mousetrap in which their characters live allows us to make the approximation. It is hard to say whether this is because scientific discipline is an indispensable point of reference in the work of both, and that they are contemporaries in that sense, or because the spiritual exhaustion of the bourgeoisie was already a common horizon for the whole planet, even if it took different shape in different places.

At the beginning of this chapter we underlined the antioligarchic animus that was associated with the entry of the new ideas into Brazil: science would supposedly provide the basis for a kind of authority more rational and civilized than patronage. In the *Memoirs,* however, we see, on the contrary, the methodical subjection of the most varied forms of modern thought to the haphazard movements of the will of the narrator and his fellows. Machado, and Brazil before him, set up a hierarchy as unconventional as it was unusual, which the book nevertheless explores with extraordinary wit and subtlety, copiously and realistically extracting some of its suggestive facets. The modern prestige pertaining to the scientific posture, aggressively opposed to the traditional mentality, fits the practical and expressive needs of the behavior we are trying to characterize like a glove. It is true that Brás Cubas's union with science is made at the price of some absurdity, but this feature itself easily fits into the milieu and contributes to rounding out the picture of a characteristic civilization, harmonious in its own way. Of course, it is understood that the agent of the corruption of modern ideas is always caprice, abstract and metaphysical, although accompanied by realistic details. In its turn, the "modified" use of these same ideas will never, at any moment, have a precise social definition. But this does not prevent the ensemble of the episodes providing the outline of a historical process, seen in terms of class: what we have is the oligarchic appropriation of progress on the level of ideas, with the accent falling on certain of its consequences.

9

QUESTIONS OF FORM

DESPITE ITS CONSTRUCTIVE AND ANALYTIC BRILLIANCE, the composition of the *Memoirs* presents difficulties. There are passages that do not work, even though they are ingenious (unless it is the critic who is mistaken, which is never improbable). At the most general level, the narrator's self-assuredly malicious tone is disproportionate to what is, after all, the devalued world of the characters, who end up looking like puppets. The ubiquitous presence of caprice and its role as a universal key bring about a certain monotony, as well as hiding the novel's realist framework. The differing dimensions of the characters are not always well integrated with each other, which makes for some uncertainty in their outlines, and so forth.

According to Adorno's sensible theoretical position, the higher the level of artistic success, the less accidental the artistic weaknesses of a work will be. These latter no longer have their cause in the author's limitations and point rather to objective impossibilities, whose foundations lie in social questions. In the eyes of a dialectical critic, fractures in the form point to historical impasses. For all their aesthetically negative qualities, they thus represent important cultural facts, which also require interpretation.[1]

At the origin of our analysis of the novel is an observation that is plausibly true but not obvious, and that could be called the thesis of this book: that everything we have said flows from the identification of the narrator as a member of a *class*. The relevance and effect of the prose, of the cast of characters, and of the general composition can all be divined from that point of view, and give a many-sidedness, breadth, and reach to the *type,* who in his turn is defined inside a system of social relationships capable of being described and made explicit. Seen in this way, in the informed light of history, the artistic tools that the narrator uses go through a corresponding process of redefinition, which reveals their unexpected usefulness as weapons of aggression. The result is a complex of historical links of scandalous import, composed of hints that in the novel, however, are scattered in the background, without an obvious structural function. Even so, once they are brought together, they provide an outline of new coordinates and make one see the unity of the *Memoirs* in different terms. Perhaps we should talk of a latent form, in opposition to the ostensible one: Brás Cubas's volubility, which at first sight is just a literary expedient, changes its aspect when we look closely at the way it operates.

Since the narrator is a *biased* element in the story, his formal procedures lack impartiality, have something of ad hoc maneuvers about them, and are placed there for practical ends, which forces one to analyze their content in terms of their immediate context. This reading is in disagreement with Brás's own instructions, for he attributes the superiority of his style — his literary and moral contraventions of the law, as well as his grand philosophical ruminations — to the superiority of the dead over the living. Instead of taking this explanation seriously, we prefer to take it as one more provocation, one among many in which the character's position of power is translated into narrative technique.

This argument thus contradicts the explicit message of the text at one point where it does not carry conviction, and, in compensation, has the considerable advantage of allowing one to see the cohesion behind the surface arbitrariness. Supposing we are right, it has to be underlined, however, that at no stage is the correspondence between narrative behavior and the portrayal of society affirmed. The relationship is a virtual one, depending exclusively on the reader's perception, on his having the courage, even, to contradict the opinion of the narrator himself. What is more, we will see that the relationship is obscured by some of the traits of the composition, which hide its presence, without lessening its effectiveness. These questions constitute the artistic heart of the *Memoirs.*

Brás Cubas's position in society stands out less than the liberties he takes with narrative conventions, with the conditions of verisimilitude, the rules of fairness, the impartiality of abstract thinking, the irreversibility of time, and so on. The character implied by his social position is historically specific, while the one implied by all these latter features, given the reputation for generality of all the rules he disrespects, might seem to be general too—something like man in his so-called absolute condition, without further qualification. We have tried to show that the narrator's pirouettes only sparkle, or, better, only avoid being insipid metaphysics thanks to the figure, lying somewhere between deplorable and specious, that they cut once one takes into account the other Brás, the member of a class, whose extremely insidious presence is nevertheless discreet. We could say that it is a deceptive distribution of the weight given to each part, which deliberately invites mistakes. It is no accident that, even recently, a reputable specialist should have published a book about Machado de Assis and philosophy, in which, at the end, the meditative sallies of the author-character are part of an anthology of serious thoughts, when all that would be necessary would be to extend the quotations by one or two sentences to see the evidence of their self-regarding, mocking, or crazed dimension.[2] Nor is it any accident that Machado de Assis sparkles in school anthologies, with official sanction, or that Rui Barbosa,* speaking in the name of the Brazilian Academy of Letters, at Machado's graveside, should have compared his prose to that of Frei Luís de Sousa.[3]*

Thus, behavior typical of a class, linked to the consequences of colonization, makes signals that go counter to the surface import of the prose. This behavior operates outside its expected sociological context and develops its potentialities on the stage of the general culture of the time, imposing itself especially on its literary conventions, or, by extension, on the norms and axioms of modern culture, which are international by their very nature. In this unexpected, rarified atmosphere, Brás's mode of existence becomes at first sight more difficult to pin down; this fact, once its strangeness has been overcome, should not stop critics from perceiving the social nature of its infractions of the norm. It is, literally, the universalization of the forms of conduct of the Brazilian ruling class, or in other words, the working out of its—disastrous—effects on the dominant patterns of contemporary civilization, beyond its immediate empirical context.

As can be seen, it is a form with immense scope and potency, whose danger lies in sliding toward serious metaphysics. Let us not speculate on the motives that may have led Machado to prefer a slippery kind of composition, in which a ferocious clarity of vision in historico-social matters is linked to a nonspecific, universalizing form of expression, out of step with the real object of study. But let us also note that the misfit between Brazilian social relations and the ideological frameworks of the bourgeois world, which latter, because of this very misfit, are transformed into rhetorical generalities, was not invented by the writer: it was the role of cultural life to give witness of the elite's modern, European links, rather than reflecting their relationships with other classes. This gives rise to the tendency for any intellectual endeavor to end up in platitudes, with their cognitive uselessness and their efficacy in bringing people together in mutual flattery. It is as if reality itself had no motive for stimulating literature to suppress these prestigious cliches, which there would seem to be no way of avoiding, except by sacrificing . . . historical accuracy. With malice and intelligence, Machado made sure he provided an abundance of cliches, always placed in compromising positions.

In the novels of Machado's first phase, there are several well-to-do young men who behave admirably and who could come out of a guide to good manners. To appreciate the novelist's about-face it can be seen that in Brás Cubas, that same social type is taken up again, only seen by an author who now gives no quarter. This view imposes itself as soon as we take into account the character's social relations as a whole: this reading, however, is not one that the book makes easy. We have seen that the passages that deal with the system of social interests are separate from one another, or lost among other material, or have their sting removed, though this doesn't stop their being powerful in themselves. And to whom could it occur to understand the butterfly movement of the narration as a strictly controlled process, the rigorous expression of a system of iniquities? The conventional, comfortable enjoyment of the *Memoirs* sticks to this elegant discontinuity, to the refined style of expression, to the rather precious disparity between contiguous moments in the novel, and doesn't ask the most revealing question of all — about the total consistency of all this. It is true that if the *Memoirs* are read in this key, Brás, though no compendium of virtues, does present a model to any reader anxious to feel he has access to privileges exclusive to superior people. To go along with this, in the passages that weigh up profit and loss, which sum matters up and are intended as counterweights to the former futility, and which are thicker on the ground in the last part of the novel — though such passages are present here and there from the beginning — what dominates is an egalitarian mockery of everything and everybody in the face of death. Thus, one of the conformist potentialities of the book could be summed up as a love of privilege, when we are dealing with the living, and of metaphysical melancholy, when we come to the unavoidable. The poetry produced by placing these two things next to one another, a pattern repeated over and over again, is cheap ideology, as can easily be seen — as long as one tries to see the unity of the book, or resists the high prestige of the formal inconsequentiality.

On the same subject, it can be seen that Brás Cubas's volubility borrows its solutions in terms of technique from *Tristram Shandy,* one of the high points of eighteenth-century *sentimentalism*. However, it avails itself of them in 1880, after Romanticism, realism, and naturalism, when they can no longer have the same meaning. In spite of the older form, this arbitrary manner and attitude toward reality and the rules for representing it converges with the antinaturalist reaction then happening in Europe. In fact, the magnification of caprice in the *Memoirs* has something of a clowning elitism about it, of a self-congratulatory, exclusive irresponsibility, of a cult of dilettantism and of the self, undertaken in an antisocial spirit, and which were part ot the aestheticism just then coming into vogue.[4]

This said, we should consider the antidotes present in the composition: the universalizing psychology, with its diction impregnated with classical French rationalism, naturally bolsters social vanity. However, since it is an ethos that doesn't allow exceptions, its pessimism includes the narrator, who tries to use it to bestow distinction on himself. Analogously, and in common accord with aestheticism, Brás cultivates doing exactly as he pleases, gives precedence to his own thoughts and emotions over objective considerations, eagerly indulges those delicious moments when the soul traces the contours of its own strangeness, and so forth. However, the realist dimension is too present for these features to dominate the novel as they might in a European context. Far from being a rare, sensitive soul, Brás Cubas is vulgarity in person, and the multiple twists and turns of his mind serve more than anything to make his presumptions preposterous. We can say then that the *Memoirs* combines a certain aestheticist view of reality — unusual and daring in its unconformity with bourgeois utilitarianism — an analytic psychology that privilege cannot penetrate, and a framework of realist fiction, in which social conflict redefines the totality of subjective pretensions and puts them in their place. With a wonderful result: here we have, identified and scrutinized, as in Nietzsche, the secret foundations of values, even of truth, which, without will and social power to impose them, would be nothing. This is a radically critical position, one, furthermore, free of the elitist airs that even today make these same contributions of aestheticism and the philosophy of the will so suspect.

How are we to interpret the words of an ill-intentioned narrator, one, moreover, whose volubility is governed by what is acceptable and unacceptable in terms of his class position? Thinking about them outside this practical bias, and of the skeptical reading that they should in principle be subjected to, can only make them seem banal. In the spirit of Marxist tradition, we can say that the question of honesty in narrative changes in quality and takes on its present-day aspect from 1848 on, when the tide of popular revolutions forced the European bourgeoisies to recognize the particular nature of their own interests.[5] France, it seems, is paradigmatic in this respect. The Paris insurrection, "an episode of proportions without parallel in the history of civil wars," fixed the parameters of the future: "the first battle had been fought between the two classes that divide modern society."[6] We should add that once the rising had been defeated, the "nation of owners" ordered the massacre of the "nation of workers"[7] with a ferocity that had also "never been seen in civilized cities."[8] The brute reality of class oppression laid bare the unreal side of the phraseology of liberty, equality, and fraternity, on which, however, the new order was based. The *Fall* had taken place, "the original sin, which took place in 1848, but which had been committed since the beginning of time — the a priori consequence of bourgeois praxis."[9] According to the famous formula, the fireworks of Romantic-liberal rhetoric, which aimed to unite workers and owners, had given way to General Cavaignac's incendiary bombs.[10] A short time afterward Marx will also say that the bourgeoisie had rightly seen that their intellectual and moral resources, forged in the name of Man, that is, against feudalism, now had turned against them and served the new enemy: "the gods that it had created had now abandoned it."[11] From the point of view of popular awareness, and of the self-awareness of the victors, the experience of the June massacres has the importance of a historic revelation. They reveal the true adversaries to each other and to themselves, linked by the chains of oppression and exploitation, which produced a rancorous intimacy, riddled with mental reservations, always on the verge of having recourse to force, and foreign to any kind of legitimacy. Bourgeois normality, and with it the whole of contemporary language, began to live in a state of siege: words became soaked with incompatible meanings, produced by social antagonism; on one side, the official acceptations, on the other, those that the words held for the defeated, which were often semi-clandestine. This was a very sharp discrepancy, in which were reflected, with an objective sarcasm, recent historical experience and the hatred characteristic of class warfare. The radical ambiguity practiced by Flaubert and Baudelaire, which makes their treatment of bourgeois existence so insulting, consists precisely in writing so as to allow the other reading, the repressed one, so giving literary expression to the historical clash. Thinking of them both, Dolf Oehler states that "it is no accident that the decisive writers of the Second Empire should be those who reflected most profoundly on the effects and importance of the June events, and, moreover, who transposed the experience of that month into the texture of their writing" (Oehler, *Ein Höllensturz*, 17–18 [*Le spleen*, 19]).

By an understandable paradox, this crisis in language's common meanings helped form the sui generis brand of objectivity of modern literary form. To face up to the prime importance of social discord, which was a new epistemological horizon, making the narrator's role a difficult one and his confidence in speaking his own mind problematic, the most rigorous and consistent novelists tried to invent technical solutions that could not be objected to as being allegedly biased. Some examples of this are the methodical effort to be impersonal (Flaubert), the attempt to give a scientific standard to fiction (Zola), the recognition of the problems connected with point of view (Henry James), the up-front use of the first-person singular—the spontaneous form of expression par excellence—but in a spirit of self-exposure, as if the third person were being used (Dostoevsky in "Notes from Underground").[12] The common denominator lies in the primacy of narrative procedure over opinions, which are banished, backed up by science, relativized by having to take turns, or distanced. The objectivity of the technical rules the artists adopts allows him to jump over his own shadow, since the status of opinions, including authorial ones, does not allow open assent. Authority and relative meaning are conferred through mediation of the literary method, above all by means of its effects of dislocation, which function as instances and allegories of the precedence that the social formation has over subjective intentions.

The crucial case for our argument is Flaubert. The discipline of his writing, which cultivated observation of reality, the mot juste, and the perceptive and suggestive potentialities of language, all pursued with equal perfectionism, resulted in an object whose concrete presence was, so to speak, unanswerable.[13] However, this solid front, with not a break in it, so peculiar to the writer, is the consequence of the simultaneous incorporation of conflicting social perspectives and not, as might seem to be the case, from their suppression. It is well known that Flaubertian impassivity is sustained by scientific impartiality, but also by hatred of the bourgeois and, in an equal dose, by contempt for the impotence of that same hatred. In brief, as for the class content of this amalgam, one can feel in it the silent presence of the "fourth estate": there was added to the disdain for utilitarian calculation, common in those with Romantic aristocratic leanings, a horror—modern beneath the surface—for a certain inhumanity of the owner class, an inhumanity whose importance came to light in the workers' repression in 1848 (which did not prevent its already affecting the connotative aura of language before that date).

However this may be, *among the basic axioms of this new literary dispensation is the bankruptcy of ideas or intentions considered in the abstract.* Flaubert had developed an extremely detailed art of plot construction, which specialized in unveiling the lies of ideology. Thoughts and emotions are qualified at every step, and in crushing fashion, by the place they occupy in the intrigue, and they exist only within that specific circumstance. The occasion, the immediate context, and the manner, thought through with an unheard-of scrupulousness, became decisive and entered the ensemble of the novel, which from then on had to be considered *objectively,* that is to say, separately from the explicit aims that make it up.[14] Thus, to the new level of class conflict there correspond new types of literary form in which, on peril of falling into anachronism or making an artistic "mistake," nothing escapes redefinition by its immanent context, always in a key of thoroughgoing ambiguity, and an enigmatic representation of contemporary history. Conforming externally to traditional genres, ideological positions, or just simply to common sense now no longer guarantees anything. Authority has gone over from the author or from his ideas into the internal consistency of the prose, which thereby becomes more dense — totally so, insofar as such a thing is possible — and an aesthetic aim in itself, leading to the novel written with all the care dedicated to poetry.

These effects reach their greatest artistic strength when anecdotes and things appear treated in a "realist" manner, that is, when they fall within the purely contingent context of individual perception, free of conventional, above all Romantic literary traits, and disciplined by an enlightened skepticism and the model of scientific observation. The shocks that the internal dynamics of the work inflict on the reality of empirical observation, however impartial this observation may be, go to make up the poetry and the lesson of this scheme of things. The form, in this system, provides the experience of the modern world and plays the part of reality, whose modern development, moreover, continuing to follow Marx's ideas, also takes place in spite of and behind the backs of its subjects. The total integrity of the composition, which takes into full account the element of chance in materials gathered from day-to-day existence, becomes the guarantee of aesthetic integrity and the privileged object of critical reflection. Flaubert's famous aspiration, to write "a book about nothing [where 'nothing' is the triviality of petit-bourgeois existence], a book with no external ties, which would sustain itself on the internal strength of its style,"[15] is the first setting-out of such a position. The reconsideration of Brazilian daily life in Machado's prose also belongs to this tendency, though in a different vein.

Taking this parallel further than might seem reasonable, let us look at some of Flaubert's other observations. "The author's reflections [those of the author of *Uncle Tom's Cabin*] irritated me the whole time. Do we really have to comment on slavery? All you need is to show it, and that's that. . . . See if usury is castigated in *The Merchant of Venice*. The dramatic form has the advantage that it removes the author. — Balzac didn't escape from this same defect, he is legitimist, Catholic, aristocratic. — The author should be in his work like God in the universe, present everywhere, but visible nowhere."[16] In principle, nothing could be more contrary to the form of the *Memoirs* than this banishment of authorial comment. The advice is linked to the demand for artistic objectivity, and perhaps to the aim of being useful to humanity without allying oneself to anyone, least of all to the reader, an irony that since then has lain behind a decisive section of modern art. But, returning to Brás Cubas's intrusions: we have seen their recurrent character, as inevitable as the stars in their courses, their psychic compulsiveness and their class bias. Far from being a prologue to the irrelevance of the writer's opinions — opinions rejected in Flaubert's ideal prose — the caprices in Machado's prose deliberately reify narrative freedom and subordinate it to a system of constraints that lowers the prestige of its narrative world, of which that pseudo liberty is a part; indeed, it is its most characteristic expression. In analogous fashion, the games with the reader do not aim to create but to destroy the idea of an enlightened understanding with the reading public, replaced by a kind of aggressively degrading complicity (after the manner of Baudelaire), whose conditioning substratum is the painful awareness of Brazil's social injustices.

So, quite differently from what one would expect, it is the constant breaks in the novel's texture that establish the relationships by means of which the characters' realist fate and the immanent presence of the fictional universe are completed and rounded out. After reminding ourselves that the narrative techniques of 1750 are used in the aestheticist spirit of 1880, we can say that this latter, without losing its tendency to dissolve, serves to characterize a specific social type, a member of a historically coherent cast of characters, and conforms to a realist literary project, characteristic of the previous European generation. In their turn, the appeals to the reader, given their provocative tone, are each a kind of expulsion of that same reader from the text, and place him harshly up against the relational universe of the novel, producing a sensation comparable to that created by . . .

Flaubertian objectivity. The systematization of the Brazilian elite's moral impasse, condemned to something like an enforced structural infraction of the rules, allowed Machado to take up the emerging aestheticism in a nonaestheticist manner. This same aestheticism was, precisely, rehearsing and stylizing its new assault on bourgeois civic guarantees—the same assault of which, on another level, the incipient new imperialism was the most spectacular manifestation.[17]

The enumeration of these historical paradoxes and combinations illustrates the complexity of the literary operation carried out in the *Memoirs*. Machado de Assis explored in detailed fashion, and to perfection, the nonbourgeois dimension of bourgeois existence in Brazil and extended it into the area of artistic convention, under the generalizing guise of transgression. Naturally, these steps were made easier by the antiliberal developments that in Europe were beginning to push in the direction of open illegality, developments from which it was possible to borrow "advanced" ideas and forms. As a result, slavery and clientelism are not shown just in their obvious aspect, that of backwardness, but also from a disturbing, more substantial side: their affinity with these new tendencies. This "modernity," which might have been useful as an alibi for a class, in Machado's universe, however, does not feed such illusions: it only makes its wretchedness worse, for, without applauding backwardness, it undermines the prestige of its progress of which that same backwardness is a part. This is a critical position not easily equaled in its power.[18]

The mediation of caprice prevents anything in the *Memoirs* from being what it seems to be at first sight. This generalized displacement, a manifestation of the divergence between the form and the common meanings of things, places the book in the modern camp. The vital information is always to be found in the deviation or the negation placed by the literary method on its materials. For Machado, it was a case of signifying, deliberately, at the expense of what is overtly said: the words give way to the composition and are placed at a lower level of complexity than that same composition, which unsays those words and frames them in a context that is tacitly understood and more negative than what is explicitly said. This theatrical or situational notion of language, with its correspondingly sharp-witted, cunning reader, makes up an entirely *artistic* method of construction, if by this adjective we understand the predominant importance of the writer's use of form. The exceptions that prove the validity of this point can be found in the half-dozen passages in which the author forgets his basic principle that the form disqualifies the matter and tries to show his authority as a witty, cultivated writer in a direct fashion. The fall in quality is immediate, and for a moment we find ourselves really and truly — unless I am blind to some hidden irony — in the presence of one of those sententious formulations that delight one section of Machado's admirers. One example that comes to mind is the moment when the narrator defines the status of his book, "a supinely philosophical work, with an uneven philosophy, at one moment austere, playful the next, something that neither builds nor destroys, neither inflames nor congeals, and all the same is more than a pastime and less than proselytism" (ch. 4). Or we can recall the regretful tone of the lines about the domestic atmosphere of Brás's childhood, in which the lecherous uncle "did not respect my youth, just as he didn't respect his brother's cassock" (ch. 11), or where the prayers taught him by his mother, deprived of the spirit that should have given them life, become "an empty formula" (ch. 11). Without irony, these expressions interrupt the course of the volubility and might make one think that youth would be pure, were it not for the uncle, or that prayers are not in vain, when they are sincere. These are exceptions to the rule of composition, artistic slipups, that is; well-behaved leftovers on which the narrative movement has not managed to impose its complexity. The most aesthetically paradoxical case can be found in the group of chapters given over to the protagonist's miseducation, which we commented on many pages back (86): remarkable as observation and social criticism, they still give an impression of being simplistic, because they back up that same bourgeois norm that the movements of the caprice question (chs. 10 and 11).

The artistic solution elaborated in the *Memoirs* marked the end of a cycle in Brazilian literature. The figure of the discredited and not very likable narrator did not lend itself to the constructive role that, for more than a century, writers of both the Arcadian and Romantic phases, permeated by the duty to affirm nationality, had attributed to literature and to themselves.[19] The break did not pass unnoticed, and José Veríssimo notes that "Never has [Machado de Assis] written beneath the title of one of his novels the habitual words 'A Brazilian Romance.'"[20] Despite his admiration, Veríssimo himself would like Machado to be more natural, popular, and patriotic, and less critical. Unless I'm wrong, behind his reservations about Machado's lack of "congenial" qualities or "charm," or about the shortage of "superior emotions" and of the "exuberance . . . characteristic of Brazilians,"[21] what was at stake was the unfortunate effect that modern literary models would have on dedicated patriots eager to contribute in exemplary fashion to the formation of national identity. At least a part of the aversion Machado's writing provokes in Sílvio Romero also had its origin there, in its incompatibility with "healthy Brazilianness" and the "shout of enthusiasm for a better future," all words with a progressive intention, whose dimension of self-delusion and apology for a certain class was naturally not apparent to those who used them. "Every Brazilian writer at the present time is charged with the overwhelming duty to tell our people the whole truth," wrote Romero,[22] at the antipodes of the individualistic radicalization of the new literature, which was advancing in an opposite direction, though with truths, by any reckoning, of equal importance: "Nothing destroys a man like having to represent a country."[23] So too, from the point of view of our naturalist critics, with their profound nationalism and vulgar materialism, it was natural that Machado should appear as a pallid creature, lacking in generosity, courage, and even sensual appetites(!).[24] Since he didn't fit into the mold of patriotic manliness, the daring of his strategies failed to impose itself, and it is a fact that his reputation as a writer was at first established on the basis of conventional merits, those of a cultured, refined person, writer of correct and elegant prose, and so forth,[25] compatible with the idea of a nationally useful kind of superiority.

As he put the character of Brás Cubas — the real target of the satire — in the position of narrator, Machado was taking a perverse, disorientating tack. Camouflaged by the first-person singular, which no one would think of using against itself and with destructive intent, the savage imitation of the elite's ways of behaving made a framework intended to produce a high degree of mystification; it is up to the reader to find out that he is not in the presence of an example of self-examination and consummate honesty, but of a devastating indictment. Judging by the critics' reactions, the disguise took almost everyone in, which doesn't invalidate a reading in social terms, though it does make one reflect on the effectiveness of such a deceitful literary form. Like Stendhal, who knew that his writings were fifty years ahead of his time, Machado was writing for a public that did not as yet exist. The very choice of pseudo memoirs is an insidious move, for although the biographical framework attenuates the gravity of the *accusations* by diluting them in the contingencies of an individual's career, it also gives them, fictionally, the inescapable status of a *confession*. It is as if, impelled by volubility, a great national figure had opened up the vices of his class, as exemplified in his own person, for public inspection. Moreover, because of what it implies in terms of an intimate relationship with despicable behavior, the sarcastic incarnation of the narrator in the ego of this fine figure of a man sets up a fight on equal terms, complex and merciless, something like an internal willingness to confront this adversary, this object of denial, in full awareness and with all the means at one's disposal. On the other hand, what are the references that introduce an element of distance into the identification, allowing for the narrative flow to be organized so that it is a self-indictment, but one that maintains the appearance of spontaneity and chance? In this character dressed up as an important personage, but pointedly aware of both the perspective of the dependents and the European bourgeois norm, Machado applied himself to observing and inventing modes of action that are, characteristically, deplorable when seen from these points of view. The results are real tours de force in the art of class betrayal. Mutatis mutandis, we can recall Walter Benjamin's description of Baudelaire as "a secret agent — an agent of the secret dissatisfaction felt by a class at its own dominance."[26] Picking up on a previous argument, we can say that by its formal complexion the *Memoirs* did not fit in with the historic pact between nationalism, enlightenment, and the elite, and, more than that, it laid bare the ideological dimension of that pact and its workings in class terms (even without these being named, that is, without forcing the reader to recognize them).

Seen in the context of the modest achievements of the Brazilian novel up to this point, the sheer number and acrobatics of the cultural references made in the *Memoirs,* particularly in the opening chapters, has something of a triumphal entry on stage about it. Here was a writer much better equipped than his contemporaries and predecessors, and, what's more, with every interest in underlining this very fact. A comparable distance appears again inside the novel itself and separates the up-to-date and universal level, on which the narrator's argument develops, from the limited space of the anecdotes, with their local flavor. We can say that the aesthetic imbalance brought a real, existing historical tension onto the level of the literary form. From the point of view of the composition, and at first sight, this disharmony brings about a certain emptying of the two poles. Finding little support in the context of the story line, reflexive activity takes on a certain gratuitous air, which allows the reader to ask, in Brás's own words, "if the previous chapter [of deliberately insulting pseudo philosophy] is merely insipid, or if it rises to the level of a joke" (ch. 32). At the same time, the episodes of the plot, ironically and arbitrarily produced in support of "superior" speculations, and so separated from any practical context, are deprived of any immanent meaning. Their relevance becomes the — *forced* — product of the narrator's speculative whims. The belittling of the characters, who in spite of their complex motivations often give the impression of being puppets, is linked to this merely illustrative function, and to the enormous distance that separates them from the effervescent up-to-dateness of the one doing the talking. Later on, at the end of this chapter, we will try to interpret the content of these mismatches; for now, let us return to their foundations outside literature. The survival of the colonial mold in the midst of modern conditions explains the world apart, foreign to contemporary civilization and its categories, the intense desire these latter provoke, and the element of skepticism that, in its turn, goes along with them. In this sense, the structural discord of the *Memoirs* reproduced objective contradictions.

Along the same lines, we can see the problem to which Brás's volubility gave a kind of solution: in the most demanding terms, free of any empathy with our narrow existence, what is the meaning of Brazilian experience? The narrator's intense to-ing and fro-ing between local facts and the prestigious perspectives of the West constructed, for literary purposes, the intimacy of Rio de Janeiro with the outside world—an intimacy that was being established in practice but that had few repercussions in consciousness, dominated by the segregated ways characteristic of the country. Dona Plácida and the Voltairean critique of Divine Providence; Virgília and the subtle ways of the reproduction of the species, on Darwin's model; a chicken wing as the final aim and explanatory key of the process of colonization: because of the wing was hunted the African, who planted the corn, which fed the chicken, whose bones Quincas Borba philosophically chews on. These are ways of removing Rio's day-to-day existence from its provincial setting, and of linking it to universal culture in its fullness, even if this is somewhat abruptly done.

It is true, of course, that the *Memoirs* is the first Brazilian novel without provincial limitations. It is not that the hypercultured narrator has identified an up-to-date vein in the local anecdotes, which establishes their relevance. On the contrary, the literary force of his explanations, which are ingenious and cleverly formulated, lies in their inadequacy. In order, we noticed first the dissonant construction of the book, then seen as a reproduction of Brazil's own impasse. The dissonance itself is born of an attempt at overcoming a practical problem in artistic terms: Brás Cubas's volubility establishes and carries through, on a personal level, the universalization of connections that slavery and clientelism impede in daily life; the profusion of cultural references makes up for the precariousness of real relationships, marked by the thinness of the plot and the anecdotes, which explains the disproportion. From this angle, the form of the *Memoirs* (a) provides a transcribed version of a historical difficulty, (b) tries to find a way out of it, and (c) underlines the sacrifice made on the level of the composition, a sacrifice that in its turn is characteristic and significant. In other words, it is a form that is rigorous, apt, and instructive in its terms and its internal logic. The breadth and density of Brás's knowledge, which presuppose as much again and then some on Machado's part, are witness to the really great cultural possibilities — which these days we are not used to thinking about — of the nineteenth-century Brazilian elite. The horrors of the country's social structure did not prevent an extensive familiarity with European intellectual life, even if they did mean displacements in the ways it was used. The deprovincializing of Brazil through volubility, that is, by the arbitrary mental associations of a cultured Brazilian who sees everything everywhere, Aristotle here, St. Augustine or Gregorovius there, is Machado's caricature of this situation, or, again, the capturing of its clownish aspect, which is still present today. Point by point, the waywardness of this process is given a discipline by its usefulness to the tacit, pedestrian aims of the narrator. Thus, the deprovincialization achieved in the *Memoirs* is not the direct, straightforward consequence of the accumulation of intellectual resources, magisterially given shape in the style of the dead author, of whom one can say without fear of contradiction that he mixed with the best circles and models in cultural terms. With notable daring (and detachment in relation to the amount of reading he has undertaken) the whole repertoire of the Enlightenment is subjected to a negative movement and treated as ideology. The realistic literary effect and the historical insight do not lie in the rightness or consequences of Brás's reflections, but in their effectiveness in avoiding the subject, and in their meaning *on another level,* which the reader must identify and construct for himself.

In Brás Cubas are combined the enlightened gentleman, the charlatan inventor, a madman's disciple, and the absurd deputy in parliament. Cotrim contains in his person a respectable businessman and smuggler who uses the whip on his slaves. In analogous fashion, hidden in the literary and philosophical pirouettes of the enlightened narrator, we can recognize the specific features of a product of the slave system. The almost-minister Lobo Neves is an eagle in politics but owes his seat in parliament to his father-in-law and refuses the presidency of a province because the appointment came out on the thirteenth of the month. And Virgília herself, so elegant and uninhibited in her adultery, has a love affair outside marriage only because "it's the will of heaven" (ch. 57), as well as reciting the whole of the catechism when it thunders. The reader will notice that the common denominator in this cast of characters lies in the contrast between the public face, marked by the atmosphere of the capital city and of modernity, and the traits in which the colonial world either is seen or can be guessed at. In the figure of Cotrim the discrepancies are explored with exceptional wickedness and brilliance, and they give us a page of great literature. Also, the oligarchic features of the narrator are delineated with extraordinary exactitude and spiritedness, but we have seen how much of this is not easily seen, which is perhaps not a fault, though it does point to something ambiguous. In the figure of Virgília another line is developed, though the same contrast is very present. We can say that Machado systematically included in his characters elements of the two spheres — with varying results, since the contrast can either be solved by a movement that explores it or place side by side elements that are not fully integrated, producing a certain lack of focus, a vacuum between the diversity of the observations and the final outline of the type.

So, the two Brazils are juxtaposed inside the characters, who are heterogeneous in the way they are constructed. They form a reasonably normal gallery of types, if they are seen from the perspective of daily life; if, however, the perspective is European, it will seem that everything is extravagant, and that we are in the company of a collection of eccentrics, bandits, credulous bigots, and the like. The vertiginous instability in our capacity to judge them repeats in its own way the country's status, whose normality, seen from the point of view of the hegemonic ideas of the time, was an anomaly. The grotesque nature of these uncertainties, given extra power by the way it is reflected in the characters' own vanity, became one of Machado's specialties. When it is treated almost exclusively within each individual's sphere, with no support in social history or the description of social formations, and above all when it is not developed any further in the plot, this disharmony appears in a moral light. However, if we pick up on the legacy of the colonial world in each character, and put all this together, we will see the subject matter of picturesque Romanticism, with an obvious collective dimension.[27] Here are slaves' punishments, traditional religious habits, extended families, clientelism, and so on. But it so happens that, taken one by one and associated to some character's pretensions to civilization, these elements become part of his inner consciousness, and so constitute a problem, or, one could say, the opposite of simple *local color*. That is where the advance is located: Machado surpasses the picturesqueness of his predecessors by *interiorizing* it, but he didn't throw their inheritance away, and perhaps one could say that he sublimated it, *or that he began to specialize in the picturesqueness of our problems of conscience.* The critics, themselves marked by the Romantic and patriotic poeticization of local color, and seeing that it was absent in Machado's fiction, pointed out the writer's preference for universal values. However, all one has to do is think of the clashing registers within the types who make up the *Memoirs* to see there an investigation of other kinds of peculiarities and historical necessity—in a trend completely contrary to nationalistic jingoism. Unlike the Romantics, for whom the picturesque functioned as a necessary backdrop, which had nothing to do with the drama of the plot itself, Machado places it right at the heart of his principal characters: after all, when you think about it, what could be more picturesque than Cotrim, Dona Plácida, Virgília, Quincas Borba, and Brás himself? And, differently from the Naturalists, who look for local peculiarities in the lower classes or in distant regions of the country, Machado found it in our frock-coated elite.

At one point, in the chapter where he corrects "Helvetius's principle," Brás Cubas observes a contradiction in his interests as a lover: *security* demands that he keep the adultery with Virgília secret, whereas *conceit,* hungry for the envy of others, wants to let the secret get out. This first interest "was reflexive, and presupposed a syllogism preceding it; the second was spontaneous, instinctive, and came from inside the person; . . . the effect of the first was remote, the second immediate" (ch. 133). Some pages later, this time talking about charity, and the sensations of vanity that it too provides, Brás also thinks that "any and all outside rewards are hardly worth anything beside the subjective, immediate reward" (ch. 157). That is, so-called enlightened self-interest, which takes reality into account, puts on a poor show beside the alacrity of imaginary satisfactions, which prevail even though they are ridiculous. The reader will have seen in this "subjective and immediate reward" the state of mind that controls volubility and dominates the world of the *Memoirs,* a world that is thus linked to a frivolous, opportunistic revaluation of the Enlightenment.

Since it is the motive of motives, or the motive that emerges from behind all the others, the quest for "some kind of supremacy, any one will do" soon crystallizes as an abstract notion, which is allegorized in the narrator's acts and those of the other characters. The first interpretation of this that presents itself belongs to a premodern horizon: there is no human being without his grain of madness. This notion is backed up by the archaic sound of the prose, loaded with figures of speech, personified abstractions, parables in the form of anecdotes, constructions that are truly allegoric, and more. Reading all this in another key, however, the preeminence of caprice can be read as a differential characterization of a nonbourgeois society in a period of bourgeois hegemony. On this reading, volubility loses some of its metaphysical status and gains validity via the complex of historical relationships it gives expression to. In analogous fashion, the apparatus of ornate language, out-of-date in the context of demands to disobey convention and be historically in tune, is reused in an ironic fashion and within a very acute realist criterion, something that in principle is its opposite. The distance that separates it from objective, sober prose alludes to the real situation of Brazilian society and to this society's relationship with its models, which are, presumably, in accordance with reason. A quasi rule of obliqueness hovers over the novel: the old-fashioned literary clothing obeys a historically specific imitation, while the ostentatiously up-to-date terminology and discourse give comic support to obsolete forms of behavior.

The voluble narrator is a literary technique, a sign of human futility, an index of historical specificity, a representation of the movements of the consciousness, whose sudden impulses gradually go to make up a world—a vast but always *internal* one. Within this space, shaken by the lively rhythms of the person's feelings about himself, the paraphernalia of classical rhetoric goes through a surprising role change. This most worn-out and public of languages works as an often direct and quite unconventional imitation of the psychic process and of the social life that inhabits its secret recesses. Although they are contrary to the spirit of modern prose, the showy effects of traditional eloquence are very suitable indeed for exhibiting volubility, for this latter, too, looks in its own way and speaks shamelessly on its own behalf. Legal cunning, abrupt interruptions, depressing comparisons, classical references, and so forth fit the expression of the inner hunger for acknowledgment and grandeur like a glove: the contrast of these demands with "external" mediocrity is a realistic effect in its own right. We are in the same climate that leads, twenty years later, to Freud's description of dreams and daydreams—which, according to the celebrated formula, are always "wish fulfillments" that take place in the presence of a censor, at the expense of reality and by means of the imagination's reuse of elements of this same reality.[28] At the level of the narrative succession one can see an analogous affinity. To the extent that they cut into the narrative sequence, the interruptions, coded intercalations, substitutions, associations, deformations, condensations, and amplifications allow us to see a kind of psychic operation, no less articulated than the more conventional one and rather similar in manner to what Freud would describe in talking about the "dream work." So, although it is immutable, human inconstancy has a philosophical and scientific aspect that is right up-to-date; and the allegorical landscape — inhabited by dead men and abstractions like time, nature, and infinity — asks to be seen as a modern, inner space.

Let us look at other examples of this figurative and obliquely *realist* use of the metaphysical world. The insouciance with which the narrator exchanges one perspective for another, however disparate they may be, whether they are on this side of the grave or the other, points to the equivalence of everything and everybody in death (the "cadaverous" — or allegorical — "twitch" that the work suffers from, according to Brás). On the other hand, the anarchic variety of motifs is soon whittled down to one single one, egotism. This reduction of the diverse to the elementary, by means of analytic ingenuity, bears the stylistic stamp of seventeenth-century rationalism and has something of *positive* knowledge about it. Its referent is the natural nature of Man, if one can put it that way, and not the condition of the sinner in this vale of tears. Also, the universalization of rivalry between individuals, embedded in the literary method, belongs to the early origins of the bourgeois order; and the generalized equivalence of everything to everything else, if we once pay attention to its note of self-interest, mixes the leveling effect of *death* with the equalization suggested by the *market,* which makes everyone into competitors. Finally, the air of extravagance surrounding these different theories highlights the element of fantasy inherent in any explanatory ambition, but this does not stop the book's aspiring to a psychological vanguard characteristic of the rigorous and quasi-scientific patterns of imaginary compensation; nor does it lose its objective of providing a caricature, linked to the more censurable peculiarities of Brazilian intellectual life. This multiplicity of possible readings, sustained by the narrative technique and given the lie by the profound structure of the book — as we will see in a moment — produces a harmony made up of clashing voices, which has a remarkable density and relevance.

Among the most spectacular aspects of the *Memoirs* is the "temperamental" treatment handed out to space and time. The *absolute* tone of volubility is, in the nature of things, due to a relative position, that is, to disrespect for realist convention, which, even though abused and insulted, is still taken for granted as the norm. And, in fact, at first sight the dead narrator and the "arbitrary" manipulation of the chronology appear to be an insult to verisimilitude and common sense, and to their correlate, the mimetic status of literature. At a second look, the emphasis will fall on the other side and focus on the daring and profundity of Machado's mimesis, which is trying to capture new historico-social objects, real, existing organizations, in which the insult to verisimilitude plays a real part. Seeing things from this angle, let us return to the chameleon-like mobility of the narrator, with its atomizing, fragmenting consequences: interrupting oneself, or others, or actions, or the prose itself, makes tiny antiunits, which are complete and psychologically intelligible, and which do not go beyond themselves — except in the direction of metaphysics, since this inconsequence functions as an *imago mundi.* The full stops at the end of each movement are arbitrarily placed, with a deliberately harmful effect on the fictional material, but according to the psychological economy of imaginary compensation, that is to say, to the perpetual urge to establish some kind of superiority over someone or something. At once absurd and easy to understand, this movement by means of small segments takes place by systematic recourse to witty interruption, which works as its punctuation; at the same time, it would seem to exclude from the scene any kind of complex wholes, endowed with breadth, contradiction, objective development, or able to include any kind of diverse reality, long stretches of time, and so forth. This is how the comic, and *mimetic,* effect comes about, because we are limited to a society that at one and the same time is self-interested and really quite simple — an excellent recipe for triviality — in which the bourgeois virtues of judging things in the longer perspective are just so many empty words.

Still focusing on the attack on differentiation that seems to be a consequence of the formal principle of the *Memoirs,* let us give our attention to some effects of the prose that, quite to the contrary, are highly differentiated and pioneering, and linked to the *numerous* character of these procedures. If we look at them all together, the instances of the voluble conduct can be distributed into different but comparable groups, where they take on a certain individuality again, acquiring a sort of presence that unites the accidental and the representative, a presence of which the absent variants are a part. The groups, in their return, seen as collections, not only exemplify human inability to stick to anything fixed; they also set up, by means of the contrast between different types of volubility, a species of historical present that is sui generis, more fluid and less factual and local than is commonly imagined, a present at whose heart there always lies another place, the distant object of envy, and a corresponding dissatisfaction (or mocking satisfaction), with the here and now. All these quests for supremacy, the liberties with narrative convention, the cruelties in the treatment of dependents and slaves, the conniving sordidness of the rich in their attitudes to one another, the misuse of the prose manner and the intellectual resources of the Enlightenment, the malign deliberateness in the aggression directed against the reader's finer feelings, and so on all appear in a large number of examples, which pile up as scattered instances of an ongoing process, as well as reciprocally reflecting and contaminating each other, going from the most insignificant to the most serious, and vice versa. It is a cumulative principle, with not much in the way of explicit articulation, and that in spite of or because of the crazy proliferation of its tiny units gives us the shape of a modern, materialist experience — reality as a flux given shape by repetitions.

As he picks his references from all the corners of the globe and of history, Brás inevitably decontextualizes them, as he decontextualizes himself when he takes them as his . . . context. This analysis has tried to construct the historical and class atmosphere of this decontextualization, a perspective we will return to later. For now, we can note that caprice would no longer be what it is if it looked at situations according to the aspect they show to the realist. The outrageousness of the narrator demands that they be separated from their foundation in history, and in doing so, and closing the circle, it prepares them for that order of freely subjective, though also disciplined, evaluations and combinations that could be called formalism or aestheticism. Thus, at one given moment Brás thanks heaven for "the gift for finding the relationships between things, the faculty of comparing them, and the talent for reaching appropriate conclusions" (ch. 127). This gratitude appears in the context of a clever and ludicrous analogy between the coquetry of Muslim women and Damasceno's distress at the death of his daughter: the former veil themselves so as to give greater value to their whole face, while the latter will not resign himself to the small number who came to the funeral, for which he had sent out eighty invitations. As the narrator argues, there is a kernel common to the two cases, since each is testimony to the importance of formality — "agreeable Formality" — which is able to wipe away "a father's tears," and to attract "a Prophet's indulgence" (ch. 127). The ostentatious ingenuity can trick the reader and lead him to quote approvingly the passage about the "gift for finding the relationships between things." He will be wrong, because what the passage exemplifies is the comparison of everything with everything else, a preposterous use of the intelligence and of abstraction, which is emphatically of the same capricious order as the anecdotes that it glosses and has pretensions to transcend. Brás Cubas's many theories, with their specious universality, come into this category. This said, the blatant multiplication of parallelisms, gradations, repetitions with different end results, differences with the same end result, and so forth—a necessary consequence of the formal principle with a single module—trains the reader's immediate sense of the *structural*. Thus, we separate from the fictional nucleus the motivations, phrase patterns, narrative solutions, situational outlines, and so on, to regroup them according to the possible correspondences between them, in an order outside time and space, which is at one moment absurd, then poetic, but always interesting, because if it so happens that it doesn't reveal "the relationships between things," it still represents a kind of functioning of the imagination, with the desires and satisfactions that go along with that. The narrator's reflections about Muslim women and Damasceno themselves serve as one illustration of this.

The offenses committed against the normal order of time are accompanied by the most varied explanations and connotations. They can manifest the breezy confidence of the dead man safely ensconced in eternity, or, better, a nineteenth-century skepticism armed with historical erudition, and with no belief in progress. But the contempt for verisimilitude and narrative convention can also represent, in the context of the relationship with the reader, a further aspect of the narrator-character's domineering class attitude: the Law exists, but only to be invoked and then disrespected by those who benefit from it. Thanks to the meditative and romantic power of the memory, free circulation between present and past can still express a victory of consciousness over the irreversibility of what has already happened. Or, finally, the break with common sense can be understood as the demolition of the system of illusions by which realism was underpinned, giving fiction back its playful, critical side, and so on. Taking the weave of the plot into account, however, the common element lies in the dissolving action of caprice, which attacks the minimal elements of unity or causality—and without them everything is called into question. For the purposes of our argument, it is important to underline the nexus between this fragmentation, caused by the many comings and goings of the plot and the commentary, and an extraordinary rearticulation that takes place on another, complementary level. The volubility undoes the rule of the clock, of conventionally sequential chains of events, of the ordering that is indispensable to active existence, but it does so in vain, for time reemerges inside the movements of volubility itself, which are impregnated with a complex, differentiated temporality, only to be found in the greatest literature. The focus of the mimesis and of the search for the historical *quidditas* is moved from what is narrated to the narrator's specific rhythm, whose implications in time, or for time, are the quintessence of the novel. It would be wrong to talk of subjectivism, since, as we have seen, volubility belongs to everyone. Putting it another way, the achievement does not lie in the premeditated defiance of normal chronology, well known to have been borrowed from Sterne, but in their adaptation to the Brazilian social structure and in the imagining of its consequences for the individual subject. Melancholy, tedium, wear and tear, collapse and nothingness — Machado's famous specialties — constitute the unwilled development, inside the narrator's own self, of the chain of arbitrary acts, socially defined, that go to make up the narration of that self. These are peculiar forms of experience of time, in which the effects of a social formation are gathered and reduced to their essence.

In the final chapter, "On Negatives," the narrator lists the things he was not: "I didn't achieve celebrity with the plaster, I wasn't a minister, I wasn't a caliph, I never experienced marriage." To capture the sardonic note in these frustrations, we must not forget the debased nature of the fame, the political career, the philosophy, and the marriages in question. The objects of the frustrated ambition are themselves paltry and cannot be maintained with conviction. The failure of the will to achieve an aim that in itself is worthless: here is a very Brazilian syndrome, with deep historical foundations, expressed in another vein by Oswald de Andrade, when he refers to the "nonexistent trail" along which he had run in the first part of his literary life.[29] As a counterpoint to these frustrations, there is "the good fortune of not having earned my bread with the sweat of my brow." An obvious enough advantage, but from the implicit point of view of the work ethic, or of Christian feeling, it is yet another minus sign, another way of not being. Underlined by the repetition, this kind of doubt reappears in the next sentence, in which Brás includes on the credit side not having suffered "Dona Plácida's death, nor Quincas Borba's semidementia" — a lack of charity in the case of the dependent, and an illusion as far as his own mental health is concerned. Sarcastically musical, the thread of the argument alternates debits and credits; unless the latter are seen from the egotistic and class-biased perspective of the character, they do not make up for the former, since they are in essence just further additions to the debit side and so make the imbalance even more striking. The tension is resolved in the famous final sentence, by means of a surplus that is the most irremediable deficit, or a deficit that is the only final balance that counts: "—I had no children, I transmitted to no one the legacy of our misery." Prepared for by the mocking crescendo on the side of the unbearable "positive" statements, highlighted by means of the dash, the sentence echoes in our minds, and it is as if it finishes the novel off with an emphatic affirmative (even though it's negative), which breaks with the constant relativization of the opinions implied in the established formal pattern of the chapter. Again, the move from the first-person singular to the plural of "our misery" seems to point to a jump up to a different and more serious plane, where the dead man finally stops evading the issues and writing literature, and assumes the responsibility of saying things as they really are. The distance between the witty routine of the narrative and this fortissimo conclusion does really seem to argue for the book's metaphysical interpretation, which, in this view, would transcend the play of fiction and of social and individual interests and reach the affirmation of the wretchedness of all human beings. On the other hand, the harmony produced by meanness and the absolute, and which involves the specious functioning of the second of these terms, is an old friend of ours. So why should we suppose that the final sentence has a different status, instead of seeing in it a drastic intensification of the preceding dynamics of the novel? The movement that prepares for this denouement revolves around the pros and cons of Brás's life, with the peculiar satirical touch that the first are no better than the second, and are simply added to the list, so suggesting an evaluation quite different from the narrator's — until this moment. The sum of the explicit and implicit negatives produces the deficit referred to in the final declaration, which, however, transfers it from Brás Cubas's account to humanity's, socializing the losses, so to speak. Is the life to which it would be better not to give succession identical with that of the species, as the final phrase suggests? A certain buffoonish grandiloquence on the part of the narrator, his taste for lugubrious farce, and the odd slap in the face force one to consider the other hypothesis, that is, that this same — spectacular — phrase puts on show the sterility and the desire to sterilize particular to the person formulating it, and so forms a natural part of the impasse that characterizes this historical destiny.

The list of what Brás was not could be lengthened, and seems to say, by extension, that he was nothing — that is, nothing *presentable,* in the bourgeois order of individual achievements, nothing that results from effort or merit. However, he must have been something, even if the novel doesn't seem to have at its disposal the terms to denote it, while developing it and setting it out all the time in narrative terms. We can say that nonbeing, here bluntly and explicitly affirmed, participates in some form of being, which is very much present, though it lacks any reflexive accompaniment to help in identifying it. The whole ensemble repeats the vicious circle imposed on Brazilian intelligence by reality: (a) the normative primacy of contemporary European terminology, (b) the ineffectuality of this same terminology to provide a descriptive synthesis of local social relations, and (c) the reflexive powerlessness of these same social relations, which lack the historical power to conceive of the contemporary world in terms of their own experience — an experience that exists but remains an empty space. The formula for this difficult process, which still characterizes our own day, was coined by Paulo Emílio Salles Gomes,* apropos of the history of the Brazilian cinema: "The painful construction of ourselves is developed in the rarefied dialectic between nonbeing and being another."[30]

What is the meaning of Brás Cubas's life, which the negatives quoted above seem to ignore, while at the same time they help in giving it shape? We have tried to find the answer to this question in the preceding chapters, studying the narrator-character's career, his ambiguous position in relation to the civilized norm, his iniquitous relationships with inferiors and dependents, his connivance with his social equals, at the heart of which lies this same iniquity. Unless we are mistaken, the result is a coherent world that is historically identified: the trajectory of the central character gives us one exploration of this world among other possible ones. This said, despite the detailed attention we have given to the internal connections in the novel, our reading does present a certain difficulty, because of its complete divergence from the narrator's own explanations. These, as we have seen, are heterogeneous, and chosen in such a manner as to allude to the totality of available intellectual resources. And indeed, Brás leaves no stone unturned to decipher and reduce to nothingness the movements of volubility, which makes for a kind of *eclectic nihilism,* not without its element of comedy. Thus, the spectacle of Rio life is made to exemplify the insignificance of our condition, explicated by the narrator in the incongruous light of Ecclesiastes, of madness as conceived by Renaissance writers like Erasmus, of the mechanical explanation of the universe, of the immensity of space, of the egotistical nature of human behavior, of the equivalence between everything and everything else, of the crushing preponderance of habit and instinct, of the peculiar dynamics of the unconscious. The list, which is extensive and could be lengthened, is defined, however, by an absence: *among the various kinds of explanation does not figure the historical one,* that is to say, a reflective process that looks for terms able to apprehend and problematize the particular form of a society, a class, a life. In a book that is in competition with Romanticism, and marked in its diction and its title by

Chateaubriand's *Mémoires d'Outre-Tombe* — one of the foundational prose works in terms of modern historical sensibility — this lacuna is not caused by mere forgetfulness. And in fact, the note of mockery that accompanies the narrator's universalizing arguments is linked to the fact that they represent a feint, or a flight from any particularized thinking that might fit their specific circumstances. So, if we are right, Machado composed a novel that was in perfect harmony with the social moment he wrote in, but by renouncing the intellectual and artistic procedures that historical consciousness had elaborated with this aim in view. As if this were not enough, he availed himself of a vocabulary, of concepts and techniques explicitly contrary to the reflexive expression of the universe of relationships where they themselves evolved and had their function. In other words, he was writing a realist novel with instruments suited to antirealist literary aims, and at the same time revealing the import of Brazilian reality outside the context of the fashionable explanations for them, simply by means of getting a fitting method of composition. Thus, the unsuitable application of recent European terminology to local society was avoided, as well as being portrayed. Also avoided was the element of poeticization and apologia almost inseparable from Romantic historicism, along with another of its characteristics, the feeling that a crisis is imminent, which in the Brazilian case perhaps constituted the most attractive promise and the greatest illusion of historicity. Among the unusual and frightening visions set up in the *Posthumous Memoirs* in fact is the possibility not only that the injustices of Brazilian society may lead nowhere but that their end is not in sight. We can also say that the universalization of volubility, despite the negative view implicit in it, maintains that the individual sphere of action is insurmountable, or, better, surmountable only by the extinction of the species. As he wrote a novel "of his time and his country," with the techniques of the previous century, Machado prevented the Romantic fusion of the individual into the collective and into the movement of history, a modern and regressive barbarism explicitly targeted in the critique of Humanitism, a philosophy in which individual pain does not exist.

Despite the taste for tricking the reader, for eccentricity, or for puzzles, the series of events that occupy the foreground of the prose are easy to follow and are easily made explicit. To understand them, all one has to do is not lose sight of their universal key, the volubility of the narrator and his demands, which are unreasonable and antirealist in their very nature. In one of the first chapters in this book we pointed out the unifying force of this movement and put it forward as the formal principle of the

Memoirs. Now we have rectified this affirmation and have located the deep form of the book in the displacement undergone by volubility and its corresponding explanations, a displacement caused by the tacit and always powerful ensemble of social relations. This adjustment takes place outside the book's sphere of explicit thought and constitutes one of those well-defined realities, without a defined name, in which the best postrealist literature would specialize. We can say, then, that the latent form makes itself manifest by removing authority from the foreground form, which is reconsidered in the light of the novelistic material. Of course, about-faces of this kind are always possibilities present in a modern reading, one that realizes that the form is something objective and does not depend on authorial intention. In Machado's case, however, it is undeniable that he had the aim of making the reader aware of an independent position, opposed to that of the narrator, by use of this new status of form. Working in this direction, among other kinds of provocation, there is the technique of aggressively twisting quotations for his own ends, so spurring the reader to check the arguments and motivations of the person doing the talking. In this context, there's no harm in reminding ourselves of chapter 35, "The Road to Damascus," in which the conversion of the biblical Paul to the Christianity of those he is persecuting serves as a model to Brás Cubas in his conversion to oligarchic egotism. Behind the narrator, and betraying him to the reader's critical sense, is the artifice of the narrative situations.[31]

The metaphysical status of volubility in the *Memoirs* is slippery. In contrast with the solidity and eternity of the raw material, or with the certainty of death, it is a nothingness, something that doesn't subsist. But it is also everything, when it makes manifest the reality of instinct and the natural rhythms of the will, as against man as a conscious, superior being. There is the possibility of heroism, when the (Romantic) imagination defeats time and present circumstances to impose on itself and on other things a particular meaning—but this is a creation that will not survive either, for it will be abandoned by human inconstancy even before time returns it to the dust. The ontological theses weigh in the balance against one another and cause one of the hesitations that mark the book, that is, the swings between spiritualism and materialism—and there is always the possibility of sensational about-faces, when the terms turn into their opposites. What could be more materialist than a "necessity of the conscience" (ch. 70), as strict as the laws of motion or the need to eat, and what could be more spiritual than observing the refined flutterings of the instincts as they look after their own interests? Having said this, the relevance of the debate in this case is not philosophical, for it owes its literary importance to another ambiguity, which really is central and gives it its ironic resonance. Thus, when it is confronted with the bourgeois, nineteenth-century demand for constancy, objectivity, and reason, volubility, which is the form in which consciousness appears in this novel, is, in a pejorative sense, nonbeing; and when it is confronted by the system of Brazilian social relationships, where personal whim is a structural fact with practical consequences, the same volubility appears as a substantive force that cannot be bypassed. Does this mean that the grave, insoluble ontological question appears now one way, now another, according to circumstance? Let us say that the nothing with which the *Memoirs* ends is complex, an expression of the pressure, at one and the same time real and innocuous, exerted by the model of contemporary civilization on the prerogatives enjoyed by the Brazilian ruling class, and that go on existing all the same. These prerogatives throw a sardonic light on the condemnation itself—and on the metaphysical debate that it obliquely touches on. The final nothing, then, feeds off the process that leads up to it, and our reading of it will be all the more instructive, the more it articulates this slow impregnation.

Within its own simple mechanism, the search for imaginary compensations remains the same from the beginning of the book to the end, imposing on it its aggressive monotony. The persistence of this basic rhythm, however, does not prevent there being interesting changes and differences. Repetition itself causes a process of wearing down, so transforming volubility, which at the beginning was an exclusive prerogative, into an inexorable fate. The contexts, also, create variety. The first phase of Brás's life, until he goes to Europe to study, passes in a universe belonging to the ancien régime, in which the desire for some kind of supremacy has something of a naive conformity about it, which venerates authority, wealth, and religion, though this doesn't prevent him from trampling them underfoot. In the subsequent phases, this same appetite will put on the modern clothes of liberal society, with its respect for citizenship, law, parliamentary politics, scientific activities, social philosophy, and the like. The result is more grotesque and less innocent, since the enthusiastic adoption of the new model, just as abject and uncritical as the other, now brings in its train moral and ideological contradictions, and a necessary increase in cynicism. The contrast between the two moments (of Brás's youth and maturity) is a result of the composition and is a very tangible, tacit historical contextualization, a fact conveyed by the form — if we can put it that way — which invites one to reflect. In the same order of changes that are given shape but not directly commented on is Brás's increasing madness, from the moment that Virgília goes away and the affair ends. Here, too, depending on the angle we look at things from, nothing new happens, for the mechanism of imaginary compensation stays the same, whether we're dealing with an enviable adultery, a seat in parliament, the philosophical key to the universe, or one's portrait in oils hanging in the sacristy of a religious brotherhood. The results, however, do differ, and the long period of amorous fulfillment between Virgília and Brás, though stuffed with crazed negotiations intended to bolster self-esteem, is nevertheless one of relative personal equilibrium. The reality of the fondness they feel and the demands of the adultery impose a certain discipline and rationality on life, which soon disappear when external prestige takes over. External, in this sense, are philosophy, politics, journalism, philanthropy, science, which might still surprise one, until we remember that in the gravitational field of volubility, which represents the spiritual life of the country, these activities take leave of the usual rules that bind them and start functioning as empty forms of prestige, doubly empty given that they pretend to substance. It is as if the development of the novel were saying that, in the absence of love and family, the inevitable search for some kind of supremacy transforms our "great men" into simpletons, admired by other simpletons, men completely lacking in inner continuity. Hence the curious, almost popular character of Brás Cubas in his final, postamorous phase, when life comes to him entirely from the outside, and his bedazzlement with various kinds of public exhibitionism gets more and more like the search for the kind of distraction that makes people with nothing better to do follow military parades or frequent parliamentary debates. Here is a last example of something hinted at in the way the novel is organized: the reader will have noticed that a fair proportion of the characters, after a while, make a brief reappearance. Toward the end, the good Eugênia is begging for alms in a slum, Dona Plácida dies in abject poverty, the lovely Marcela in a hospital, Quincas Borba returns to poverty, the ex-slave Prudêncio becomes a master in his turn and takes out on his slave the drubbings he had received from Brás, Virgília has the composure of a woman with an immaculate reputation, and Cotrim is still wheeling and dealing, getting more and more prosperous. There is no lack of mobility among the characters, and yet the ensemble reveals no particular tendency; at the same time, this same ensemble is morally conclusive, and this is precisely what is most intolerable about it.

The lesson of the total form of the novel has to do with an organization of collective aspects of life, their existence in time, their rhythm, direction, problematic character, and so on. At the same time, the antics in the foreground, which take place in rapid succession and have crystal-clear motivation (even when that motivation is hidden), bring their own conclusions with them, or go beyond this only to confirm the general way in which mind operates in the novel. The objects targeted in these two cases do not belong to the same sphere. It is as if the instructions to the reader emitted by the narrative prose were conflicting, and appeal to disparate forms of receptivity, which from the aesthetic point of view can be disorienting. We have to engage our imagination at one moment in recognizing and sounding out a form of historical existence; at the next, to solving a puzzle with no transcendent meaning at all, and whose clues are all laid out on the table in front of us. An example is the difficult riddle in chapter 71: "Miserable leaves of my cypress tree, you must fall, like all the others, shiny and beautiful though they may be." This passage is only a small distance from a particularly malicious paragraph about Dona Plácida, and possibly indicates that not even cynics are eternal. However, a little further on, the narrator observes that in these lines there figures "a phrase very like a nonsense," and the reader is challenged to find it. And in fact, if we take the trouble to go back, we will remember — with a weak smile — that the cypress is evergreen and does not have leaves but needles. With a strongly critical outcome, the riddle has debased the melancholy consolation, according to which the abjectness of the rich will also end — "you will fall" — and has made one think that considerations of this type might also be no more than "nonsense." However, in spite of the interesting effect, it must be conceded that this point of view, suggested by the social system and the alterations it imprints on general propositions, is not immediately obvious. The cleverness of the riddle, the challenge to the reader, and the insult to Dona Plácida are more easily grouped under the universalizing instance of the quest to elevate oneself by demeaning others. We can say that the narrator's tricks can be appreciated only if one pays a great deal of detailed attention, which in its turn gets in the way of the more open, meditative attitude required to understand the overall movement — and vice versa. The dysfunction inherent in this mesh impairs both perspectives, and the more complex of the two is the one more damaged. The humorous tone that invades everything settles the reader into a kind of laughter that contains no novelties, with a short life, and shuts his eyes to the broader rhythms, which give dynamism to the relationship between the part and the whole, give the lie to fixed formulas, and bring to the surface, in witty sallies like this, a mordacity that has a different, higher quality, and that the first reading does not register. Access to this dynamism depends on one's reaction to the repetitive sameness of the other perspective, on distancing oneself from the narrator, and, paradoxically, on greater attention paid to the details, to the differences and changes hidden or revealed by Brás Cubas's insistence on everything always being the same.

Finally, it should be said that Machado did not invent the technique of the voluble narrator, which, however, he appropriated with a discernment amounting to genius and to which the complexity of the novels of his second phase is intimately connected. A decisive intuition told him that Sterne's self-indulgent humor could be adapted to the universe of Brazilian class domination, which could thus be transposed into fiction in an elegant, pitiless manner, full of crucial meanings. The English predilection for eccentric characters and for whimsicality, linked to the emergence of democratic culture in Britain,[32] would be put to use to express the eccentric position — if I can put it that way — of our elite, linked to the modern bourgeois model but diverging from it in a scandalous manner on the level of sociological relationships. In Europe the literary value given to caprice had been linked to the Enlightenment and to the struggle "for the autonomy and spontaneous expression of the feelings."[33] Brought to Brazil, it allowed a close-up view of a completely unenlightened freedom, but one in daily operation and crucial to the country, in which a given individual, especially if he belongs to the upper classes, arbitrarily decides if he is going to think of his fellow citizen in terms of equality before the law, or according to the gamut of relationships inherited from the colonial period, or, again, as the latter disguised by the former. Thanks to this historical relocation, volubility and its many formal possibilities begin to produce dividends on a realist level, in an implicit manner, as we have seen.[34] In an analogous perspective, we should remember that Machado investigated the quantitative, account-keeping dimension of the movements of the conscience, whose continual dissatisfaction is governed by the demands of pleasure and the avoidance of its opposite — even if for this purpose it has to abandon the real world for imaginary compensation. Adopted as the basic single cell of the narrative prose, and of the conduct of the characters, these compensatory transactions incorporate into the novel a reflection on psychological questions that is as advanced as one could wish, has affinities with science, and differs widely from the religious or moral evaluations of the inner life. It so happens that, in the absence of these latter standards, paternalism loses any possible acceptable justification and is reduced simply to the will of the owners. Yet, the hypothesis of a strictly economic dynamics of the mind has not only a critical role but one of apologia, for it frees the beneficiaries of the social order from responsibility for their dependents — a mere illusion, according to this line of thinking. From still another angle, because of its aspect of inconsistency, volubility at every moment allows the narrator to invoke, wittily and on a grand scale, the Western literary tradition, in which anecdotes, phrases, and reflections on human imperfections are ten a penny. The result is a gallimaufry of rhetorical fireworks, absurdities, and weighty arguments, with a cultured, universal flavor, that is also picturesquely accurate as far as the cultural style of our elite is concerned. Finally, there is no need to comment on the demeaning effect of volubility and its consequences for the universe they characterize, right in the heart of the nineteenth century. But we have also seen the corresponding advantages, the regressive forms of pleasure linked to a continuous, unpunished breaking of the rules, though this does not affect the nothingness they end up in. Under the sign of the narrator's volubility, a literary disposition was established, in which the status of the individual, the law, the scientific spirit, the tradition of elegant writing, and philosophical arguments all spin out of their normal, accepted axes, at the same time obeying other rules, those of a social formation. This "relocated" form of motion allows one to look, from innumerable perspectives, at a historical situation inside the system linking modern nations, as well as — and above all — a possibility, a group of problems, and one of the destinies of this same system. Some pages back we suggested that Machado had deepened and reduced to its essence the program of his Romantic predecessors when he took the investigation of the picturesque inside his characters' and narrator's makeup, inventing a kind of moral picturesque, the exact correlative of a social structure.[35] However, let us forget previous Brazilian literature (without which, of course, these configurations could not find a form) and adopt the perspective of a general history of the novel. Instead of a satire on local types and their incongruous desire to emulate the modern bourgeois model, we see emerging the elasticity with which this same model confers distinction, associating itself with the progress of exotic calamities like those we have exemplified and of which, in theory, it should be the critic. Into the foreground comes *the formalism of bourgeois civilization,* its adaptability to the most extravagant of roles. In other words, Machado's parsimony in the use of local color, which critics sometimes point to as an advance in the direction of a view of Man's problems *tout court,* is a step in making picturesque, or, better, in relativizing, bourgeois universalism itself, whose overweening pretensions at this time had in Brazil — and in the other countries on the periphery of capitalism — one of their moments of truth.

In a famous letter, not without its touch of dogmatism, Marx would claim as one of his contributions to science the demonstration of the *historical* character of the civilization of capitalism, which is not eternal — as was thought then — nor is it an expression of human nature, much less a complete summary of it.[36] Unerringly, by concentrating on the internal and external thresholds of the bourgeois order, the advanced literature of the second half of the nineteenth century dedicated itself to showing this same relativity and usurpation. This vanguard still has a validity today, and Machado de Assis is a part of it.

II

LITERARY ACCUMULATION IN

A PERIPHERAL COUNTRY

10

LITERARY ACCUMULATION IN

A PERIPHERAL COUNTRY

[T]he appearance of *Brás Cubas* modified the established order: the positions of José de Alencar, Manuel Antônio de Almeida, Taunay, Macedo — until then the big names in our fiction — had to be appreciably altered. — Lúcia Miguel-Pereira, *Prosa de ficção de 1870 a 1920*

If, however, we turn to look at Machado de Assis, we will see that this admirable master meticulously imbibed the work of his predecessors. His line of development shows a highly self-conscious writer, who understood what was right, definitive, in Macedo's predilection for describing customs, in the wholesome, colorful realism of Manuel Antônio, in José de Alencar's vocation for analysis. Machado presupposes the existence of his predecessors, and this is one of the reasons for his greatness. In a literature in which, in each generation, the best begin all over again, da capo, and only mediocre writers simply continue the past, he applied his genius to assimilating, deepening, fertilizing the positive legacy of previous experiences. This is the secret of his independence vis-à-vis his European contemporaries, of his aloofness from French and Portuguese literary fashions. This, too, is the reason why many critics have not known where to classify him. — Antonio Candido, *Formação da literatura brasileira*

THE DISCONTINUITY BETWEEN THE *Posthumous Memoirs* and the somewhat colorless fiction of Machado's first phase is undeniable, unless we wish to ignore the facts of quality, which after all are the very reason for the existence of literary criticism. However, there is also a strict continuity, which is, moreover, more difficult to establish. These two features were pointed out in Machado's lifetime, and since then have been commented on, each separately, in the illusory context of his biography. The crisis of his fortieth year, his problems with his sight, his encounter with death, or a sudden burst of genius explain the break; increasing maturity and constant effort account for the uninterrupted progress. Taken onto the objective level of the comparison of the novels, the question changes its aspect and the two points of view are no longer mutually exclusive. Instead of an individual's career, in particular his psychological or philosophical development, we can observe the changes by which a first-rate work arose from a series of middling, provincial narratives. In what terms can we conceive of the difference? To explain the importance of the question, we can say that it requires us to reflect on the way the form, content, and perspectives of the novel were given greater depth, and so showed themselves capable of correcting the irrelevance of a part of our culture, or of overcoming its narrowness. The central question is to specify what it is that changes and what stays the same, always in terms of a preexisting literary impasse that has to be overcome, and which underlies the transformation, giving it pertinence and truth value.

The newness of the novels of the second phase lies in their narrator. For many critics, the English humor and the literary inspiration that apparently knows no limits seemed to suggest, for good or ill, a creative space lacking any Brazilian landmarks. In the preceding chapters we have argued in the opposite direction, trying to highlight the realist function of the novel's universalism, which is steeped in the contemporary world by dint of being refracted in the class structure typical of Brazil. In analogous fashion, the relatedness of the narrator of the *Memoirs,* so metaphysical in his tone, and the narrow and moralistic world of the early novels does not strike the eye immediately but can be demonstrated.

We have seen that Brás's literary practice — his volubility — consists, at every instant, of contradicting and failing to obey the rules that he himself has just stipulated. Now, if one subtracts the rapidity of the process, this same behavior already figured in the novels of the first period, *in the guise of the subject matter.* From *Ressurreição* (1872) to *Iaiá Garcia* (1878), the narratives have as their object the harm caused by the unpredictable capricious will of a member of the owner class. From *The Hand and the Glove* (1874) onward, the class framework of the theme comes into the foreground and begins to determine the novel's structure. The question is seen from the point of view of the young woman, very deserving but poor and dependent, for whom the arbitrary — apparently generous — decisions of the young man of the family, or a rich widow, have in store a choice between humiliations and misfortunes, or the possible prize of cooptation. The moral aspects dissected by the analysis are above all two, strictly complementary to each other, at opposite poles of the relationship: (a) given the imbalance of means between the member of the owner class and his pro-tégés, how much margin for maneuver do these latter have, if they refuse to behave in an undignified fashion or be treated insultingly, but still, in spite of this, want to have access to the benefits of modern living? and (b) how can our privileged class avoid being ignoble, as well as *mad,* if a promis-cuous relationship between hidden desires and social domination, which impedes any kind of objectivity, is the structural consequence of others' lack of rights? The viewpoint of these novels is a civilizing one, for it tries to make these relationships less barbaric for the dependents, and less sterile for the wealthy, all by means of an enlightened understanding of the inter-est of the two parties, each of whom is confused by the effects of arbitrari-ness, which is the real thing to be corrected.[1]

Considered together, the novels of the first phase explore the di-lemmas of the free, poor man and woman in a slave-owning society, in which goods have a mercantile form, the masters aspire to contemporary civilization, the ideology is Romantic and liberal, but the labor market is no more than a hypothesis on the distant horizon. If there is no way of escap-ing from relationships of dependency and favor, even though one may be aware that they are historically anachronistic, might there be any way of avoiding their humiliating and destructive effect? Guided by a very strin-gent self-criticism, the progress made from book to book is remarkable. This period culminates with *Iaiá Garcia.* Here the liberal-clientelist system is amply exposed to view, expressed in its own terminology, and given substance in a whole gallery of relevant, differentiated characters, organized according to the practical and moral conflicts specific to them, and backed up, finally, by a dramatic disposition of a plot that is made to measure. An adjustment to the peculiar nature of the country is a result of a wide-ranging effort to absorb the empirical facts, and, what is no less important, to displace and nullify the Romantic models, whether liberal or derived from the melodramatic feuilleton plot, which are seen as deluded. At this point, the quantity of the social and psychological observations, critical reflections, and formal solutions found already represents a very respect-able assemblage in realist terms—neutralized, despite everything, by the conformist framework.

In its most complex version, laden with moral, ideological, and aes-thetic resonance, the impasse given shape in *Iaiá Garcia* is linked to the dependents' demand for dignity. They don't want to owe favors to anyone, since "their cup of gratitude is full to the brim" (ch. 3). But that doesn't stop their giving and receiving courtesies, since the social space they live in offers no other means of survival. However, they discharge their role coldly, without personal involvement, trying to thwart the game of warmth, congeniality, and reciprocity, as well as of indebtedness, which is inseparable from the practice of favor. This attitude of reining oneself and others in should not be taken simply as a psychological matter, for it represents the end product of a class experience, a kind of heroism of renunciation, of a particular, considered kind, one suited to its historical circumstances. The coldness, paradoxically, is a response to the hypothesis most favorable to the dependents, according to which, though without rights to protect them, they would be treated as equals — because the person with the power on his side wanted it that way. Conditioned by an unacceptable element of caprice, this favorable hypothesis would be the greatest courtesy of all, and for that reason the greatest abuse and humiliation. *The subjection of dignity, of Romantic and liberal values, to the impudence of a member of the owner class is the characteristic nightmare to which the poor person's deliberate reserve should put an end, even if it has the price of not changing their situation one iota.*

The main artistic limitation of *Iaiá Garcia* is its prose, which fails freely to verbalize the conflict that is laid bare in the plot. This deficiency is caused not by lack of resources but by the ideological restriction imposed by the aim of having a civilizing effect without being disrespectful. Yet, this restriction has a practical basis in the position of the inferiors, who do not have the independence necessary to allow them to criticize; this gives a contextualized, realistic note to the conventionality of the terms used. Even so, the injustice in the relationships somehow puts pressure on the well-behaved model of the writing, for its inadequacy is objective and makes one long for a narrator who would be less inhibited when faced by the owner class. This is the more so as the novel ends with the heroine looking to salaried work as a remedy for the "life of dependency and servility" (ch. 17) that paternalism obliges the poor to live. The position had been reached from which the insouciant effrontery of the wealthy could be looked at without subservience, nailed down in its backwardness and its embarrassing link with slavery. Thus, the last novel of the first phase had inscribed on itself, like a photographic negative, another book — the next one? — in which the superseding of personal dependence by free labor, a historical advance, would allow one to expose, without mincing one's words, the unacceptable, destructive character of the power relationships typical of the *previous* period. We know, however, that Machado did not write this work, and that the road taken by Brazil itself would be different.

It is a notorious fact that, as the years went by, the end of slavery did not turn slaves and dependents into citizens, and that the dominant note of the process that took place was, on the contrary, the grafting-on of precarious types of wage labor to old relationships of property and authority, which thus entered the new age barely affected. At some moment before the *Memoirs* and after *Iaiá Garcia,* with a decade to go before Abolition, the novelist must have fully appreciated this depressing but vitally important trend. The civilized reorganization of the relationships between the owner class and the poor, which had been the focus of literary attention in the first phase, was put off indefinitely. From now on Machado would insist on the regressive potentialities of modernization as the dominant, grotesque trait of progress in its Brazilian form. Going back to *Iaiá Garcia,* the European pattern embedded in its plot, linked to the moralizing dynamics of free labor, was out of the reckoning.

If we are right, this picture allows us to appreciate the genius involved in the about-face that takes place in the *Memoirs.* Now, it is no longer a question of looking for an — unreal — brake on the irresponsibility of the wealthy, but of throwing that irresponsibility into relief, giving it total freedom of action with nothing to impede it, though it will be no less unacceptable for that. The social type of the owner, treated before as one topic among others, and as the origin of varied kinds of affronts, could now move into the (trustworthy?) position of narrator. Or, to put it another way, the censurable (but uncensured) behavior of the owner class reappeared, transformed into a narrative method in which the to-and-fro between willfulness and enlightened discourse, itself the cause of the poor's practical and moral discomfort, was universalized and affected the whole of the novel's subject matter. Adjusting the focus better, we can say that the narrative volubility confers the generality of the form, and all the foreground, on the most intolerable aspect of relationships of favor, in which, according to the convenience or whim of the moment, respectable folks either do or do not let themselves be ruled by the civilized norm and decide the fate of a dependent "between two cups of coffee" (ch. 16). Exit the embarrassed, constrained narrator of the first novels, whose decorum was dictated by the precautions necessary to his subaltern position, and enter the brazenness characteristic of the second phase, the "free form of a Sterne or a Xavier de Maistre"* ("To the Reader"), whose ingredient of systematic contravention of the rules reproduces a structural fact about the situation of our elite. There is, then, an obvious though complex link between questions of literary form and social class: the point of view changes places and leaves the inferior, respectful position for the superior, lordly one, though only to prepare the case for the indictment of the latter. In other words, Machado was appropriating the figure of the class enemy, only to ill-treat him, documenting with examples in the first-person singular the gravest accusations that the dependents could make against him, whether from the traditional angle of paternalist obligations or the modern one of the bourgeois norm. Previously we have seen the owners from the resentful viewpoint of the dependent; now we have the dependent seen from the mocking perspective of the member of the owner class, *who makes a spectacle of himself.*[2] In a biographical context, perhaps one could say that Machado had completed his social ascent but had no illusions about it, and did not forget the troubles of the previous situation. This reorganization of the literary universe is profound and laden with consequences, some of which we will examine.

The narrative volubility makes the moral and ideological ambiguity of the owner class a matter of routine, in contrast to what happens in the early novels, where this same feature came as a moment of exception and revelation, as a crucial moment in the dramatic progress of the book. The methodical, continual reversibility between the normative and transgressive postures now became the general atmosphere of life. The long-drawn-out processes of conflict, with an ideological framework and representing an objective crisis, typical of European realism, became impossible; they are replaced by an overall movement that is sui generis and whose historical foundations are no less strong — instead of dialectics, the gradual wearing down of the will. The literary normalization of a structural fact about Brazilian society, however, did not mean that it was being justified. On the contrary, the indefensible nature of volubility stands out at every moment, whereas, out of prudence, it was not given prominence in the previous novels. In these novels, the desire was to remedy it, whereas in the *Memoirs,* where no way out is in sight, the objective is to see it in its full glory, and in the extent of the damage it causes.

What is the nature of the self-imposed reserve of the narrator of the early novels? As far as the relationship between owners and dependents is concerned, moderation lies in not commenting with any brio on the most perverse examples of direct personal domination, and, as far as the contemporary meaning of this same relationship is concerned, in not exposing respectable people to the bourgeois criterion that would condemn them. However, as he avoided the modern point of view in deference to the wealthy, whose dignity, very much emphasized, seems to have no connection with the abuses they practice, Machado was setting his novel in an apologetic and provincial terrain: he was constructing a place apart, protected from contemporary judgment. It was as if this latter had been locally deactivated. The voluble narrator puts an end to this protective segregation. By ostentatiously breaking the rules of equity and reason, he recognizes them and gives effect to them, making obvious, all along the line, the discrepancy between our social forms and the model of bourgeois civilization.

In the same way, the novels of the first phase have little room for the most spectacular manifestations of the new epoch, such as parliamentary politics, the cultivation of science, capitalist enterprise, the philosophy of evolution, or material progress. This almost complete absence is caused not by lack of interest but by the evidence for the precarious nature of such activities in Brazil, since they are difficult to reconcile with the forms of domination in force. Yet, they could not be completely absent, since they were indispensable to nineteenth-century verisimilitude and to the civilized pretensions of refined people. With the sense of realism necessary for idealization, Machado treated interest in mathematics, poetry, civil engineering, historical research, or the Chamber of Deputies as simple complements of aristocratic elegance. The secondary position of these indices of modernity allowed one to bypass, in these early works, the backward aspects of our most "advanced" representatives, though at the price of a certain generalized note of irrelevance and datedness, which destroy the novels as a whole. From the *Memoirs* on, however, when the dignity of the masters comes in for questioning and is no longer taboo, there will be a switch of signals and of proportions. As we have had occasion to see, the novelties of bourgeois civilization now come to the forefront. There they are, center stage, recent philosophical systems, scientific theories, pharmaceutical inventions, projects for colonization and building railways, and along with them, liberalism, parliament, the political press, and so on, even though they are always disfigured by their subordination to a certain class impudence, which is the true nature, seen critically, of the dignity proper to the owner class, still aspired to in the novels of the first period. *Literary deprovincialization happens on a grand scale, whether it be by lowering the status of local social relationships, which are confronted by or exposed to the norm and the progress of bourgeois civilization, and never get away without some embarrassment; or whether it be by attacking the reputation for unconditional truth of this same progress and these norms, which, in context, are made to take on displaced roles, contrary to their own idea of themselves.*

The narrative freedoms peculiar to the second phase begin under Sterne's wing, as Machado himself tells us. We should note, however, that at this time this whimsical prose was an old acquaintance, not only of the novelist but also of many Brazilian writers, who practiced it in their weekly newspaper columns [*crônicas*], imitating French models.[3] This miscellany made up of parliamentary reports, theater reviews, book news, social chitchat, and all kinds of anecdotes, whose object was entertainment, was a well-established genre — with a "nonserious" status. Perhaps because of this doubtful standing, several of its formal properties ended up constituting elements in the new period of Machado's writing, for reasons we will see.

Political subjects, for instance, asked for a concise setting-out of positions, which could be spiced up when the latter were absurd, ridiculous, demeaning, and so forth. In their turn, the very *modern* disparity between the different problems arising inside parliament, which parallels their irrelevance for each other, and the incongruity of subjects coming from all over the world, stuck together with no particular order on a front page or in the space of a newspaper column, was an incitement to take a loftily Olympian view. The random ordering of the topics, their great number, the inevitably arbitrary passage from one to another, introduced an element of the bazaar and of caprice. Expressive of the contingent and splenetic situation of the contemporary individual, this same caprice lent itself to poetical treatment, and to acting as a decoy, fulfilling the commercial necessity of grabbing the reader's attention. In fact, in the imaginary atmosphere originated by the press and intensified in such columns, the public was invited to behave as a consumer on a planetary scale. And the columnist, exploiting variety, novelty, liveliness, price, exclusivity, and more to attract the reader, transposed the practical demands of salesmanship into prose techniques.

The list of features common to the weekly column and the *Posthumous Memoirs* could be lengthened at will. With different functions, the amalgam of up-to-dateness and frivolity is present in both cases. However, if Machado had, already as a young man, mastered this technique, intimately linked, as we have seen, with the superiority of his "second manner," why was he only now bringing it into the ambit of the novel? It is an interesting question, for it allows us to detail in unforeseen ways the steps in an undeniable *literary progress*. In the 1870s, when he was writing his first four novels, weaker than the later ones and almost lacking in contemporary atmosphere, Machado was already well trained in the petulant, cosmopolitan pirouettes of these *crônicas*. What was missing to complete his mature artistic form was not the narrative procedure, therefore. The impending about-face, which would allow him to incorporate an available technique, common to many writers, into the execution of his novels, was of an ideological nature. In a general way, one can imagine that journalistic writing, *frivolous and a little cynical,* might seem incompatible with serious artistic ambitions. More decisively, these *defects* represented everything opposite to the *faithfulness* and *rectitude* that one would almost have to demand of the owner class as the only sure protection against their abandoning their dependents. Thus, the historical way out that the novels of the first phase try to find presupposed a moral commitment and dedication to the social progress of the poor, above all to the most gifted among them, a commitment and dedication that had to have unquestioned precedence over the *bourgeois* definition of interest, which, however, the owners could not fail to obey. When he sees how unfounded this presupposition is, Machado realizes the literary relevance of the ways of lowering the tone to which the *crônica* gave prestige, and turns them into the spiritual atmosphere of his writing. The new types of consumption and property, in the face of which the impoverished dependent is, in the nature of things, unprotected, emerge from the shadows and begin to set the tone. Under the prestigious sponsorship of Sterne, and of the antisocial behavior cultivated and given aesthetic form in journalism, the narrative volubility joins and alternates with the outbursts of patriarchal domineering and the I'm-all-right-Jack of the modern owner class, the whims of the old slave-owning oligarchy, and the irresponsibility of the new forms of wealth. Machado was putting on-stage the characteristic ambiguity of the Brazilian ruling class and holding it up to the condemnation of those perspicacious enough to understand.[4]

Thus, the formal principle developed in the *Memoirs* solves the impasses defined in Machado's early novels and lifts them up to a new level. The dialectic of content, social experience, and form is rigorous and brings with it a truly immense gain in terms of artistic quality, historical accuracy, depth, and breadth of vision. To appreciate the scope of this process, whose critical and accumulative aspects depend on each other, we must take a step back and see things from a distance.

From the point of view of Brazilian literary evolution, the narrowness of the novels of the first period was not merely a defect, as our observations might have led one to think. Elsewhere, we have shown that these works were a discerning response to a certain failing in the realism practiced by Alencar, which they escaped, though at the cost of giving rise to another kind of defect, perhaps even a less attractive one. Indeed, studying *Senhora,* we were able to describe a whole system of ideological and aesthetic mal-adjustments.[5] Unless we are wrong, this is the consequence of the uncritical acceptance of a formula of European realist fiction, linked to the liberal and romantic conception of the individual, and which, because of this, is not suited to reflect the logic of paternalist relationships. The innocent combination of local subject matter and a new European form heeded the more informed reader's desire to be up-to-date but was ignorant of the chemistry inherent in this mixture. As a consequence, the details of social life, that is, the society actually observed, have little interaction with the main lines of the plot, and the two remain separate from one another, which does not prevent them, on the general level of the composition, from mutually discrediting one another. The result is a fractured literary universe, in which romantic demands—the mainspring of the action—always have something ridiculous, false, and *imported* about them. Thus, when Machado in his first phase retreated from the so-called contemporary terrain and practically excluded the new and critical discourse of individual freedoms and the right to self-fulfillment from his novels, he was fleeing from the false position in which liberal ideology and the conspicuous virtues of progress found themselves in the Brazilian context. Once this position of discernment is established, it will permit him, from the *Memoirs* on, to reintroduce the presumptions of modernity, only now explicitly marked by belittlement and dislocation, as was demanded by the circumstances. He thus solved the artistic problem set up by Alencar's urban fiction, one that he avoided, at the cost of confining himself to the sphere of intrafamily dominance, in his own works of the first phase.

In turn—though this does not prevent them being naive—Alencar's realism in his "profiles of women" can be seen as a considered reply to previous novels by Joaquim Manuel de Macedo, and they represent a step forward in relation to them. For comparison, we can take chapter 4 of *O moço loiro* (1845), where two charming young ladies are sitting at the window of a suburban house, contemplating the moonlight and the sea. They discourse on the hardships of being an heiress: how can they believe in their suitors' declarations of love, when these latter will inevitably be motivated by her parents' money and other, even more cynical thoughts. Macedo had pinned down the poetic resonance, which was greater than might seem, of the combination of patriarchal atmosphere, the landscape of Rio de Janeiro, and ultraromantic cliches, which was profitably taken up by his successor. The charm of the scene lies in the artificiality of the ideas, blatant even if the girls have "twice the education that our Brazilian girls usually do" (*O moço loiro,* ch. 4). The function of the disillusioned speeches of the two girls is not critical but flattering, or, to put it another way, it is not there to reveal the outlines of the situation they find themselves in but to show off their links with modern civilization. With less desire to please, or with another kind of desire to please, the same atmosphere and a comparable topic are set out in *Senhora,* in which the several stages of the purchase and ultimate redemption of a husband are laid out. The book is organized with an ostentatious clarity, divided into four parts — "The Price," "Receipt," "Possession," and "Redemption" — according to the terminology of commercial transactions. In this way, Alencar brought an analytical (if somewhat absurd) rigor and the seriousness of moral indignation (itself a little out of focus) into the universe of his predecessor, which could be described as coquettish and avid for novelty. For all this, the strongly underlined rationality and dignity, in turn, had their own coquettish side, proofs of progress and Europeanism rather than real efforts to think clearly — and so repeated, on a more elaborate level, the set of ideas that needed to be superseded. The specious operation of moralistic anger and analytic enthusiasm, all twisted by having their foundations in elitism, and that are so uncomfortable to encounter in Alencar, will later constitute some of the great finds of the *Memoirs,* where they are a systematic part of the literary material. As he underlines their immediate and compensatory motivations, which give the lie to their gestures in the direction of enlightenment, Machado reconstitutes, on another level and given a new charge by moral discernment and the hard work of the intelligence, which had both been spinning out of axis, the easy inconsequentiality that moves Macedo's prose along.

A current of much more open, popular comedy is formed by França Júnior,* Manuel Antônio de Almeida, and Martins Pena. Their distinctive trait lies in the extraordinary insouciance with which the central ideas of the nineteenth-century bourgeoisie are treated, or ignored. These authors have no trouble in admitting the precarious position of the new civilized norms in Brazil, and in fact they see something cheery in this, a freedom from constriction. This can be seen, in the case of França Júnior's *crônicas,* in the picturesque mixture of European pretensions and the realities of slavery, clientelism, and the old patriarchal family, a mixture that is, already, the same that Machado de Assis will practice, though with a critical awareness absent in the former case.

In *O inglês maquinista* [The English Engineer], by Martins Pena, written before the end of the transatlantic slave trade, everything depends on the deliberate lack of decorum of the thematic combinations. Thus,

Mariquinhas's three suitors are a poor cousin, honest and patriotic, a slave smuggler, with a beard that even grows into his eyes, and an English con-man, as dishonest as the smuggler; the girl's mother beats the slaves to relieve her emotions, makes silk dresses for dress shops owned by French modistes but cheap cotton ones for her friend Merenciana, is a past master at using her influence to use the slaves from the public penitentiary, and naturally prefers suitors with money. And even though there are no doubts about where good and evil lie, the former does not enjoy different literary treatment and exists on the same level and in complete intimacy with bar-barism and transgressions of all kinds. The equanimity, embedded in the sprightly rhythm of the play, could be explained by the genre—farce—which, however, would be to ignore Martins Pena's historical sense. We can say, then, that the climate of farce allowed the playwright to give artistic shape to some of the most scandalous features of normal Brazilian life.[6]

The solution found by Manuel Antônio de Almeida in his *Memoirs of a Militia Sergeant* (1854–55) is less obvious but related. Antonio Candido has pointed out the easy familiarity of bonhomie and cynicism in his prose, whose rhythm opens room for both sides of every question, which are seen at one moment from the angle of the social order, at the next from that of the transgression of that same order. There is thus a certain suspension of moral judgment and of class perspective, in delightful contrast with the *critical* tone developed by the Romantics, above all Alencar, imbued with a rather pharisaical indignation and by pretensions to personal superiority. Antonio Candido also notes the "unobtrusively fabulous" resonance of this rhythm, which suggests a "world without guilt," "a universe which seems free of the weight of error and of sin."[7] To link these observations—which have provided a great deal of the inspiration for this argument—to our out-line, we can add that the narrative takes place in a semifantastic ancien régime, contrasting with the contemporary period, which is the *norm*. "It was in the king's time" when the bailiffs and other functionaries dressed and acted according to the majesty of their position, not like today's equivalents, who "have nothing imposing about them, in either their demeanor or their dress" (ch. 1). Of course, the charm of olden days is due not just to the clothes they wore or their colorful customs but above all to the tangible absence of the modern sense of morality, which, for those who are subject to its dictates, takes on a utopian connotation. Thus, one cannot say that there is no tension between the moral consciousness—of which the prose com-position tacitly reveals awareness, even if it is only to bypass it—and the world of deals struck between individuals, favored by clientelism. The sub-tly modern comedy of the book depends on this form of distancing.

We can say, then, that notwithstanding their different emphases, the trends we have described explore and develop a single problematic, whose origins lie outside literature and which is posed by the major features of Brazilian reality and its insertion in the contemporary world. The practical matrix had been formed at Independence, when there was a perverse conjunction between the aims of a modern state, linked to world progress, and the permanent social structure, created in colonial times. Between this setup and that of the advanced capitalist countries lies a fundamental difference. Inscribed in the framework of the new international division of labor, with its equivalent division of prestige, this difference took on a negative connotation: it signified backwardness, characteristic picturesque features, the irrelevance of modern issues, and being stuck in problems of no contemporary relevance. Though caught in this tangle, which was alienating in the true sense of the word, the role of artistic production and historico-social reflection would be to undo this compartmentalization and discover, or construct, the universal contemporary relevance of huge chunks of collective experience, stigmatized and denied as peripheral.

Recapitulating, our argument has as its starting point the peculiar, disconcerting kind of polarization Brazilian life imposed on a collection of categories that belong to modern experience. This social peculiarity has been noted and reflected on in innumerable ways, going from everyday thought, which left no record, to others conserved in newspapers or books. In the artistic field, in tune with more immediate and popular ways of reacting, we have seen that there is a small tradition of comic literature, unpretentious but remarkably irreverent. Guided by the Romantic sense of historical peculiarity and aware that, in such local circumstances, adhering to the model of the human personality proper to this same Romanticism was an imposture, these writers treat so-called advanced points of view and customs with no deference at all, and above all they do not privilege them over the nonbourgeois and nonprestigious daily life of Rio de Janeiro. The critical relevance of this vein of humor, its links with the colonial period, and its modern extension in Mário de Andrade's *Macunaíma* and Oswald de Andrade's *Serafim Ponte Grande* have been pointed out by Antonio Candido ("Dialectic of Malandroism," 101). In contrast, the Macedo-Alencar line adapted the complications of subjective aspirations, of the inner sanctum of the mind, of liberal sentiment, or, more generally, of the individual self that wants to be autonomous, to the familiar day-to-day life of Rio — which leads to the clashes we have already studied, and which, in the novels of his first phase, Machado would try to repress. In the *Posthumous Memoirs,* finally, this movement reached a higher synthesis, which recuperates its bad and its good moments and transforms them into great triumphs. The inner man is shown working at full capacity, full of hidden spaces and revelations, but with nothing of the chic, the superiority, and the reformist potential that, in differing degrees, Macedo and Alencar had attributed to him. Treated as a box of imaginary compensations, and harmonizing with decisive advances in the scientific concept of man, this inner universe does not push forward in any progressive direction. It adjusts itself to the lively merry-go-round, with no intention of reforming itself, that the literary tradition of a popular inspiration succeeded in inventing, molded on the true dynamics of Brazilian society. The rhythm of Martins Pena and Manuel Antônio de Almeida is taken up again in *Brás Cubas,* only now it is brought up the Alencarian heights of a demanding, contemporary self-awareness, which condemns that rhythm emphatically, though this does not stop it making a secret pact with it. High seriousness proves to be a farce and is condemned in its turn.[8]

Thus, the narrative technique of the *Memoirs* resolved questions posed by forty years of Brazilian fiction, and, above all, found rhythms and arguments suited to the moral and ideological destiny implied in the organization of Brazilian society. As can be seen, the aesthetic problems have an objectivity engendered by the history of literature and history itself. As he faces these problems, even in the purified, abstract shape of a formal equation, the writer works on a substratum that goes beyond literature, and it is to this substratum that the solutions achieved owe whatever strength and appropriateness they have. The formal questions are not reduced to linguistic ones, or they are linguistic questions only to the extent that this linguistic dimension implies others in the practical domain. In their simple layout, the elementary cells of Machado's tempo presuppose, in their widest implications, a judgment on contemporary bourgeois culture, and on the specific situation of the Brazilian ruling class, combined in the inexorable, to some degree automatic, discipline of a technique and a style, to which the historical meaning of this clash gives its unique ring.

The materialist tendency of this book will not have escaped the reader's attention. The road I have taken, however, goes in a different direction from the usual one. Instead of the artist imprisoned in social constraints, which he cannot escape from, we have shown his methodical, intelligent effort to capture them, come close to them, understand their implications and assimilate them as the conditioning context of the writing, to which they give *real* weight and a solid frame. This prose, given discipline by contemporary history, is a great writer's end point, his objective, not his starting point, which is always lacking in force in modern society because of the contingent nature and isolation of the individual.

Returning to Machado de Assis, we have seen that his narrative formula is a meticulous reply to the artistic and ideological questions of the Brazilian nineteenth century, themselves linked to the country's peripheral position. The palpable hits of his predecessor and contemporaries, their impasses, the moments when they are too narrow for their topic or simply ridiculous, are none of them wasted; everything is put together again and transfigured into an element of truth. Furthermore, far from representing a limitation, the formalization of Brazilian class relations gives a realistic basis to the caricatural universalism of the *Memoirs,* one of the aspects of its true universality. The demands of volubility, with a well-defined Brazilian and class aspect, stamp their own historical movement and meaning onto the apparently anti-Brazilian repertoire of forms, references, topics, and so forth, whose artistic interest lies in this same deformation. Machado's remarkable independence and breadth in his literary dealings with the Western tradition depend on the exact solution he elaborated to imitate his historical experience.

Finally, let us remember the note of mystification that accompanies the interminable maneuvers, or transgressions, of the "dead man who has become a writer": the norm that is being mocked has real validity (otherwise the intended clash would not happen), yet is still the law of the foolish. Put in this predicament, how are we to react? Do we enroll in the school of mean tricks of this prose, or do we distance ourselves from it and transform it into a content whose context it is up to us to construct? With a heightened but enigmatic profile, in the manner of Baudelaire and Flaubert, Dostoevsky and Henry James, the artistic method deliberately places itself on the surface, as itself a part of what is in question. It does this not because literature should take itself as its own subject, as is often said these days, but because in the arena opened up in the middle of the last century, whose final cause is social antagonism, every representation began to carry, in the implications of its form, a political ingredient. Literary audacity consisted in putting this very fact into relief and aggressively attacking the conditions that allowed trusting, passive reading, or rather, it consisted in trying to wake the reader up.[9] As is well known, the *Memoirs*'s most obvious debt in terms of technique lies in the eighteenth century, but this cannot be the essence of the novelty of a writer of the last quarter of the nineteenth. The faithful imitation of the impudence of the Brazilian ruling class — the acute sense of its contemporary meaning and harmful effects, complete uncertainty about how long it will last, and — the greatest daring of all — about the superiority of the civilization that served as its unattained model: the specifically modern preeminence of Machado's form, so clear and so disorienting, is attributable to this complex and highly mature ensemble of features. This narrative method purged the amiable and trite feelings our elite held toward any kind of elegant literary or patriotic self-congratulation (when it didn't have the opposite effect), and this same elite thus saw themselves transformed, with total implacability, into a mere cipher in the destiny of bourgeois civilization. Contrary to what the present vogue for antirealism might make one think, historical mimesis, duly imbued with critical sense, did not lead to provincialism, nationalism, or backwardness. And if one part of our intelligentsia imagined that the most advanced and universal of Brazilian writers passed by, at a considerable distance, from the systematic injustice thanks to which their country was inserted into the contemporary world, it must be thanks to a blindness that is also historical, a more or less distant relative of the impudence that Machado *imitated*.

NOTES

Introduction

1 More biographical detail can be found in the introduction to *Misplaced Ideas,* a collection of Schwarz's essays published in 1992. The first eight (of sixteen) essays in this book are of immediate interest to *A Master.* Two are chapters from *Ao vencedor as batatas,* the "first part" of this book; three deal with the question of misplaced ideas; and four are about Machado de Assis.

2 The title phrase is a reduction of the doctrine of "Humanitism" as expounded in *The Posthumous Memoirs of Brás Cubas* (ch. 117): it sums up its crude, parodied social Darwinism. The words themselves, which become an ironic refrain, appear only in the sequel novel, *Quincas Borba* [translated as *Philosopher or Dog?, The Heritage of Quincas Borba,* and *Quincas Borba*] (1892).

3 There is no space to go into detail here on this subject, which of course is part of wider social and political shifts touched on in this introduction. Just as an indication, one could mention the building of Brasília, the invention and growing popularity of bossa nova, and in literature, the works of Clarice Lispector and João Guimarães Rosa.

4 Schwarz's title takes up a suggestion of Benjamin's, according to which Baudelaire was "a lyric poet in the era of high capitalism." Obviously, in both cases an element of paradox and tension is involved. See the interview "Um mestre na periferia do capitalismo" [Brazilian Sequences] in Schwarz's *Seqüências brasileiras,* 220.

5 A more extended treatment of Schwarz's thought, primarily in a Brazilian context and less centered on Machado, can be found in Paulo Arantes, *Sentimento da dialética na experiência intelectual brasileira* [The Feeling for Dialectic in Brazilian Intellectual Experience].

6 One of the best guides to the period between the two "coups" in Schwarz's own essay "Culture and Politics in Brazil, 1964–1969," in *Misplaced Ideas,* 126–59.

7 Roberto Schwarz, "Um seminá rio de Marx," in *Seqüências brasileiras,* 86–105.

8 Although not published until 1979, the doctoral thesis on which Novais's book is based was successfully defended in 1973 and was "conceived in the years of the seminar" ("Um seminário," 96).

9 Fernando Henrique Cardoso and Enzo Faletto, *Dependency and Development in Latin America.*

10　The importance of Carvalho Franco to Schwarz's thinking is testified to by a passage in a very interesting "debate" about *A Master* with several intellectuals from Schwarz's generation, published in *Novos estudos (Cebrap)*, which I quote more than once. Toward the end, he says:

> I'll tell you the story of how I arrived at the construction of my little pattern. I had already more or less set up my analysis of Machado de Assis's voluble narrator, and was racking my brains to find out what this had to do with Brazilian reality, because I had the impression that it had something to do with it, but I couldn't find the link. At the time, I was reading a lot of Sérgio Buarque [de Hollanda], and Fernando Henrique [Cardoso], *Capitalism and Slavery,* and couldn't get any further, because I only had the slavery business in my head. Then I read Maria Sylvia's book, *Homens livres na ordem escravocrata.* . . . She makes an observation that enlightened me and put my study on the right track. . . . At one given moment, she says more or less the following: the plantation owner — who has these people living on his land, his dependents — when it suits him, acts according to his moral ties, that is, acts in a paternalist manner to his dependents, as a protector. However, when he needs to do business, when the protector role doesn't suit him, he sells the land and they're done for. Then I understood the movement. In São Paulo, the plantation owner acted like a bourgeois or a paternalist landlord, whichever was more convenient." (82–83)

Carvalho Franco's book is of course by no means the only one to deal with the phenomena of dependency and clientelism. In the nineteenth century, the abolitionist leader Joaquim Nabuco dealt with the topic in his essay *O abolicionismo,* arguing that this crushing dependency was one of the evils of the slave system. Schwarz is a great admirer of this essay.

11　The question of the supposedly conciliatory tradition in Brazil's history, which according to some masks a pervasive violence, is the subject of José Honório Rodrigues's *Conciliação e reforma no Brasil: Um desafio histórico-político* [Conciliation and Reform in Brazil: A Historico-Political Challenge], significantly published during the same period, in 1965.

12　"Dépendance nationale, déplacement d'idéologies, littérature," *L'homme et la société* 26 (Paris, 1972).

13　On the *malandro,* see especially the work of anthropologist Roberto daMatta, *Carnaval, malandros e heróis* [*Carnival, Rogues, and Heroes*], ch. 3.

14　"Within Marxism, also, we should make distinctions: although the vocabulary is quite different, we are in the ambit of the German tradition and the influence of Lukács, whose aesthetic constructs depend, precisely, on the objectivity and historicity of social forms. In contrast, for the Althusserians, as for the positivists, the form is a scientific construct without an independent reality." Schwarz, "Presuppositions," 142.

15　Candido in fact regretted that decision, as he says in the preface to the first edition, though he also justifies it by citing the book's unity. He also says there that he thought he might remedy the omission, but he never did.

16　I have argued this point in the context of Machado's last novel, *Counselor Ayres' Memorial,* often seen as his swan song, or reconciliation with life, which in fact is anything but. See "The Last Betrayal of Machado de Assis: *Memorial de Aires.*"

17　"Nowadays, a hundred and ten years after the novel's publication, in spite of all the changes that have taken place, a substantial part of those terms of domination still remains in place, with its accompanying sense of being the accepted norm."

18 "A nova geração" [The Present Generation], in *Obra completa,* 3:813. This edition will henceforth be referred to as *OC.*

19 Maria Sylvia de Carvalho France, "As idéias estão no lugar," 61–64.

20 Roberto Schwarz, "Beware of Alien Ideologies: An Interview with *Movimento,*" in *Misplaced Ideas,* 33–40.

21 One curious case, exceptional but no less interesting, is that of Machado himself. How did his own acute awareness of the phenomenon affect his own intellectual life? Did he, for instance, see something particularly suited to Brazilian reality about the (remarkable) selection of writers he was influenced by? Sterne? Schopenhauer? Gogol? As Schwarz says in chapter 8 of this book, Machado appropriated the essentials of the scientific spirit at a level that in Brazilian terms was an achievement in its own right (111).

22 In an interesting article that owes a great deal to Schwarz but takes his arguments further in some respects, Sidney Chalhoub argues that the analysis of the devious routes by which the dependent figures express themselves and manipulate their "betters" in more subtle than even Schwarz has seen. "Dependents Play Chess: Political Dialogues in Machado de Assis," in *Machado de Assis: Reflections on a Brazilian Master Writer.*

23 See *A Master,* ch. 6. The word in fact is different in Portuguese, *arbusto* in *The Hand and the Glove* and *moita* in the *Memoirs,* but the point stands.

24 In Schopenhauer's case, this can be seen above all in the remarkable chapter 44 of volume 2 of *The World as Will and Representation,* "The Metaphysics of Sexual Love," to which Machado refers more than once.

25 Many critics, notably Eugênio Gomes in "Schopenhauer e Machado de Assis," have noted Schopenhauer's influence. It can be seen, for instance, in the famous chapter 7 of the *Memoirs,* the "Delirium," which by Schwarz's own confession is not one of his favorites.

26 See note 2 to ch. 6.

27 In a lecture given in 1989, and whose text has been published recently, Schwarz says the following, in dealing precisely with the question of the historical transition that didn't happen: "You know that even today the world of labor is not entirely governed by the law, and that the great novelty of the PT [Partido dos Trabalhadores or Workers' Party, founded in the early 1980s], for example, in our time, is just that: it's the party that defends workers' rights to an existence in law." "A novidade das *Memórias póstumas de Brás Cubas,*" 59.

28 He is included, for instance, among the luminaries of "misty Albion," in the Visconde de Taunay's first novel, *A mocidade de Trajano* [Trajano's Youth] (1871), and called "the inventor of sentimentalism" (59).

29 This is made most explicit in note 2 to ch. 2, in which he acknowledges the quality and insights of Augusto Meyer's work on Machado.

30 The clearest guide to Machado's own reading and his thoughts on that matter appear in this — ironic — advice in "Education of a Stuffed Shirt": "Only, you must never make use of irony, that vague movement at the corner of the mouth, full of mystery, invented by some decadent Greek, caught by Lucian, passed on to Swift and Voltaire, a trait befitting skeptics and men without illusions" (*OC,* 2:294).

31 See Jean-Michel Massa, "La bibliothèque de Machado de Assis."

32 There is an essay on my work on Machado in Schwarz's *Seqüências brasileiras,* 106–12.

33 For a highly appreciative study of Schwarz's importance in discussion of these ques-

tions, which deals primarily with his essays on twentieth-century culture, see Neil Larsen, *Modernism and Hegemony,* ch. 4 ("Modernism as *Cultura Brasileira*").

Preface

1 Machado de Assis, "Notícia da atual literatura brasileira — Instinto de nacionalidade" [An Account of Contemporary Brazilian Literature: The Instinct for Nationality (1873)], in *Obra completa,* 3:817. This edition is henceforth referred to as *OC.*

2 Quoted in Raymundo Magalhães Júnior, *Vida e obra de Machado de Assis,* [The Life and Work of Machado de Assis] 4:376.

3 Walter Benjamin, *Charles Baudelaire: A Lyric Poet in the Era of High Capitalism,* 104, and *Das Passagen-Werk.* For an excellent discussion of the theme, see Dolf Oelher, *Ein Höllensturz der Alten Welt.*

4 [Tr.: See my introduction for a discussion and summary of this earlier book, parts of which exist in English translation.]

5 [Tr.: Here the author is referring to the military coup of April 1964 and the subsequent repression of the Left and much intellectual life, which hardened further in 1968 and only began gradually to lift in the mid-1970s. Schwarz's "Culture and Politics in Brazil, 1964–1969" (*Misplaced Ideas,* 126–59), first published in French in 1970, is fundamental to understanding this period.]

6 [Tr.: This seminar has been described recently in some detail in Schwarz's essay "Um seminário de Marx," in *Seqüências brasileiras,* 86–105. See also my introduction.]

1 Initial Observations

1 [Tr.: This dedication is missing in the translation of *Memórias póstumas de Brás Cubas* with the title *Epitaph of a Small Winner.*].

2 [Tr.: This was worth about $160,000 at the time. Brás is rich.]

3 [Tr.: For information on translations of the novel and different editions, see the translator's introduction, 000.]

4 "Machado is a writer in whom the strongly rhetorical aspect of the style, far from diminishing, in fact *reinforces,* the mimetic energy of the language, its power to effectively recreate in fiction the actual variety of life." José Guilherme Merquior, *De Anchieta a Euclides,* 174.

5 [Tr.: It is impossible to get the symmetry of the opposition in the original into English, since in Portuguese *defunto* and *autor* can be both adjective and noun, and so by switching order, switch the meaning.]

6 Antonio Candido, "An Outline of Machado de Assis," 109. For eighteenth-century English prose, see Ian Watt, "The Ironic Voice."

2 A Formal Principle

1 Augusto Meyer, "O homem subterrâneo," in *Machado de Assis, 1935–1958,* 13.

2 Augusto Meyer, "De Machadinho a Brás Cubas," 15. Meyer's observations and deductions, in this and other studies, are the high point of criticism on Machado. They still have a remarkable power to reveal, despite the fact that their theoretical framework has aged, which shows the relative lack of connection between the concepts adopted,

and literary perception and the ability to put it into words. This book owes a great deal to Meyer's formulations.

3 The Practical Matrix

1 Antonio Candido, "Dialectic of Malandroism," 95.
2 Theodor Adorno, "Rede über Lyrik und Gesellschaft," 49, and "Ideen zur Musiksoziologie," 19.
3 See Luiz Felipe de Alencastro, "La traité négrière et l'unité nationale brésilienne," and Fernando Novais, "Passagens para o Novo Mundo" [Passages to the New World]. My arguments owe a great deal to these two studies.
4 The British and French examples of national sovereignty with widely spread citizenship had reached the status of a paradigm; this produced international resentments of all kinds. On this subject, see Hannah Arendt, *The Origins of Totalitarianism,* pt. 2, and Eric Hobsbawn, *The Age of Empire,* ch. 1.
5 "[T]he Brazilian from the coastal region and the city lived, during the first half of the nineteenth century — really, during the whole of it — with an obsession with 'foreign eyes.' . . . And 'foreign' eyes meant those of Europe. They were the eyes of the West. Of the bourgeois, industrial, coal-mining West." Gilberto Freyre, *The Mansions and the Shanties,* 2:426. For a recent discussion of the theme, see Florestan Fernandes, "As implicações socio-econômicas da independência" [The Socioeconomic Implications of Independence]; Emília Viotti da Costa, "Liberalism: Theory and Practice;" José Murilo de Carvalho, "A política da abolição: O rei contra os barões" [The Politics of Abolition: The King Against the Barons]; and Alfredo Bosi, "A escravidão entre dois liberalismos" [Slavery between Two Liberalisms].
6 The expression is Trotsky's; he expounds and uses it in the first chapter of his *History of the Russian Revolution.*
7 Ellen Meiksins Wood, "Capitalism and Human Emancipation," 5–6.
8 Apropos of modern colonization, Marx observes that the realities of the colonies have much to teach us about the *relative* nature of free labor in the metropolis. *Capital,* vol. 1; ch. 25.
9 Quoted by Manuel de Oliveira Lima, *O império brasileiro* [The Brazilian Empire], 142. The speech is from 1843.
10 Antonio Candido points out the link between the philosophical exhibitionism and the state of national culture: "One could say that he [Machado de Assis] flattered the average public, critics included, giving them the sensation that they were intelligent for a modest outlay." "An Outline of Machado de Assis," 107.
11 [Tr.: In English in the original.]

4 Some Implications of the Prose

1 [Tr.: The author is here referring to one of Machado's most famous short stories, "Teoria do medalhão" (first published in 1881, and thus from the same period as the *Memoirs*). It has been translated into English as "Education of a Stuffed Shirt," in *The Psychiatrist and Other Stories,* 113–22.]
2 On the dialectics of mimesis and construction, see Theodor Adorno, *Aesthetische Theorie,* 72–74 [*Aesthetic Theory,* 79–83].

3   Related by Araripe Júnior, *Obra crítica,* 4:282. In the original: "Tudo! meu amigo, tudo! menos viver como um perpétuo empulhado!"

5   *The Social Aspect of the Narrator and the Plot*

1   On the dynamizing formal function of characters of the "Napoleonic" type in the European realist novel, see Georg Lukács, "Dostoevsky" and "Balzac and Stendhal."

2   [Tr.: A *compadre* is the godfather of one's son or daughter.]

3   [Tr.: Brazilian independence came in 1822. The first emperor, Pedro I, abdicated in 1831; his son, Pedro II, reached an anticipated majority at the age of fifteen and came to the throne in 1840. The Conciliation ministry (1853–1857), headed by the marquis of Paraná, was widely held to have laid the basis for the stability of the Empire. The Law of the Free Womb, which declared in 1871 that all slaves born after 28 September that year would be freed when they were twenty-one, made it certain that slavery would end; full abolition came on 13 May 1888. The Empire was overthrown and the Republic declared on 15 November 1889.]

4   John Gledson, *Machado de Assis: Ficção e História,* especially the introduction and the chapters concerning "Casa velha" and "Bons dias!" The former chapter was published in English as "*Casa velha:* A Contribution to a Better Understanding of Machado de Assis."

5   Otávio Tarqüínio de Sousa, *A vida de D. Pedro I* [The Life of Dom Pedro I], 1:240 ff. [Tr.: The Spanish Constitution referred to here is that of the Cortes of Cadiz (1812).]

6   This question has been amply treated by John Gledson, *The Deceptive Realism of Machado de Assis.* See also Silviano Santiago, "Retórica da verossimilhança" [The Rhetoric of Verisimilitude].

6   *The Fate of the Poor*

1   [Tr.: Tijuca is an area of Rio, not far from the center, which in the nineteenth century was a rural retreat with its steep jungle-covered hills.]

2   The peculiar position of the poor in rural Brazil was frequently commented on throughout the nineteenth century. "The agricultural classes, who cannot afford the necessary capital to have land of their own, live as dependents on the great owners of the soil, and by a *precarious* contract: that is, they may be expelled when it suits the landowner." In return, there was political loyalty expressed in votes: "The great owners of the soil still allow the presence of dependents because our electoral system demands it." L. Peixoto de Lacerda, Werneck, *Idéias sobre colonização* [Ideas on Colonization], 36 ff. Or, as Joaquim Nabuco* sums up the matter:

> An important class whose development is impeded by slavery is that of the landless farmers and the rural and backland inhabitants in general. We have already seen to what level this abundant part of our population has been reduced. For them, lacking independence, reliant as they are upon the chance whims of others, the words of the Lord's Prayer, "Give us this day our daily bread," have a real and concrete meaning. We do not refer here to workers who, released from one factory, find work in another, or to families who can emigrate, or to manual workers who offer their services in the labor market. We are dealing here with a population without resources, without assistance, a population taught to think

of labor as an activity suitable only for slaves. We are referring to a population without markets for its products, far from the realm of wages — if such an El Dorado even exists in our country — and therefore without any alternative but to live and raise its children in the conditions of dependence and misery in which they are allowed to vegetate. (*Abolitionism,* 123)

Beneath the class of sharecroppers, there are still others who "own nothing, who inhabit the land and have nothing to sell to the proprietors, who lead a vagabond existence remote from all social responsibility and beyond the government's protection" (*Abolitionism,* 124). A sociological systematization of the question can be found in Maria Sylvia de Carvalho Franco's very useful book *Homens livres na ordem escravocrata.* Antonio Candido, in his "Dialectic of Malandroism," has established the importance of this theme for understanding decisive aspects of Brazilian fiction.

3 [Tr.: There is an untranslatable pun here in the Portuguese. The word *coxa* means "thigh," but is also the feminine of the adjective *coxo,* meaning "lame."]

4 In *Sonhos d'ouro* [Dreams of Gold, a novel published by José de Alencar in 1872), which Machado undoubtedly read very attentively, Alencar had already tried to link class guilt and sadism. The rich girl in the novel cannot stand the sight of poverty, which exacerbates her urge to be cruel. Thus, when her little dog kills one by one a clutch of chicks belonging to an impoverished family, the girl snaps her fingers with pleasure. Immediately afterward, she amuses herself by making her elegant English horse trample on the humble crockery of this same family, destroying it. When this affront has been carried out, the heroine haughtily undoes these misdeeds, which indeed had a noble motive, for they were aimed at giving self-respect to a family crushed by defeatism (ch. 6). The viewpoint of the deserving poor also appears: Ricardo — who considers himself "a black butterfly" in relation to the girl (!) — was an excellent student. "But what good is that to him, if no one knows him? It would be much better if he had half the talent he has, with another half of patronage." Later: "So a poor person cannot have a relationship with rich people without flattering them? What a doctrine!" Concerning the drawbacks of love between people of unequal rank, the "daughter of a millionaire" explains to the "obscure pauper": "imagine the agreeable amusement each of us would have, you crushed by my wealth and generosity, I, riddled by the darts of your dignity. After a month we would be unable to stand one another; and would have the lowest possible opinions of each other" (chs. 5, 7, 10, 17).

5 [Tr.: The Portuguese word is *pateada* and literally means "stamped"; a way of showing disapproval of a play was to stamp on the floor. The English equivalent of course is "booed."]

6 Here, too, the joke that is being rewritten in appropriate terms is provided by Alencar, who in *A pata da gazela* [The Gazelle's Foot, 1870] refers to a misshapen foot with obvious delight, as "an enormity, a monster, a deformity," "a pedestal, a plank, a tree-bole." "This aberration of a human figure, though only at one point, seemed to him the symptom, if not the effect, of a moral monstrosity . . . that foot was full of bumps, like a tuber, . . . it was a slab of meat, a log!" (ch. 6). Later on we will see the hard fate of Dona Plácida, another case in which Machado critically rectifies the Brazilian literary tradition: like the hero of the *Memoirs of a Militia Sergeant* (1855), by Manuel Antônio de Almeida, the poor woman is the product of a "conjunction of idle lusts," of a "dig in the ribs and a pinch on the backside." In Machado's character's case, however,

the irregular birth does not mean a bit of fun or a merry accommodation to life's travails, and only leads to an accumulation of terrible hardships and humiliations. *Memórias de um sargento de milícias,* ch. 1, and *Memórias póstumas de Brás Cubas,* ch. 75.

7   Supposedly out of philanthropic feelings, Baudelaire advised his readers to beat beggars they found in the street, as the only way to force them to rediscover their lost dignity—since at some moment they would try to get revenge. "Assommons les pauvres!" [Let's hit the poor!]. *Le spleen de Paris* (1869), in *Oeuvres complètes,* 348. For a political analysis of this *petit poème en prose,* see Dolf Oehler, *Pariser Bilder, 1830–1848,* 155–60 [*Quadros parisienses,* 161–65].

8   [Tr.: This name of a thoroughfare that really existed means literally "Louse Street."]

9   Are men bourgeois by nature? Or because of circumstances? Brazilian society, with its partial and peculiar links to the international economy, caused people's judgment to waver, as in the case of Luís d'Alincourt (1787–1841), a Brazilian army officer who traveled around the country and for whom "the generality of the people, since they cannot export and are not motivated by self-interest—the real spur of the human heart—has given itself over to indolence and laziness, with fatal effects on the population." Alincourt, *Memórias sobre a viagem do Porto de Santos à Cidade de Cuiabá* [Memoirs of a Journey from the Port of Santos to the Town of Cuiabá], 65, quoted in Ilmar Rohloff de Mattos, *O tempo saquarema* [The Time of the *Saquaremas* (the nickname of the Conservative Party)], 122.

10 For a contrast between the Eurpean and Brazilian situations, as to what was obvious and what had to be demonstrated, one should read the first paragraphs of the "Critique of the Gotha Program" (1875). There, Marx criticizes the mythical valorization of labor within the labor movement itself, calling attention to the fact that it is an expression of bourgeois interests.

11 The philosophical import of Mário de Andrade's interest in sloth was pointed out to me by Gilda de Mello e Souza.

12 Carlos Drummond de Andrade, "Elegia 1938," from *Sentimento do mundo,* in *Obra completa,* 115.

13 Karl Marx, *Capital,* vol. 1, pt. 3, "The Production of Absolute Surplus-Value."

14 The discrepancy between the modernity of the observation and the "old fatalistic language, which comes from *Ecclesiastes,* the cynics, Machiavelli, and the French moralists," has been pointed out by Alfredo Bosi. See "A máscara e a fenda" [The Mask and the Crack], 451.

15 [Tr.: The writers referred to here, according to the author, were, in their different ways, Alfredo Bosi and Marilena Chaui. For Schwarz's view of the first of these writers in a more recent article, which tackles parallel questions, see "Discutindo com Alfredo Bosi," in *Seqüências brasileiras,* 61–85.]

16 See the study by Vilma Arêas, "No espelho do palco" [In the Mirror of the Stage].

7   The Rich on Their Own

1   [Tr.: Brazil signed a treaty with Britain in 1825 by which the transatlantic slave trade was to be abolished by 1831. In fact, the trade increased after this date and was only concluded in 1850, after an increase in British pressure. Thus, after 1831, all slaves brought in were technically smuggled.]

2   Gilberto Freyre, *Sobrados e mucambos,* 1:xcii. The preface to the second edition, from which this quotation is taken, is not in the English translation.

3   "The distance between Machado de Assis and writers contemporary with him is, in the end, the result as much of his intrinsic superiority as of the fact that he followed the social and political rhythm of the ruling classes, while the others remained in a backward state, lost in the search for what was typical." Lúcia Miguel-Pereira, *Prosa de ficção de 1870 a 1920* [Prose Fiction from 1870 to 1920], 68.

4   Eusébio de Queirós, the minister of justice who presided over the termination of the transatlantic slave trade in 1850, after having protected it for many years as Rio de Janeiro's chief of police, explained himself on the subject in parliament in 1852:

> Let us be frank. In Brazil, the traffic was linked to the interests, or, more correctly, to the presumed interests of our planters. And in a country in which agriculture has so much power, it was natural that public opinion . . . would express itself in favor of the traffic. Why does it then surprise us that our politicians bowed before that law of necessity? Why is it surprising that all of us — friends or enemies of the traffic — bowed to that necessity? Gentlemen, if this was a crime, it was a very widespread crime in Brazil. But I maintain that when in a nation all the political parties hold power, when all of its politicians have been called to exercise that power, and all of them agree on one policy, that policy must have been based on very powerful considerations. It cannot possibly be a crime, and it would be bold to call it a mistake.

Quoted in Joaquim Nabuco, *Abolitionism,* 69.

5   We are thinking of the acute understanding that Stendhal, Machado, and Brecht had of the social significance present in an ideology's way of expressing itself.

6   The liberal and constitutional model of the nation-state was not confined to the "developed" world. It also corresponded to the aspirations of every other country, at least of those that did not deliberately intend to avoid modern progress. See Eric Hobsbawm, *The Age of Empire,* 22.

7   See Fernando Novais, "Passagens para o Novo Mundo."

8   For a historical interpretation along different lines, see Raymundo Faoro, *A pirâmide e o trapézio* [The Pyramid and the Trapeze]. Faoro conceives of Machado's prose as an immense expanse of situations, anecdotes, and formulations, whose historico-sociological commentary he tries to gather, setting aside the boundaries between individual works and genres. This procedure has a price, since it marginalizes the meaning of the artistic forms, which is tacitly present and decisive. Yet, it eases the freedom of movement from one work to another, which allowed Faoro to refute once and for all the general opinion according to which Machado had little interest in Brazilian matters, particularly politics. As it moves through the vast range of connected questions, the book shows not only the quality but also the enormous quantity of observations made by the novelist. Faoro also brings out, so to speak, their differential historical spirit: these large changes are seen through the perspective of details. What might be more questionable is the general point of view of the essay, which makes of Machado's work a mural of the *transition* from a society ruled by an aristocratic social stratum to a class society, from a dispensation in which solidarity rules to a contractual one. The melancholy penumbra of the fiction is, on this reading, due to the irrevocable waning of the old world, which the writer thought of as authentic, and the advance of the bourgeois world, which he did not understand and was horrified by. If Faoro's reading were right, the meaning of Machado's novels would be elegiac.

9   Friedrich Meinecke, *Historism: The Rise of a New Historical Outlook,* ch. 2; Erich Auerbach, *Mimesis,* ch. 15.

10   Max Horkheimer, "Authority and the Family."

11   Marx, "The Eighteenth Brumaire of Louis Bonaparte," ch. 1.

8   *The Role of Ideas*

1   Sílvio Romero, "O Brasil social de Euclides da Cunha," 163.

2   The good sense and discernment with which Machado confronted the models of novelistic organization with their empirical raw material is well illustrated in his study of Eça de Queirós:*

> Everybody recognizes that Sr. Eça de Queirós is the disciple of the author of *L'assommoir. O crime do Padre Amaro* [The Crime of Father Amaro] is an imitation of Zola's novel *La faute de l'Abbé Mouret.* An analogous situation, the same tendencies; a difference in the milieu; different denouements; an identical style; some direct echoes, as in the chapter at Mass, and others; lastly, the same title. Whoever has read both novels certainly could not contest Sr. Eça de Queirós's originality, because he possessed that originality, and still does, and deliberately shows it; I even think that this same originality lies at the source of the greatest defect in the conception of *O crime do Padre Amaro*. Sr. Eça de Queirós naturally altered the circumstances surrounding Father Mouret, the spiritual mentor of rural parish, flanked by an austere, harsh priest; Father Amaro lives in a provincial town, among a group of women, and by the side of colleagues who are only priests in the sense that they wear the cassock and collect their wages; he sees that they are lecherous and live in quasi marriages, without losing the smallest bit of influence and respect. Since this is so, one cannot understand Father Amaro's terror, on the day when a child is born as a result of his lapse: still less can one understand why he should kill it. Of the two forces contending in Father Amaro's soul, one is real and present: the feeling of paternity; the other is fantastic and impossible — his terror of public opinion, which he has seen to be complicit and tolerant in his colleagues' transgressions; and yet, it is this latter force that wins the day. Is there any moral truth here? (*OC,* 3:904)

It is a shrewd observation and makes one think about the problems concerned in adapting French artistic models in Portugal. It also, naturally, makes one reflect about Portuguese society itself. To complete the demonstration of independence, the lack of "moral truth" was also part of a — questionable — objection made to Zola's school, whose emphasis on external conditioning, it was said, transformed the characters into puppets, destroying their functioning as moral agents.

3   Paul Bénichou, "La démolition du héros"; C. B. Macpherson, "Hobbes's Bourgeois Man": "As motivating forces, Hobbes gives approximately equal emphasis to greed and glory, lust and vanity" (240). Macpherson underlines the modern import of universalized competition. On the evolution of the problem, see Albert O. Hirschman, *The Passions and the Interests.*

4   [Tr.: In English in the original.]

5   [Tr.: "Ordem e progresso" is a Positivist motto that is still found on the Brazilian flag. It was placed there because of the importance of the doctrines at the time of the Republic's founding in 1889.

6   Richard Hofstadter, *Social Darwinism in American Thought,* 35.

7   Marcel Proust, "À propos du 'style' de Flaubert." See also the comparison between Balzac's and Flaubert's styles, also in *Contre Sainte-Beuve,* 268–69.

1 Theodor Adorno, "Ideen zur Musiksoziologie," 21.

2 Miguel Reale, *A filosofia de Machado de Assis* [The Philosophy of Machado de Assis].

3 Rui Barbosa, "Machado de Assis," 254.

4 "Understanding *dilettantism* is easier than defining it. Rather than a doctrine, it is a very intelligent, and at the same time very voluptuous, kind of disposition, that inclines us alternately to different forms of life and makes us lend ourselves to all them without giving ourselves over to any. . . . Dilettantism then becomes a refined science of emotional and intellectual metamorphosis. Some superior men have provided illustrious examples of the type, but the very agility that they manifested gave the imprint of something unsettled and disquieting to their achievement." Paul Bourget, "M. Ernest Renan," 55–56.

5 The classic views of Lukács, Walter Benjamin, and Sartre have been taken up again recently in two instructive books, to which this argument owes a great deal: Dolf Oehler, *Pariser Bilder* and *Ein Höllensturz der Alten Welt.* [Tr.: See list of works cited for the French and Portuguese translations of these books.]

6 Karl Marx, "The Class Struggles in France, 1848 to 1850 (I: The Defeat of June 1848)," 58.

7 Marx, "Die Junirevolution," 133.

8 Friedrich Engels, "Der 24 Juni," 125.

9 Jean-Paul Sartre, *L'idiot de la famille,* 2:401.

10 Marx, "The Class Struggles in France, 1848 to 1850 (I: The Defeat of June 1848)," 59.

11 Marx, "The Eighteenth Brumaire of Louis Bonaparte," 189.

12 The use of the first person with a historico-sociological aim, can also be observed in the introductory note to "Notes from the Underground:"

> Both the author of the *Notes* and the *Notes* themselves are, of course, fictitious. Nevertheless, such persons as the author of such memoirs not only may, but must, exist in our society, if we take into consideration the circumstances that led to the formation of our society. It was my intention to bring before our reading public, more conspicuously than is usually done, one of the characters of our recent past. He is one of the representatives of a generation that is still with us. In this extract, entitled *Underground,* this person introduces himself and his views and, as it were, tries to explain those causes which have not only led, but were also bound to lead, to his appearance in our midst. In the subsequent extract (*Apropos of the Wet Snow*) we shall reproduce this person's *Notes* proper, dealing with certain aspects of his life.

Fyodor Dostoevsky, "Notes from the Underground," 107.

13 The surprise caused by *Madame Bovary* and by the new technique can be observed in the critical commentary of Duranty, ironically one of the paladins of realism.

> They say that the book took many years to compose. And it is true that the enumeration of the details is done one by one, without distinguishing between their relative importance. There is no emotion or feeling or life in this novel, but there is a great mathematical power, which has examined and collected everything possible in the way of gestures, actions, or geographical accidents in the characters, the events and the places. The book is a literary application of the calculus of probabilities. . . . The style has the uneven features characteristic of a man who — artistically, and devoid of feeling — writes pastiches, then lyrical pas-

sages, but nothing personal. I repeat: always material description, never impressions. It seems to me useless to examine the point of view of the work, from which these defects remove any possible interest. Before its publication, it was thought that the novel would be much better than it is. A great deal of study is no substitute for spontaneity, which comes from the feelings.

Quoted in René Dumesnil, *Le réalisme et le naturalisme*, 31.

14 For a careful analysis of these methods of composition, see chapter 7 on Flaubert in Oehler's *Ein Höllensturz*.

15 Gustave Flaubert, letter to Louise Colet (16 January 1852), in *Correspondance*, 2:31.

16 Flaubert, letter to Louise Colet (9 December 1852), in *Correspondance*, 2:204.

17 Writing about the musical character of Richard Strauss, Adorno observes that "his intuitionism, the *élan vital* that is opposed to systematic, routine musical logic, along with a certain brutality and basic coarseness, are like the expansionist mentality of the German industrial haute bourgeoisie." "Ideen zur Musiksoziologie," 19. "One of the disturbing aspects, never sufficiently examined, of aestheticism is its affinity with violence. One of the foundations of aestheticism is the principle of the arbitrary transposition of reality, the faculty of transforming everything into everything else with the help of analogy, which is a less innocent principle than it might seem to be, since it always involves a moment at which reality is violated. The crisis of the bourgeois individual at the end of the nineteenth century seems to produce structures of behavior that, though one cannot speak of an immediate economic causality, show a surprising analogy with imperialism." Peter Bürger, "Naturalismus-Ästhetizismus und das Problem der Subjectivität," 45–46.

18 Although linked to eighteenth-century English humor and nineteenth-century aestheticism, Machado's sense of the outlandish allowed him to capture some of the truly incredible peculiarities of Brazilian society, which are the products of the colonial past and are perhaps even capable of producing shock in our own day. The hypothesis is somewhat enigmatically formulated by Araripe Júnior. "Well, it was precisely [Machado's] attraction to the dark sides of humanity that I needed in order to appreciate his discovery, or, rather, his exaggeration of certain new aspects that I suspect exist completely hidden in Brazil. / Yes. I firmly believe that the slow processes of almost four centuries have made such extraordinary things germinate, that there is no imagination capable even of measuring or weighing them. / And yet, these same things exist, happen daily around us, jostle one another. . . . / Just to think of the twentieth century makes me tremble. / What will Brazil be? what will have emerged from this enormous growth of the unconscious?" *Obra crítica*, 1:350–51.

19 Antonio Candido, *Formação da literatura brasileira*, especially "Uma literatura empenhada" [A Committed Literature] (vol. 1, introduction, pt. 2) and "O nacionalismo literário" [Literary Nationalism] (vol. 2, ch. 1, pt. 1).

20 José Veríssimo, "Alguns livros de 1895 a 1898" [Some Books from between 1895 and 1898], 159.

21 Ibid., 157. In the 6th series of Veríssimo's *Estudos*, see "Machado de Assis" and "Livros e autores de 1903 a 1905" [Books and Authors from between 1903 and 1905], especially 103, 105, and 119.

22 Sílvio Romero, *História da literatura brasileira* [History of Brazilian Literature], 1:99.

23 Jacques Vaché, letter to André Breton (29 March 1917), in *Lettres de guerre*, 44.

24 With characteristic infelicity, Araripe Júnior regrets the lack of the indispensable *odor*

di femmina in Machado's heroines, though this is natural, according to him, given that the writer was "a hermit who lived among his books, withdrawn from the world in his study." *Obra crítica,* 2:294. Writing about the prostitutes painted by the modernist Di Cavalcanti, Gilda de Mello e Souza points to another moment in this same model of male potency, in which patriarchal brutality, a naturalist thematic, and national feeling join hands, with the last of these functioning as an alibi and a means of glorifying the rest. See her *Exercícios de leitura,* 274.

25 Antônio Candido, "An Outline of Machado de Assis," 107.

26 Quoted in Oehler, *Pariser Bilder,* 15 [*Quadros parisienses,* 16].

27 [Tr.: Here Schwarz is thinking of Macedo, Martins Pena, and perhaps painters like Debret.*]

28 See also the important role that Freud attributes to *Selbsterhöhung,* the imaginary quest for supremacy, in *Creative Writers and Day-Dreaming.*

29 Oswald de Andrade, *Serafim Ponte Grande,* 9 [*Seraphim Grosse Pointe,* 3].

30 Paulo Emílio Salles Gomes, *Cinema: Trajetória no subdesenvolvimento,* 77.

31 Machado's use of quotations, which is always distorting, deserves a special study. The French quotations in the *Posthumous Memoirs* have been suggestively examined in Gilberto Pinheiro Passos's thesis, *A poética do legado* [The Poetics of the Legacy]. [Tr.: A summary of part of this thesis can be found in Passos's afterword to the Oxford University Press translation of the novel. See bibliography.]

32 Ian Watt, Introduction to *The Life and Opinions of Tristram Shandy, Gentleman,* by Laurence Sterne, xv.

33 Georg Lukács, "Il romanzo come epopea borghese," 158.

34 This redefinition of the form of *Tristram Shandy* in the Brazilian context of the last quarter of the nineteenth century has been well pointed out by José Paulo Paes. See "A armadilha de Narciso" [Narcissus's Trap], 47–48.

35 "The Machadian sense of secrets of the soul is often connected to an equally profound comprehension of social structures, which function in his work with . . . [a] powerful immanence." Candido, "An Outline of Machado de Assis," 117.

36 Karl Marx, letter to J. Weydemeyer, *Marx and Engels: Basic Writings on Politics and Philosophy,* 494–95.

10   Literary Accumulation in a Peripheral Country

1 For a more detailed analysis, see Roberto Schwarz, "O paternalismo e sua racionalização nos primeiros romances de Machado de Assis" [Paternalism and Its Rationalization in Machado de Assis's Early Novels], in *Ao vencedor as batatas,* 63–72.

2 Alfredo Bosi refers to the "tone of pseudo conformity — in fact, of mockery — with which [the narrator] discourses on bourgeois normality." "A máscara e a fenda," 457.

3   The feuilletoniste originates in France, where he was born, and where he lives at his ease, snug as a bug in a rug. From there, he has spread throughout the world, or at least in those parts where the great vehicle of the modern spirit — I speak of the newspaper — has taken on a great importance . . . the feuilleton was born of the newspaper, and in consequence, the feuilletoniste of the journalist. It is this intimate affinity that produces the main features of the physiognomy of this modern creation. The feuilletoniste is the admirable fusion of the useful and the trivial, the curious, strange birth of the serious, mixed in with the frivolous.

These two elements, as distant from each other as the North and South poles, as different as water and fire, are perfectly married in the organization of this new animal.

Machado de Assis, "O folhetinista" (1859), *OC,* 3:959. There is ample treatment of this theme, with a great deal of documentation, in Marlyse Meyer, "Voláteis e versáteis: De variedades e folhetins se fez a chronica" [Volatile and Versatile: The *Crônica* is Made of Miscellaneous Events and *Feuilletons*].

4 The newspaper column as a meeting place of modernity and tradition has been studied by Davi Arrigucci Jr., "Fragmentos sobre a crônica" [Fragments on the Crônica].

5 Roberto Schwarz, "The Importing of the Novel to Brazil and Its Contradictions in the Work of Alencar," in *Misplaced Ideas,* 41–77.

6 On this topic, see the numerous observations of Vilma Arêas, in *Na tapera de Santa Cruz* [In the Ruins of Santa Cruz (an old name for the territory that is now Brazil)].

7 Antonio Candido, "Dialectic of Malandroism," 97, 101. [Tr.: The "king's time" mentioned below is that of the Portuguese king Dom João VI, who spent the period between 1808 and 1821 in Rio de Janeiro, in flight from Napoleon's invasion of Portugal. Rio became the capital of the Luso-Brazilian Empire.]

8 In a study of one of Machado's short stories, "O diplomático" [The Diplomatist], Vinícius Dantas has commented on the differences and continuities between Machado's mature prose and the popular comic vein of the 1830s and 1840s, as it was cultivated in the press. "O narrador cronista e o narrador contista" [The Narrator of *Crônicas* and the Narrator of Short Stories] (course essay, Unicamp, 1984).

9 "Si tu n'as fait ta rhétorique / Chez Satan, le rusé doyen / Jette! tu n'y comprendrais rien / Ou tu me croirais hystérique" [If you haven't learnt rhetoric / With Satan, that subtle teacher / Throw the book away! You'd not understand a word / Or you'd think me hysterical]. Baudelaire, "Épigraphe pour un livre condamné" in *Oeuvres complètes,* 237. These lines are addressed to the "Lecteur paisible et bucolique / Sobre et naïf homme de bien" [Placid, bucolic reader / Sober, naive, respectable man].

GLOSSARY

This glossary is intended to give basic facts about the subjects listed as they relate to this book. Individuals are alphabetized by the last part of their surname.

JOSÉ DE ALENCAR (1829–1877). Novelist, dramatist, and politician. Alencar's most famous novels include the so-called Indianist works *O guarani* (1857) and *Iracema* (1865), which dramatize the process of colonization. The first was turned into a successful opera (*Il guarani,* 1870) by the Brazilian composer Carlos Gomes. Alencar was also the author of several novels set in modern times, in both rural and urban settings. These novels and his plays often try to engage modern issues, in particular, slavery and the relation between money and morality. The urban novels — for example, *Lucíola* (1862), *Diva* (1864), *Sonhos d'ouro* (1872), and *Senhora* (1875) — most engaged Machado as admirer, critic, and, as Schwarz reveals, parodist. Machado's relation with the older man was complex: Alencar was also his personal friend and protector, and in later years he practically adopted his son, Mário, as his own. When Alencar died, Machado became, by common consent, the leading Brazilian writer.

MANUEL ANTÔNIO DE ALMEIDA (1831–1861). Novelist and journalist. He befriended Machado at the National Typography, where he was an administrator and Machado an apprentice in the late 1850s. His only considerable work — all the more important for being an exception in its time — is the novel *Memórias de um sargento de milícias,* first published in 1854–55. Set in Rio de Janeiro, it recounts the comic adventures of the rogue Leonardo Pataca, surrounded by an extensive gallery of other popular types. Almeida died tragically young, in a shipwreck.

CARLOS DRUMMOND DE ANDRADE (1902–1987). Poet and journalist. Generally regarded as the greatest Brazilian poet of the twentieth century, his output is large and varied. From about 1935–45, in such books as *Sentimento do mundo* [The Feeling of the World] and *A rosa do povo* [The People's Rose], he developed an intense but self-critical poetry of social criticism and political commitment.

MÁRIO DE ANDRADE (1893–1945). Poet, musicologist, fiction writer. He was one of the leaders of Brazilian modernism, which began in the early 1920s. He published his experimental "rhapsody" *Macunaíma: The Hero without a Character* in 1928; it is an attempt to write a representative work about Brazil as a whole, based on myths and folklore from around the whole country. The hero, who in some way represents the nation, has a catchphrase, "Ai, que preguiça," roughly "God, how lazy I feel."

OSWALD DE ANDRADE (1890–1954). Poet, novelist, dramatist. Along with Mário de Andrade (no relation), he was one of the leaders of the Brazilian modernist movement. He is perhaps best known for founding, in 1928, the "anthropophagist" movement, which advocated what he called a "cannibalistic" attitude toward European culture. In the 1940s and 1950s, in such works as *A crise da filosofia messiânica* [The Crisis of Messianic Philosophy], he speculated on new kinds of social arrangements for Brazil ("Pindorama" is an alternative, indigenous name for the country). A permanent rebel, his reputation rose in the 1960s; in particular, he was lionized by the Concretist poets (Haroldo and Augusto de Campos, and others). Schwarz's analysis of one of his poems in "The Cart, the Tram, and the Modernist Poet" places his work in a social and historical context.

JOAQUIM MARIA MACHADO DE ASSIS (1839–1908). Novelist, short-story writer, poet, dramatist, and journalist, Machado was the son of a house painter and an Azorean woman in the service of an important Rio de Janeiro family. He lived his early years to some extent under their protection. He was plainly mulatto, though his ancestors had probably been free for two generations. He began work as a typographer in 1855 and gradually worked his way into journalism and literature. Through friends and protectors, he finally achieved a post in the civil service in 1867. He married Carolina Xavier de Novaes, the sister of a Portuguese poet friend, in 1869. In 1872 he published his first novel, *Ressurreição,* followed by three more in the 1870s. In 1880 came *Memórias póstumas de Brás Cubas,* which, although some critics found it mystifying, confirmed his position as the most distinguished writer of the time. Four more novels were published between the *Memoirs* and Machado's death, the most famous of which are *Quincas Borba (Philosopher or Dog?)* (1891) and *Dom Casmurro* (1899).

RUI BARBOSA (1849–1923). Brazilian politician who generally espoused liberal causes and was minister of finance in the early years of the Republic. He was a founding member of the Brazilian Academy of Letters, of which Machado de Assis was the first president. In literature as in politics, he is a polemical figure, revered by some for his impeccable style, abhorred by others for his rhetorical pomposity.

RAUL BOPP (1898–1974). Poet and member of the "anthropophagist" movement led by Oswald de Andrade. His most famous work is *Cobra Norato* [Norato the Snake] (1931), set in a hot, steamy, snake-ridden Amazon rain forest.

VISCONDE DE RIO BRANCO (José Maria da Silva Paranhos) (1819–1880). Politician and diplomat. One of the leading figures of the Second Reign (that of Pedro II, 1840–89), his name is particularly associated with the passing of the Law of the Free Womb (1871), by which all children born of slaves after 28 September that year would be freed at the age of twenty-one. Since the law made the ultimate end of slavery inevitable, it was surrounded by violent controversy.

ANTONIO CANDIDO (1918–   ). Schwarz's principal mentor, Candido — his full name is Antonio Candido de Mello e Souza — began his academic career as a sociologist but in the 1950s, already renowned as a newspaper critic, he moved to literary criticism, and became professor of literary theory at the University of São Paulo, publishing his acclaimed *Formação da literatura brasileira* (1959). He has been vastly influential, as both a writer and a mentor, on succeeding generations of literary scholars: his approach, although almost always concerned with the links between literature and society, is undogmatic and free of jargon. Candido has always maintained a strong commitment to the left in politics. Four essays on him open Schwarz's most recent book, *Seqüências brasileiras.*

CRÔNICA. A daily or weekly column in the Brazilian newspapers that has traditionally been a very popular form of reading matter and a way for writers to earn a living. Part of its attraction is that it varies in topic, tone, and structure, though it is almost always witty or humorous. Among its greatest practitioners have been Alencar, Machado de Assis, and Drummond de Andrade.

JEAN-BAPTISTE DEBRET (1768–1848). French painter and draftsman who came to Brazil in 1816 with the French artistic mission at the invitation of King João VI. He stayed in the country until 1831 and is most famous for a series of vivid paintings and drawings of everyday life in Rio of great verve and documentary value.

JOAQUIM JOSÉ DE FRANÇA JR. (1838–1890). Dramatist and journalist. He was a very popular *cronista,* who specialized in the caricature of typical figures of the time. His plays continued the comic and farcical traditions of Martins Pena.

GILBERTO FREYRE (1900–1987). Anthropologist, historian, essayist. Born in the northern state of Pernambuco, he studied anthropology with Franz Boas at Columbia University. His reevaluation of the colonial plantation system in *Casa-grande e senzala* [*The Masters and the Slaves*] (1933), which gave a more positive role to the black slaves and argued that Brazilian society is relatively free of racism, has been enormously influential, though criticized as reactionary and nostalgic.

PAULO EMÍLIO SALLES GOMES (1916–1977). Film critic and novelist. A colorful, polemical figure who was a communist in the 1930s, he was a theoretician of cinema, in particular the Cinema Novo of the 1960s and 1970s, in his famous article "Cinema and Underdevelopment." His only novel, *Três mulheres de três PPPés* [*P's Three Women*], appeared in 1977; Schwarz published a long article on it in *O pai de família* [The Father of the Family] (1978).

SÉRGIO BUARQUE DE HOLLANDA (1902–1982). Historian, sociologist, and literary critic. He was the leading historian of his generation. In 1936, he published the celebrated *Raízes do Brasil* [The Roots of Brazil], which argued that Brazilians were characterized by what he called "cordiality," which meant that they were excessively ruled by their emotions. The author of many important books, in particular on the colonization and exploration of Brazil, he directed the multivolume *História geral da civilização brasileira* [General History of Brazilian Civilization] for which he wrote a volume on the transition from the Empire to the Republic (1868–89).

JOAQUIM MANUEL DE MACEDO (1820–1882). Novelist, journalist, dramatist, the most popular and prolific of his generation. His first novel, *A moreninha* (1844) is a light-hearted romantic tale about adolescent students and their loves, set in Rio de Janeiro and an island in Guanabara Bay, and is still widely read. Machado's respect for Macedo was qualified: he recognized his importance, but regarded him as the eager victim of his own popularity. By the early 1870s, despite attempts to update himself with abolitionist works like *As vítimas-algozes* [The Victim-Executioners] (1869), Macedo's heyday was past.

MACUNAÍMA. See Mário de Andrade.

XAVIER DE MAISTRE (1763–1852). Younger brother of the famous conservative philosopher Joseph de Maistre. He is most famous for the short novel *Voyage autour de ma chambre* (1795), the style of which owes a great deal to Laurence Sterne.

JOSÉ GUILHERME MERQUIOR (1941–1990). Literary critic, theorist, diplomat. Merquior was one of the most distinguished and prolific writers of his generation, often engaged in controversy. He was an opponent, in particular, of Western Marxism, on which he published a book in English (*Western Marxism*, London: Paladin, 1986); this did not prevent his admiring Schwarz's work. His own approach to Machado was concerned with matters of genre, concentrating in particular on his affinities with the Menippean satiric tradition.

AUGUSTO MEYER (1882–1970). Literary critic and poet. Meyer began his career as a modernist poet. From 1937–66 he was director of the National Book Institute in Rio de Janeiro. His important book of essays on Machado de Assis was published in 1935, with additions in 1958. In essays such as "The Underground Man," "The Mirror," and "In the Green House" [Na Casa Verde], he revealed Machado as a much more conflict-ridden and disturbing writer than he had hitherto been thought to be.

JOAQUIM NABUCO (1849–1910). Politician and historian. The son of a distinguished senator, whose political biography he wrote under the title *Um estadista do império* [A Statesman of the Empire], Nabuco is most famous as the leader of the movement for the abolition of slavery, eventually successful in 1888. His book *Abolitionism* (1883) is a penetrating analysis of the pervasive ill effects of slavery on Brazilian society. He was a long-standing friend of Machado's.

LUÍS CARLOS MARTINS PENA (1815–1848). The first Brazilian dramatist of any stature, Martins Pena wrote both "serious" drama and comedies, but the latter, twenty-two of them altogether, assured his enduring popularity. His plays are for the most part lively farces, involving a mass of contemporary characters of all kinds from city and country (including foreigners), and with plots surrounding courtship, marriage, dowries, wills, and the like.

JOSÉ MARIA EÇA DE QUEIRÓS (1845–1900). Novelist. A member of the Portuguese 1870 generation, he adhered to a combative realism in the 1870s, particularly in *O crime do Padre Amaro* and *O primo Basílio*. His work had enormous impact in both Portugal and Brazil. Machado's attacks on him, in two articles published in 1878, may have been one of the factors that resulted in a move away from dogmatic, Zola-inspired Naturalism, evident in his greatest novel *Os Maias* [*The Maias*] (1888).

RECIFE SCHOOL. A group of intellectuals based in the late 1860s and 1870s around the Law School in Recife, the capital of the northern state of Pernambuco, and who were among the first to introduce positivism and evolutionary philosophies into Brazil. Its most famous figures are Tobias Barreto (1839–1889) and Sílvio Romero.

SÍLVIO ROMERO (1851–1914). Literary critic and historian. He was one of the foremost members of the Recife school and an adherent of evolutionary philosophy, particularly that of Herbert Spencer. Romero was Machado's most vehement critic. In a book published in 1897, he accused the novelist of being alienated from his Brazilian roots, "morbid," and "riddled with incurable indifference."

FREI LUÍS DE SOUSA (c. 1556–1632). Portuguese writer and monk, author of historical and religious works, and thought of as one of the most perfect stylists in the language.

BERNARDO PEREIRA DE VASCONCELOS. (1795–1850). Politician and one of the most powerful figures of the early years of Brazilian independence; he was a minister four times during the Regency period (1831–40). Vasconcelos was a brilliant orator and most famous for having quite openly and consistently in his own view moved from a liberal position to a conservative one, fearing the consequences of "disorder and anarchy."

José Veríssimo (1857–1916). Literary critic and historian. One of the foremost critics of his time, he was a friend and admirer of Machado de Assis: his essays on him have some important insights. Veríssimo was a rival of Machado's enemy, Sílvio Romero, and wrote the famous and still valuable *História da literatura brasileira* [History of Brazilian Literature] (1916).

BIBLIOGRAPHY

Adorno, Theodor. *Aesthetische Theorie.* In *Gesammelte Schriften,* 7:0–0. Frankfurt am Main: Suhrkamp, 1970. [*Aesthetic Theory.* London and New York: Routledge and Kegan Paul, 1984.]

——. "Rede über Lyrik und Gesellschaft." In *Gesammelte Schriften,* 11:0–0. Frankfurt am Main: Suhrkamp, 1974.

——. "Ideen zur Musiksoziologie." In *Gesammelte Schriften,* 16:9–23. Frankfurt am Main: Suhrkamp, 1990. [Also in *Klangfiguren,* 9–31. Frankfurt am Main: Suhrkamp, 1959.] Portuguese trans. (by Roberto Schwarz): "Idéias para a sociologia da música." In *Os pensadores: Benjamin, Habermas, Horkheimer, Adorno,* 259–68. São Paulo: Abril, 1983.

Alencar, José de. *Lucíola,* and *A pata da gazela, Sonhos d'ouro.* In *Obra completa,* 1:229–331, 407–87, 489–660. Rio de Janeiro: Aguilar, 1965.

Alencastro, Luiz Felipe de. "La traité négrière et l'unité nationale brésilienne." *Revue française d'histoire d'Outre-Mer* 66, 244–45: (1979): 395–419.

Alincourt, Luís d'. *Memórias sobre a viagem do Porto de Santos à Cidade de Cuiabá.* Belo Horizonte: Itatiaia, 1979.

Almeida, Manuel Antônio de. *Memórias de um sargento de milícias.* Rio de Janeiro: Instituto Nacional do Livro, 1969. [*Memoirs of a Militia Sergeant.* Trans. Linton L. Barrett. Washington, D.C.: Organization of American States, 1959.]

Andrade, Carlos Drummond de. *Obra completa.* Rio de Janeiro: Aguilar, 1967.

Andrade, Oswald de. *Serafim Ponte Grande.* São Paulo: Global, 1984. [*Seraphim Grosse Pointe.* Trans. K. D. Jackson and A. G. Bork. Austin: Nefertiti Head Press, 1979.]

Arantes, Paulo Eduardo. *Sentimento da dialética na experiência intelectual brasileira: Dialética e dualidade segundo Antonio Candido e Roberto Schwarz.* Rio de Janeiro: Paz e Terra, 1992.

Araripe Júnior, Tristão de Alencar. *Obra crítica.* 4 vols. Rio de Janeiro: Casa de Rui Barbosa, 1966.

Arêas, Vilma. "No espelho do palco." In *Os pobres na literatura brasileira,* ed. Roberto Schwarz, 26–30. São Paulo: Brasiliense, 1983.

——. *Na tapera de Santa Cruz: Uma leitura de Martins Pena.* São Paulo: Martins Fontes, 1987.

Arendt, Hannah. *The Origins of Totalitarianism*. New York: Harvest Books, 1973.

Arrigucci Jr., Davi. "Fragmentos sobre a crônica." In *Enigma e comentário,* 51–66. São Paulo: Companhia das Letras, 1987.

Assis, Joaquim Maria Machado de. *Obra completa*. 3 vols. Rio de Janeiro: Aguilar, 1959.

——. *The Hand and the Glove [A mão e a luva]* [1874]. Trans. Albert I. Bagby Jr. Lexington: University Press of Kentucky, 1970.

——. *Helena* [1876]. Trans. Helen Caldwell. Berkeley: University of California Press, 1984.

——. *Yayá Garcia* [1878]. Trans. Albert I. Bagby Jr. Lexington: University Press of Kentucky, 1977.

——. *Epitaph of a Small Winner [Memórias póstumas de Brás Cubas]* [1881]. Trans. William Grossman. New York: Noonday Press, 1952.

——. *The Posthumous Memoirs of Brás Cubas* [1881]. Trans. Gregory Rabassa. New York: Oxford University Press, 1997.

——. *Philosopher or Dog?* (*Quincas Borba*). [1891]. Trans. Clotilde Wilson. New York: Farrar, Straus, and Giroux, 1954.

——. *Dom Casmurro* Trans. Helen Caldwell. [1900]. New York: Farrar, Straus, and Giroux, 1953.

——. *Dom Casmurro* [1900]. Trans. John Gledson. New York: Oxford University Press, 1998.

——. *Counselor Ayres' Memorial* [1908]. Trans. Helen Caldwell. Berkeley: University of California Press, 1972.

——. *The Psychiatrist and Other Stories*. Trans. William L. Grossman and Helen Caldwell. Berkeley: University of California Press, 1963.

Auerbach, Erich. *Mimesis: The Representation of Reality in Western Literature*. Trans. Willard R. Trask. Princeton: Princeton University Press, 1953.

Barbosa, Rui. "Machado de Assis." In *Novos discursos e conferências*. São Paulo: Livraria Acadêmica, 1933.

Baudelaire, Charles. *Oeuvres complètes*. Paris: Pléiade, 1951.

Bénichou, Paul. "La démolition du héros." In *Morales du grand siècle*. Paris: Gallimard, 1948.

Benjamin, Walter. *Charles Baudelaire: A Lyric Poet in the Era of High Capitalism*. Trans. Harry Zohn. London: NLB, 1973.

——. *Das Passagen-Werk, Gesammelte Schriften*. Frankfurt am Main: Suhrkamp, 1988.

Borges, Jorge Luis. "El escritor argentino y la tradición." In *Discusión,* 151–62. Buenos Aires: Emecé, 1964.

Bosi, Alfredo. "A máscara e a fenda." In *Machado de Assis,* ed. Alfredo Bosi et al., 437–57. São Paulo: Ática, 1982.

——. "A escravidão entre dois liberalismos." In *Dialética da colonização,* 194–245. São Paulo: Companhia das Letras, 1992.

Bourget, Paul. "M. Ernest Renan." In *Essais de psychologie contemporaine* [1883]. Paris: Plon, 1919.

Bürger, Peter. "Naturalismus-Ästhetizismus und das Problem der Subjectivität." In *Naturalismus/Ästhetizismus,* ed. Christa Bürger et al. Frankfurt am Main: Suhrkamp, 1979.

Candido, Antonio. *Formação da literatura brasileira*. São Paulo: Martins, 1959.

——. "Dialectic of Malandroism." In *On Literature and Society,* trans. Howard S. Becker, 79–103. Princeton: Princeton University Press, 1995.

——. "An Outline of Machado de Assis." In *On Literature and Society,* trans. Howard S. Becker, 104–18. Princeton: Princeton University Press, 1995.

Cardoso, Fernando Henrique. *Capitalismo e escravidão no Brasil meridional: O negro na sociedade escravocrata do Rio Grande do Sul.* São Paulo: Difusão Européia do Livro, 1962.

Cardoso, Fernando Henrique, and Enzo Faletto. *Dependency and Development in Latin America.* Trans. Marjory Mattingly Urquidi. Berkeley: University of California Press, 1979.

Carvalho, José Murilo de. "A política da abolição: O rei contra os barões." In *A construção da ordem: Teatro de sombras,* 269–302. Rio de Janeiro: Editora UFRJ/Relume Dumará, 1996.

Chalhoub, Sidney. "Dependents Play Chess: Political Dialogues in Machado de Assis." In *Machado de Assis: Reflections on a Brazilian Master Writer,* 51–84. Austin: University of Texas Press, 1999.

Costa, Emília Viotti da. "Liberalism: Theory and Practice." In *The Brazilian Empire: Myths and Histories,* 53–77. Chicago: University of Chicago Press, 1985.

daMatta, Roberto. *Carnival, Rogues, and Heroes: An Interpretation of the Brazilian Dilemma.* Notre Dame: University of Notre Dame Press, 1991.

Dostoevsky, Fyodor. "Notes from the Underground." In *The Best Short Stories of Dostoevsky,* trans. David Magarshack, 107–240. New York: Random House, n.d.

Dumesnil, René. *Le réalisme et le naturalisme.* Paris: del Duca et de Gigord, 1955.

Engels, Friedrich. "Der 24 Juni." In *Werke,* by Karl Marx and Friedrich Engels, 5. Berlin: Dietz, 1973.

Faoro, Raymundo. *A pirâmide a o trapézio.* São Paulo: Companhia Editora Nacional, 1974.

Fernandes, Florestan. "As implicações socio-econômicas da independência." In *A revolução burguesa no Brasil.* Rio de Janeiro: Zahar, 1981.

Flaubert, Gustave. *Correspondance.* 4 vols. Paris: Pléiade, 1980.

Franco, Maria Sylvia de Carvalho. *Homens livres na ordem escravocrata.* São Paulo: Instituto de Estudos Brasileiros, 1969.

——. "As idéias estão no lugar." *Cadernos de debate* 1 (1976): 61–64.

Freud, Sigmund. *Creative Writers and Day-Dreaming* [1908]. Standard ed. Vol. 7. London: Hogarth Press, 1959.

Freyre, Gilberto. *Sobrados e mucambos: Decadência do patriarcado rural e desenvolvimento do urbano.* 2 vols. Rio de Janeiro: José Olympio, 1977. [*The Mansions and the Shanties: The Making of Modern Brazil.* Trans. and ed. Harriet de Onís. New York: Knopf, 1963.]

Gledson, John. "*Casa velha:* A Contribution to a Better Understanding of Machado de Assis." *Bulletin of Hispanic Studies* 90 (1983): 31–48.

——. *The Deceptive Realism of Machado de Assis: A Dissenting Interpretation of* Dom Casmurro. Liverpool: Francis Cairns, 1984.

——. "The Last Betrayal of Machado de Assis: *Memorial de Aires.*" *Portuguese Studies* 1 (1985):121–50.

——. *Machado de Assis: Ficção e história.* Rio de Janeiro: Paz e Terra, 1986.

Gomes, Eugênio. "Schopenhauer e Machado de Assis." In *Machado de Assis,* 84–90. Rio de Janeiro: Livraria São José, 1958.

Gomes, Paulo Emílio Salles. *Cinema: Trajetória no subdesenvolvimento.* Rio de Janeiro: Paz e Terra, 1980.

Hirschman, Albert O. *The Passions and the Interests: Political Arguments for Capitalism before Its Triumph.* Princeton: Princeton University Press, 1977.

Hobsbawm, Eric. *The Age of Empire.* New York: Pantheon, 1987.

Hofstadter, Richard. *Social Darwinism in American Thought.* Boston: Beacon Press, 1955.

Horkheimer, Max. "Authority and the Family." In *Critical Theory,* trans. Matthew J. O'Connell et al., 47–128. New York: Continuum, 1989.

Larsen, Neil. *Modernism and Hegemony: A Materialist Critique of Aesthetic Agencies.* Minneapolis: University of Minnesota Press, 1990.

Lima, Manuel de Oliveira. *O império brasileiro.* São Paulo: Melhoramentos, 1927.

Lukács, Georg. "Dostoevsky." In *Dostoevsky: A Collection of Critical Essays,* ed. René Wellek, 146–58. Englewood Cliffs: Prentice Hall, 1962.

——. "Balzac and Stendhal." *Studies in European Realism,* 65–84. New York: Grosset and Dunlap, 1964.

——. "Il romanzo come epopea borghese." In *Problemi di teoria del romanzo.* Turin: Einaudi, 1976.

Macedo, Joaquim Manuel de. *A moreninha* [1884]. Rio de Janeiro: Ediouro, n.d.

——. *O moço loiro* [1845]. São Paulo: Ática, 1994.

Macpherson, C. B. "Hobbes's Bourgeois Man." In *Democratic Theory.* Oxford: Clarendon Press, 1975.

Magalhães Júnior, Raymundo. *Vida e obra de Machado de Assis.* 4 vols. Rio de Janeiro: Civilização Brasileira, 1981.

Marx, Karl. "The Class Struggles in France 1848 to 1850." In *Surveys from Exile (Political Writings,* vol. 2), ed. David Fernbach, 35–142. Harmondsworth: Penguin, 1973.

——. "Die Junirevolution." In *Werke,* by Karl Marx and Friedrich Engels, 5. Berlin: Dietz, 1973.

——. "The Eighteenth Brumaire of Louis Bonaparte." In *Surveys from Exile (Political Writings,* vol. 2), ed. David Fernbach, 143–249. Harmondsworth: Penguin, 1973.

——. *Capital.* London: Lawrence and Wishart, 1983.

——. "Critique of the Gotha Program." In *Marx and Engels: Basic Writings on Politics and Philosophy,* ed. Lewis S. Feuer, 153–73. London: Fontana, 1984.

——. "Letter to Joseph Weydemeyer, March 5, 1852." In *Marx and Engels: Basic Writings on Politics and Philosophy,* ed. Lewis S. Feuer, 494–95. London: Fontana, 1984.

Massa, Jean-Michel. "La bibliothèque de Machado de Assis." *Revista do livro* 6 (March–June 1961): 195–238.

Mattos, Ilmar Rohloff de. *O tempo saquarema.* São Paulo: Hucitec, 1987.

Meinecke, Friedrich. *Historism: The Rise of a New Historical Outlook.* Trans. J. E. Anderson. London: Routledge and Kegan Paul, 1972. [*Die Enstehung des Historismus.* Munich: R. Oldenbourg, 1965.]

Merquior, José Guilherme. "Gênero e estilo nas *Memórias póstumas de Brás Cubas.*" *Colóquio/Letras,* 8 (1972): 12–20.

——. *De Anchieta a Euclides.* Rio de Janeiro: José Olympio, 1977.

Meyer, Augusto. "De Machadinho a Brás Cubas." *Revista do livro,* 11 (September 1958): 9–18.

——. *Machado de Assis, 1935–1958.* Rio de Janeiro: Livraria São José, 1958.

Meyer, Marlyse. "Voláteis e versáteis: De variedades e folhetins se fez a chronica." In *As mil faces de um herói-canalha e outros estudos,* 109–96. Rio de Janeiro: Editora UFRJ, 1998.

Miguel-Pereira, Lúcia. *Prosa de ficção de 1870 a 1920.* Rio de Janeiro: José Olympio, 1973.

Nabuco, Joaquim. *Abolitionism: The Brazilian Anti-Slavery Struggle*. Trans. Robert Conrad. Urbana: University of Illinois Press, 1977.

Novais, Fernando. *Portugal e Brasil na crise do antigo sistema colonial, 1777–1808*. São Paulo: Hucitec, 1979.

——. "Passagens para o Novo Mundo," *Novos estudos Cebrap* 9 (July 1984): 2–8.

Oehler, Dolf. *Pariser Bilder, 1830–1848*. Frankfurt am Main: Suhrkamp, 1979. [Portuguese trans.: *Quadros parisienses: Estética antiburguesa, 1830–1848*. Trans. José Marcos Macedo and Samuel Titan Jr. São Paulo: Companhia das Letras, 1997.]

——. *Ein Höllensturz der Alten Welt*. Frankfurt am Main: Suhrkamp, 1988. [French trans.: *Le spleen contre l'oubli, juin 1848: Baudelaire, Flaubert, Heine, Herzen*. Trans. Guy Petitdemange. Paris: Payot et Rivages, 1996. Portuguese trans: *O velho mundo desce aos infernos*. São Paulo: Companhia das Letras, 1999.]

Paes, José Paulo. "A armadilha de Narciso." In *Gregos e bahianos*, 37–48. São Paulo: Brasiliense, 1985.

Passos, Gilberto Pinheiro. *A poética do legado: Presença francesa em Memórias póstumas de Brás Cubas*. São Paulo: Anneblume, 1996.

——. "Cosmopolitan Strategies in *The Posthumous Memoirs of Brás Cubas.*" Afterword to *The Posthumous Memoirs of Brás Cubas*, by Machado de Assis, 205–19. New York: Oxford University Press, 1997.

Proust, Marcel. "À propos du 'style' de Flaubert." In *Contre Sainte-Beuve*, 586–600. Paris: Pléiade, 1971.

——. "Contre Sainte-Beuve." In *Contre Sainte-Beuve*, 211–312. Paris: Pléiade, 1971.

Reale, Miguel. *A filosofia de Machado de Assis*. São Paulo: Pioneira, 1982.

Rego, Enylton de Sá. *O calundu e a panacéia: Machado de Assis, a sátira menipéia e a tradição luciânica*. Rio de Janeiro: Forense Universitária, 1989.

Rodrigues, José Honório. *Conciliação e reforma no Brasil: Um desafio histórico-político*. Rio de Janeiro: Civilização Brasileira, 1965.

Romero, Sílvio. *História da literatura brasileira*. 5 vols. Rio de Janeiro: Garnier, 1902.

——. "O Brasil social de Euclides da Cunha." In *Realidades e ilusões no Brasil*, ed. Hildon Rocha. Petrópolis: Vozes, 1979.

Santiago, Silviano. "Retórica da verossimilhança." In *Uma literatura nos trópicos*, 29–48. São Paulo: Perspectiva, 1978.

Sartre, Jean-Paul. *L'idiot de la famille*. 3 vols. Paris: Gallimard, 1972.

Schopenhauer, Arthur. *The World as Will and Representation*. Trans. E. F. J. Payne. 2 vols. New York: Dover, 1966.

Schwarz, Roberto. *Ao vencedor as batatas: Forma literária e processo social nos inícios do romance brasileiro*. São Paulo: Duas Cidades, 1977.

——. "Pressupostos, salvo engano, de 'Dialética da malandragem.'" In *Que horas são?* 129–55. São Paulo: Companhia das Letras, 1987.

——. "Machado de Assis: um debate. Conversa com Roberto Schwarz." *Novos estudos Cebrap* 29 (March 1991): 59–84.

——. *Misplaced Ideas*. Trans. with introduction by John Gledson. London: Verso, 1992.

——. "A novidade das *Memórias póstumas de Brás Cubas.*" In *Machado de Assis: Uma revisão*, ed. Antônio Carlos Secchin, José Maurício Gomes de Almeida, and Ronaldes de Melo e Souza, 47–64. Rio de Janeiro: In-Fólio, 1998.

——. *Seqüências brasileiras*. São Paulo: Companhia das Letras, 1999.

Sousa, Otávio Tarqüínio de. *A vida de D. Pedro I.* 3 vols. Rio de Janeiro: José Olympio, 1957.

Souza, Gilda de Mello e. *Exercícios de leitura.* São Paulo: Duas Cidades, 1980.

Taunay, Visconde de. *A mocidade de Trajano* [1871]. São Paulo: Academia Paulista de Letras, 1984.

Trotsky, Leon. *History of the Russian Revolution.* Trans. Max Easton. London: Gollancz, 1934.

Vaché, Jacques. *Lettres de guerre.* Paris: Eric Losfeld, 1970.

Veríssimo, José. "Alguns livros de 1895 a 1898." In *Estudos de literatura brasileira,* 1st series, 135–79. Belo Horizonte: Itatiaia, 1976.

———. "Machado de Assis" and "Livros e autores de 1903 a 1905." In *Estudos de literatura brasileira,* 6th series, 103–8 and 109–39. Belo Horizonte: Itatiaia, 1977.

Watt, Ian. Introduction to *The Life and Opinions of Tristram Shandy, Gentleman,* by Laurence Sterne, vii–xxxv. Boston: Houghton Mifflin, 1965.

Werneck, L. Peixoto de Lacerda. *Idéias sobre colonização.* Rio de Janeiro: Eduardo e Henrique Laemmert, 1855.

Wood, Ellen Meiksins. "Capitalism and Human Emancipation." *New Left Review* 167 (January–February 1988): 5–6.

INDEX

Roberto Schwarz is Professor Emeritus of Brazilian
Literature, Department of Literary Theory, Universidade
Estadual de Campinas, Brazil. He is the author of, among
many other books, *Misplaced Ideas: Essays on Brazilian
Culture* (1992).
John Gledson is Emeritus Professor of Brazilian Studies,
University of Liverpool.

Library of Congress Cataloging-in-Publication Data
Schwarz, Roberto.
[Mestre na periferia do capitalismo. English]
A master on the periphery of capitalism : Machado de Assis /
Roberto Schwarz ; translated by John Gledson.
p. cm. — (Latin America in translation/en traducción/
em traduçao) (Post-contemporary interventions)
Includes bibliographical references and index.
ISBN 0–8223–2210–2 (cloth : alk. paper)
ISBN 0–8223–2239–0 (pbk. : alk. paper)
1. Machado de Assis, 1839–1908. Mâmorias pâstumas
de Brâs Cubas. I. Gledson, John, 1945– II. Title. III. Series.
IV. Series: Post-contemporary interventions
PQ9697.M18 M537 2001   869.3′3 — dc21   2001033782